THE LITTLE OL' REGISTER

Dollars & Cents in Starting and Raising Your First Business

By Dimas Arquimedes Suarez

This book is written as a source of information only.
The information contained in this book should by no means be considered a substitute for the advice, decisions, or judgment of the reader's financial, psychological, or other professional advisor.

All efforts have been made to ensure the accuracy of the information contained in this book as of the date of publication. The author and the publisher expressly disclaim responsibility for any adverse effects arising from the use or application of the information contained herein.

The **Little Ol' Register**.
Copyright © 2024 by Dimas A. Suarez
Illustrations by Dimas A. Suarez

All rights reserved. No part of this publication may be reproduced or transmitted in any form or by any means, electronic or mechanical, including photocopy, recording, or any information storage and retrieval system, without the prior written permission of the publisher except in the case of brief quotations embodied in critical articles and reviews.

Produced and published in conjunction with:
Elysian Technology Corporation - Intellectual Publishing Division
LittleOl' books may be purchased for educational, business, or sales promotional use. For information, please contact the Special Markets Department at **info@LITTLEOL.com**

First Edition

College Station, Texas

Library of Congress Control Number: 2024925400

Available in audio, ebook,
paperback (ISBN: 979-8-30-106591-0),
and hardcover (ISBN: 979-8-30-107859-0) editions.

Printed in the United States of America

DEDICATION

To the spirited youth of today's generation, especially those with the entrepreneurial flame burning within, and for those who navigate the journey without guidance. May this book ignite your passion and empower you to chase your dreams.

Infinite gratitude and love to my unwavering parents, who provided me with every opportunity from the earliest age, fostering an environment where growth knows no bounds. They encouraged me to sit at the big kids' table, regardless of age, and for that, I am eternally grateful. Your belief in me has inspired me to reach for the stars.

This book is a testament to the spirit of the young forging their paths, armed with determination and resilience to pursue their dreams of entrepreneurship.

This book is dedicated to all those who dare to dream and strive to make a difference. **Carpe diem** - seize the day and make your mark on the world.

CONTENTS

Introduction 1
   Congratulations 3
   The Little Ol' Analogy 5
      Blind men 6
      Paradigms 7
      Nothing New 11
Part 1: Defining the Register 15
   The Mindset: Founder vs Worker 17
      Chicken is Chicken 17
      Wants-Needs 22
      Rich Thinking 25
   The Storefront: Defining Your Business 29
      River for Water 29
      System 31
      End in Mind 36
   The Cash Register: Your Business's Heartbeat 43
      Solving the Solution 43
      Register 47
      Mind-Killer 49
Part 2: Building the Register 55
   Going to the Market: Knowing the people 57
      Think Customer 57
      King of My Own Domain 59
      High Horse 63
   Setting Up Shop: Creating a Business Plan 67
      Why 67
      Sim 71
      Sh*t Happens! 74
   Foundational Framework: Creating Your Business 81
      Genesis 81
      Vehicle 88
      Hats 102
Part 3: Programming the Register 109
   Managing the Store: Leadership and Governance 111
      Blink 111
      Chess 116
      Take my Job 122
   At the Water Cooler: Conveying the Feeling 131
      Pyramid 132
      Kool-Aid 134
      Look up 138

> **Introduction**

    In front of the Counter: Sales & Marketing 143
        Milking 144
        Shiny 149
        Sounds Good 153

Part 4: Working the Register 161
    Behind the Counter: Daily Business Operations 163
        Never Say No 163
        Warriors 168
        Games 173
    Customer Service: Satisfying Your "Customers" 179
        True Power 179
        The Sweetest Thing 185
        Peanut Butter 188
    Checking In: Monitoring and Evaluation 193
        Count your Steps! 193
        Stickers 203
        Landmines 205

Part 5: Counting the Register 213
    Counting the Drawer: Financial Management 215
        100 Pencils 216
        Count your Pennies! 222
        Know your Numbers 230
    Side work: General & Administrative 239
        Pushing Paper 241
        Killing a Tree 248
        The Bar 250
    Growing Your Business: Investing and Expanding 255
        Broke til' Midnight 255
        More Money More Problems 259
        Going Vertical 264

Summary and Conclusion 271
    Closing the Register: Reflecting on Business Success 273
        Dog and Pony Show 273
        Never Burn a Bridge 275
    Appendices and Resources 279
        Acknowledgments 280
        Citations 280
        Publisher's Notes 288

Introduction

"Whether you think you can or think you can't —you're right."

– Henry Ford,
Founder of Ford Motor Company

LEARNING OBJECTIVES, THE SELF

At the dawn of each part in this book, lies a treasure map leading to personal growth and professional prowess in the realm of business management and entrepreneurship. These learning objectives aren't just signposts; they're GPS beacons guiding you towards introspection, strategic thinking, and tangible actions for continuous improvement. Consider them as invitations to unlock your full potential, fortify your resilience, and chart a course towards your desired future.

So, muster your courage, stand up, hook up, shuffle to the door! We're going to jump right out of your perfectly safe plane, into the thrilling world of business—unleashing your inner business guru. Prepare for this daring leap for it's time to transform from a mere amateur to a seasoned aficionado, armed with wit and wisdom to conquer every challenge that comes your way!

■ **Self-Reflection and Awareness:** Develop a deeper understanding of yourself as an entrepreneur, leader, and individual by engaging in self-reflection exercises and increasing self-awareness of your strengths, weaknesses, values, and goals.

■ **Personal Development and Growth:** Explore strategies for personal development and growth to enhance your leadership skills, emotional intelligence, resilience, and overall well-being, allowing you to navigate the challenges and opportunities of entrepreneurship more effectively.

■ **Mindset and Belief Systems:** Examine the role of mindset and belief systems in shaping your attitudes, behaviors, and outcomes, and learn how to cultivate a growth mindset and positive belief systems to overcome obstacles and achieve success.

Introduction

- **Goal Setting and Achievement:** Learn how to set SMART (Specific, Measurable, Achievable, Relevant, Time-bound) goals and develop action plans to achieve them, leveraging your strengths and resources to make meaningful progress towards your aspirations.

- **Time Management and Productivity:** Acquire time management and productivity skills to optimize your use of time, prioritize tasks effectively, and maintain focus and motivation amidst competing demands and distractions.

- **Communication and Relationship Building:** Enhance your communication skills and relationship-building abilities to foster effective interpersonal connections, collaborate with others, and build strong networks and partnerships.

- **Decision Making and Problem Solving:** Develop critical thinking, decision-making, and problem-solving skills to analyze complex situations, evaluate options, and make informed and strategic decisions in the face of uncertainty and ambiguity.

- **Adaptability and Flexibility:** Cultivate adaptability and flexibility to navigate change, embrace uncertainty, and pivot when necessary, enabling you to respond proactively to evolving circumstances and market dynamics.

Notes:

CONGRATULATIONS

Innovation! In the vast expanse of the unknown, where dreams merge with the possibilities of tomorrow, we find ourselves on the precipice of a new era. Here, amidst the wonders of emerging technologies, the boundless depths of the human mind, and the infinite realms of intelligence, we dare to venture into uncharted territories. As we gaze upon the vast expanse of space, our imaginations are ignited by the possibilities that lie beyond. With each new discovery, each bold leap forward, we inch closer to unlocking the secrets of the universe.

And now, as you stand at the threshold of innovation, holding in your hands the seeds of a new idea, know that you are embarking on a journey unlike any other. With hopes, dreams, and ambitions intertwined, prepare yourself for the exhilarating ride that lies ahead. Hold on with both hands, for the adventure of a lifetime awaits.

Let's get this out of the way so the lawyers can be happy: nothing herein shall be construed as legal or professional advisement. Please consult with your own legal counsel and licensed professionals in your jurisdiction, this is for <u>information purposes only.</u> The names may have been changed to protect the innocent and maybe the guilty.

When someone asks me do I have children, I speak somberly in jest, "Yes quite a few and they are experts in whining, complaining, and trying to monopolize my time. Oh, and they're quite skilled at trying to get away with things too. You know how it is, they think they deserve the world, especially because they're staffed with so many needy employees." Chuckles and laughter ripple through the room as I continue, "That's why I decided to make their employee folders purple; they're constantly trying to leave me black and blue." The heads agree, and the eyes give a wink in solidarity, as most have felt this pain, even if it is just a colleague that they must work next to all day. If you found yourself smiling or smirking, even just a little, rest assured—you're well on your way to being a fantastic parent to your new business, and like every great parent, no one is going to love and care for your new business, your **little ol' register**, more than you are.

At the heart of any business is the **register**, the central machine of the company, and what keeps all the gears of the **system** in line. This book is not a deep dive into any one aspect of running a company, yet it is a cursory overview of some of the base principles and individualized concepts to be guided by on your voyage.

Introduction

The book's structure is organized around the five fundamental perspectives of a company: founder (owner), governing body (board), executive (salesperson), operations (manager), and finance (accountant). Each perspective is further explored in dedicated chapters, delving into the nuances and intricacies of each role. Through a handcrafted curation of sections, the book presents colloquial adages enriched with thought experiments, straightforward universal principles, anecdotes, and parables. These serve as invaluable navigational aids on your journey towards achieving your ultimate objectives, equipping you with essential tools to add to your toolkit.

These are enduring, time-tested principles, not mere contemporary sales tactics, or fleeting strategies, but rather the foundational fundamentals drawn from the wisdom accumulated over the past few centuries and even millennia from ones wiser than ourselves. They encapsulate abridged philosophical principles many miss that can swiftly set your business in motion ahead of the competition.

This isn't just a book about business; it's a journey of self-discovery. As you embark on this voyage, you'll unlock the secrets to harnessing your inner entrepreneur, developing a winning mindset, and overcoming challenges with resilience. By the time you finish reading, you'll be equipped to turn your dreams into reality and create a business that not only thrives but inspires.

You'll learn how to navigate the intricate universe of entrepreneurship, from crafting a compelling business plan to managing finances and building a strong team. This book will serve as your curio cabinet of knowledge each on its own pedestal, providing you with practical insights, actionable strategies, and invaluable resources. By the time you reach the final pages, you will emerge with the confidence and expertise needed to address many questions or hurdles that may arise along your entrepreneurial path, empowering you to turn your vision into reality and embark on a fulfilling and successful journey in the world of business.

It is with great honor and privilege that we welcome you to embark on this remarkable expedition into the promising new era of humanity. Within these pages, you will discover a wealth of words and wisdom carefully gathered to illuminate your path forward. As we journey together, let us navigate the twists and turns of life with collective wisdom and grace, embracing each challenge as an opportunity for growth and enlightenment. Together, we will chart a course towards a brighter future, guided by the light of knowledge and the spirit of unity. So, let's dive in and unlock your full potential. **The future of your business—and your life—awaits.**

THE LITTLE OL' ANALOGY

And in the ever-evolving world of entrepreneurship, where big, scary business concepts loom like giants, it's often more palatable to break them down into simpler, more relatable forms, even for the well-seasoned. This is where the **little ol'** principle comes into play—taking complex notions and rendering them harmless through analogy and with a twist of anthropomorphism, giving life to abstract ideas in the style of a trusted companion, your **little ol'**.

Imagine, in fact, your business as a living organism, a tiny idea constantly multiplying and surrounded by the predators of the market. Just like any living entity, it experiences growth, faces challenges, and makes innovative discoveries every hour. Ideas, like prey, are ready to be devoured and redefined in the ever-evolving landscape. It's a jungle out there, with survival of the fittest at the core. Your business, much like a **little ol' register**, thrives on constant learning and growth, getting bigger and stronger with each passing day.

But what does it take to navigate this bustling jungle of business? All you need is the willingness to dream and the dedication to keep moving forward. In the upcoming sections, we'll delve into the initial steps, providing you with insights to help you decide which paths to take. Remember, the next steps are yours to determine, and the journey is as unique as your **little ol' register** that inspires and guides you through the exciting terrain of entrepreneurship.

As we embark on this entrepreneurial voyage, it's essential to establish some prerequisites, assumptions, or fundamental premises that will serve as the guiding stars of our journey. Consider these as the sexton for your exploration into the vast ocean of business. These foundational principles will help shape your perspective, enhance your decision-making, and ensure a smoother traverse through the challenges and opportunities that lie ahead.

We'll start by diving into a few base premises, addressing key aspects that will serve as cornerstones for your understanding of business dynamics. Then, from the principles of **counting your pennies** to the art of **pushing paper**, we'll equip you with more tools and insights needed to navigate this concrete jungle confidently.

So, fasten your seatbelt, and your **little ol' register** in the car seat, as we venture into the heart of entrepreneurship, where these fundamental principles will be your steadfast companions on the exciting road to success. Together, let's uncover the secrets, decode the patterns, and master the art of this **little ol'** thing we call business.

Introduction

BLIND MEN

As we hedge forward on this safari, it's crucial to take an initial step in introspection and exploration of various perspectives. An Indian folk tale serves as an illuminating example, showcasing the impact of diverse viewpoints on interpretations. The narrative of the **blind men** and an elephant unfolds as a group of blind individuals, unacquainted with elephants, strive to grasp the nature of this creature solely through their heightened sense of touch. This tale encapsulates the essence of understanding through distinct lenses and sets the stage for our exploration of diverse viewpoints in the entrepreneurial realm.

A group of **blind men** heard that a strange animal, called an elephant, had been brought to the town, but none of them were aware of its shape and form. Out of curiosity, they said: "We must inspect and know it by touch, of which we are capable." So, they sought it out, and when they found it, they groped about it. The first person, whose hand landed on the trunk, said, "This being is like a thick snake." For another one whose hand reached its ear, it seemed like a kind of fan. Another person, whose hand was upon its leg, said, "the elephant is a pillar like a tree-trunk." The blind man who placed his hand upon its side said the elephant, "is a wall." Another who felt its tail described it as a rope. The last felt its tusk, stating "the elephant is that which is hard, smooth, and like a spear." [1]

One of the earliest versions of this story can be found in the Buddhist text Tittha Sutta, Udāna 6.4, Khuddaka Nikaya—inspired utterances. Each blind man feels a different part of the elephant's body, but only one part, such as the side or the tusk. They then describe the elephant based on their limited experience and their descriptions of the elephant are different from each other. [2] In certain renditions of the story, suspicion of dishonesty arises between them, escalating to physical conflict. The underlying lesson of the parable is the inclination of humans to assert absolute truths rooted in their constrained and subjective perspectives, often disregarding the equally valid subjective experiences of others. Truth is all based on one's limited perspective or what Nietzsche sometimes calls "perspectivism."[3]

How might the responses vary if we posed a different inquiry to these blind men? Imagine if we asked them whether I should embark on a business venture. Do you anticipate receiving consistent replies? Now, what if there were 20 of these individuals? Alright, let's expand the scenario to 100 or even 1000 blind men. Let's delve deeper into this tangent and explore its implications.

In this particular situation, a jar filled with an unknown number of balls is presented to a group of people. Each person is asked to guess the number of balls in the jar. While individual guesses may vary widely and might be inaccurate, the average of all the guesses tends to be remarkably close to the actual number of balls if not the exact number itself. This story is an illustration of the concept known as the "wisdom of the crowd." [4, 5]

This phenomenon is a statistical principle based on the law of large numbers. Individually, people may make errors or have subjective and biased estimations, but when you aggregate a large number of diverse guesses, the errors tend to cancel each other out. The average of the group's estimates becomes a surprisingly accurate approximation of the true value.[6]

Our collective intelligence and diverse perspectives within a group suggest that a group's collaborative judgment can be more accurate than that of any individual member.[3] It has implications in various fields, including decision-making, problem-solving, and market predictions, where leveraging the collective wisdom of a diverse group can lead to more accurate and reliable results.

We start with the premise that there are "no facts, only interpretations." Then take as many nuggets as possible of wisdom you can, from all different opinions and perspectives, and in maternal words "Take what you want and leave the rest." Never just disregard the perceptions or judgments based on others' experiences for buried within all that hay maybe that needle you may have been looking for all this time.

PARADIGMS

In the intricate web of human perception, as illuminated by the tale of the **blind men** and the elephant, lies the profound power of **paradigms**. Dr. Covey, a trailblazer in personal development, brought this term to the forefront, derived from the Greek root paradigma, signifying a pattern, model, or representation. **Paradigms** encapsulate our lenses of perception—our frames of reference, worldviews, and value **systems** that shape the meaning we ascribe to the world. They influence how we interpret our surroundings, engage with experiences, and navigate our relationships with others.[7]

Consider, for a moment, a scenario unfolding on the bustling New York subway. After a taxing day, we find ourselves surrounded by the worn echoes of the subway car. Amid the clamor, two unruly adolescents disrupt the peace, their primal energy reverberating through the bars. The walls of the car around us echo every sound. Our attention is brought forth by the screams and rowdiness of these two adolescent primates on the bars hollering and shouting as if their primal instincts were uncontained by any social norms. The agitation within

Introduction

us boils to the point of lashing out, urging action to quell the disturbance. Elbowing you with a nod of action to address the issue. Playful shoves convey the responsibility to address the issue that I should take the initiative. The fellow sardines packed around us, our sights met with disapproving glances from fellow passengers in utter dismay at the lack of parental guidance. As we summon the courage to confront the father of the rowdy duo, we discover a profound truth.

His gaze toward the floor, hands within his lap in solace, and even lack of his own prodigy's disturbance did not disturb this statue. What kind of father just sits there letting this happen? What kind of person is oblivious to his surroundings? His demeanor continues only stoking the inferno now blazing in us. I reach over touching the man on his shoulder looking sternly into his eyes excuse me Sir can you please control your kids they are out of control. His eyes arise to mine, somber and steeped in lonely despair, he utters the words "Oh I'm so sorry, Sir, I can't believe I didn't even realize it we just got back from the hospital where my wife suddenly and unexpectedly passed away and I haven't even told them yet." His demeanor, initially perceived as neglectful, transforms into a stoic façade masking immense grief. He reveals that his wife has just passed away unexpectedly, an agonizing reality he has yet to share with his oblivious children.

Did you feel it? This moment is a testament to the power of a **paradigm** shift—a 180-degree transformation of perception. The initial agitation gives way to empathy, disgruntlement yields to compassion, defensiveness evolves into openness. You just experienced a "**paradigm** shift." A transformation that allows you to widen your view and to shed new light on something. By adjusting your map of perception, this concept coined by the American physicist and philosopher Thomas Kuhn describes a fundamental change in our beliefs about the world.

This technique has been exploited by psychologists and therapists like a favorite pair of comfy socks. They call it cognitive behavioral therapy, which basically means we're on a mission to kick those dysfunctional emotions, behaviors, and thoughts to the curb.[8] It's all about interrogating those negative or irrational beliefs, shining a spotlight on them, and saying, "You're not welcome here, buddy!" So, get ready to roll up your sleeves and dig deep into the messy garden of your mind. We're about to unearth some funky old beliefs and plant some **shiny** new ones in their place.

We can now become more aware of how our actions are instinctively attached to our preconceived perceptions. As we delve into this exploration, be prepared for a challenge to your existing **paradigms**, a gentle nudge towards transformative, solutions-oriented thinking. And hey, if you're feeling a little skeptical or hesitant, just remember—every great adventure starts with a single step, usually followed by a trip and a faceplant. But hey, that's what makes it an adventure, right?

Cognitive Behavioral Therapy (CBT) serves as a practical application of the principles underpinning **paradigm** shifts. In the psychobabble of therapy, CBT operates as a powerful tool to address and alter maladaptive thought patterns that arise in the **blink** of an eye.[9] For instance, if an individual struggles with persistent negative thoughts about their abilities, a CBT practitioner may guide them to identify these thoughts, challenge their accuracy, and reframe them in a more constructive light.[10] This process mirrors the essence of a **paradigm** shift, where entrenched beliefs are questioned and replaced with more adaptive perspectives.

Navigating this path is not without its challenges, often marked by what psychologists term "cognitive dissonance"—a state of discomfort, anxiety, or mental tension that arises when our beliefs or attitudes conflict with our actions or other beliefs.[11] In confronting this dissonance, we may find ourselves rationalizing our choices or even undergoing behavioral changes to alleviate the tension.

However, by recognizing the intricate interplay between our thoughts and behaviors, both Cognitive Behavioral Therapy (CBT) and **paradigm** shifts present pathways toward deep personal transformation. As one engages in CBT techniques, they may find themselves on a parallel journey of self-discovery, gradually dismantling old **paradigms** and constructing new, more empowering ones. A well-known scenario can be recounted to observe this unfolding.

In the cozy corner of a bustling restaurant, two individuals, each navigating their own worlds, had an unexpected encounter that would unravel a **paradigm** shift in their perspectives. Sarah, engrossed in a book, was blissfully unaware of her surroundings. Meanwhile, James, in a rush to grab a quick lunch, accidentally tripped over Sarah's extended foot.

The momentary chaos left James flustered, and a reflexive apology tumbled from his lips. Surprisingly, Sarah looked up from her book with a warm smile, assuring James that no harm was done. As James hesitated, expecting annoyance or frustration, Sarah continued with genuine empathy, sharing a humorous story of her own clumsiness. The tension diffused instantly.

This encounter sparked a cognitive shift for both individuals. Instead of dwelling on assumptions and negative interpretations, they found a connection through shared vulnerability. Sarah's understanding response encouraged James to

Introduction

rethink his initial embarrassment, and, in turn, James' genuine apology affirmed Sarah's belief in the kindness of strangers.

In this unexpected dance of empathy, the restaurant transformed into a stage for a change in basic assumptions. What could have been a moment of irritation turned into a lesson on the power of compassion, altering the way both Sarah and James perceived and reacted to the unexpected quirks of life.

We must be acutely aware of the interconnectedness of thoughts, emotions, and behaviors, aiming to identify and modify negative thought patterns to promote healthier responses. Similarly, **paradigm** shifts involve a fundamental change in one's worldview or perspective, challenging ingrained beliefs and fostering a new understanding of reality.

In your mind's eye, amidst the rigid precision of marching drills on the parade deck, a young marine, shoulders squared, and face locked in disciplined focus, found himself immersed in the cacophony of barked orders from the drill instructor. As the harsh commands echoed, a sudden shift in the atmosphere occurred. A sweet fragrance, from miles away, wafted through the air, momentarily diverting the marine's attention.[12]

The intoxicating scent teased his senses, a tantalizing distraction from the rigorous training. A silent symphony of olfactory delights swept across the parade deck, suggesting the unexpected presence of visitors, specifically those of the female persuasion emersed in his mind. In that fleeting moment, the disciplined marine, usually impervious to distractions, felt a surge of empathy for the allure of the unseen, realizing that perception goes beyond the visual, encompassing the sensory reality that shapes our understanding of the world. The juxtaposition of military discipline and the alluring scent created a **paradigm** shift, revealing that even in the most structured environments, the human experience is rich with nuanced perceptions.

An individual walked by the pungent odor of burnt tobacco trailing in their wake, unbeknownst to them that their scent lingered long after their passing. As a non-smoker, the billowing smell continued to permeate the air, evoking a subtle reflection on the power of scent undenounced to our own senses. The dichotomy between the transient nature of the smoker's experience and the enduring impression it left on the non-smoker highlighted the intricate interplay between self-perception and the perception of others.

Days later, the non-smoker found themself catching whiffs of that familiar scent, a subtle reminder of the encounter with the tobacco-laden passerby. The persistence of the odor served as a poignant illustration of how sensory experiences could linger in our subconscious, influencing our perceptions and interactions with the world around us. In this olfactory journey, the **paradigm** of perception extended beyond the immediate moment, leaving an indelible mark on the non-smoker's memory, showcasing the intricate ways in which our senses shape our understanding of reality.

Taking a deep inhalation of the sweet smell of Cinnabon that wafted through the mall, tapping into those signals of gratification and indulgence. As the irresistible aroma permeated the air, it triggered a cascade of signals in the brain, sparking a Pavlovic hunger even in those who were already full. The olfactory allure of cinnamon and sugar mingling in the air created a sensory symphony that played on the strings of desire, compelling passersby to entertain the thought of a delectable treat.

The enticing scent acted as a silent persuader, luring individuals towards the source with an almost magnetic pull. Rationality seemed to succumb to the aromatic enchantment, as hunger pangs teased even those who had just enjoyed a satisfying meal. It was a testament to the power of sensory perception and how external stimuli, in this case, the alluring scent of Cinnabon, could momentarily hijack our senses and influence our behavior. The sweet aroma not only enhanced the atmosphere of the mall but also became a symbol of the intricate dance between our senses and the temptations of the external world.

As we draw the curtains on this exploration of shifting perspectives for a solutions-oriented approach, let us embrace the notion that **paradigms** are not permanent fixtures but dynamic frameworks subject to evolution. The richness of our collective experience lies in our willingness to step outside the confines of our individual convictions and savor the subtle flavors that surround us. By fostering an environment where diverse perspectives are not only acknowledged but celebrated, we unlock the potential for innovation and collective growth. Let the tapestry of varying viewpoints weave together, creating a mosaic that reflects the adaptability and resilience of your **little ol' register**. Here's to a future where open-mindedness becomes the compass guiding us through the intricate landscapes of problem-solving and progress.

NOTHING NEW

Certainly, exploring your passion may present challenges. The business you aspire to launch might seem daunting, facing tough competition or operating in a saturated market. However, remember, it's never crowded at the top, as the **blind men** would tell you. You have the capability; someone cracked the code. How did they achieve it a thousand years ago? It requires breaking free from

Introduction

conventional thinking, a mindset not typically instilled in ordinary individuals. [13] Shifting from "I can't" to "I can," transitioning from a worker to a founder, and embracing positivity over negativity are the keys to unlocking potential.

Undoubtedly, the patterns of innovation often follow a familiar trajectory. Before the era of Facebook and Meta, Myspace reigned supreme, and before Myspace, there was Prodigy. Preceding Snapchat, there was Twitter, and before Twitter introduced direct messaging, there was AOL Instant Messenger—anyone heard of the 1900's telegram. Even before the age of online searches to obtain someone's address for doxing, people simply consulted the white pages of the phone book, engaging in analog pranks like leaving a flaming bag of mischief on someone's doorstep. The digital landscape frequently draws parallels from its analog predecessors. As technology continues to evolve, it's clear that history often repeats itself, albeit in new and exciting ways.

We have all heard the expression "Nothing new under the sun." This encapsulates the idea that while advancements and innovations continually shape our world, the fundamental aspects of human existence, experiences, and challenges remain enduring and universal. In other words, **chicken is chicken**. This phrase draws attention to the cyclical nature of history, where patterns, ideas, and themes tend to reoccur across time. It suggests that, despite the ever-evolving nature of technology and society, the core aspects of human nature, relationships, and struggles persist.

This perspective encourages reflection on the shared and timeless aspects of the human experience, reminding us that, beneath the surface of novelty, there exists a thread of continuity connecting the past, present, and future. It's all been done before; just **shiny** look here, more about the things that are **shiny** and **sound good** in Part 4: Working the Register.

The past can be daunting, yet realizing that an estimated a weeks' worth of the New York Times contains more information than a person was likely to come across in a lifetime in the 18th century shows, how much knowledge and information can be at every fingertip and already is.[14] This stresses the importance and imperative of adapting to the current times. Not just in infrastructure but mindset as well. We can look at Myspace as an example. Having over 200 million registered users at one point, and evaluated as a country would have been the fifth largest in the world between Indonesia and Brazil.[14] We can see that Myspace is now forgotten and dominated by the 2.989 billion on Facebook. [15] Let us not be forgotten or left in the dark; only inspire achievement through excellence and adaptation.

The concept of "**nothing new**" emphasizes that many challenges and problems we encounter today have likely been faced and solved by individuals throughout history. For instance, if someone, over 4,500 years ago, could conceive and construct something as intricate as the **pyramids**, it implies that the knowledge and solutions exist, waiting to be rediscovered and applied in our modern context.[16] This idea encourages a perspective that embraces the wealth of human knowledge accumulated over centuries, suggesting that the principles and solutions to many problems are timeless and can be accessed with the right inquiry and understanding. In essence, it invites us to tap into the collective wisdom of humanity to overcome present challenges and achieve new heights.

Debatable with today's youth, the idea is not necessarily that people in the past were inherently smarter, but maybe rather that they were more resourceful, creative, and found effective solutions with the knowledge and tools available to them in their respective times. The point is that the capacity for problem-solving, innovation, and achieving remarkable feats has been a consistent trait throughout human history. By acknowledging this, we can draw inspiration from the achievements of our predecessors and apply their problem-solving approaches to address contemporary challenges, demonstrating the enduring nature of human ingenuity across different eras.

Of course, at a certain juncture, we passionately believed the Earth was flat, that the sun orbited our planet, and even the origin of life spawned from inanimate matter. It's a testament to our evolving understanding that we now acknowledge these beliefs as **blind men's** misconceptions. Recognizing our fallibility becomes more apparent when we observe a collection of errors that share common characteristics. The age-old nursery rhyme question, " One of These Things is Not Like the Others," serves as a simple yet effective tool to highlight and rectify cognitive missteps in our thought processes.[17] The aim is to enhance cognitive skills and promote critical thinking, pattern recognition, and observational skills playfully and engagingly.

In closing the pages of "Nothing New," let us be reminded of Harry S Truman's insightful words, "There is nothing new in the world except the history you do not know." Even as we navigate the uncharted waters of discovery, every revelation, every truth, has its roots intertwined with the familiar. It is through our understanding of the past that we find the compass guiding us in the creation of the new. The threads of similarity weave through time, connecting the old to the new, forming a forest of knowledge that binds generations together. Embrace the wisdom of the ages, for therein lies the key to unlocking the mysteries of innovation and progress.

Part 1: Defining the Register

Part 1: Defining the Register

"Don't limit yourself. Many people limit themselves to what they think they can do. You can go as far as your mind lets you. What you believe, remember, you can achieve."
– Mary Kay Ash,
Founder of Mary Kay Cosmetics

LEARNING OBJECTIVES, A FOUNDER'S PERSPECTIVE

For the Founder's Perspective, starts at the 35,000-foot view with a deep dive into the mindset and strategies essential for laying the groundwork of a successful venture. Here, you'll uncover the secrets of visionary leadership, strategic planning, and navigating the unpredictable currents of entrepreneurship. From defining your *mission* and *vision* to crafting a robust **system**, each learning objective is designed to equip you with the tools and insights necessary to transform your innovative ideas into thriving enterprises.

■ **Understanding Entrepreneurial Vision:** Explore the significance of having a clear entrepreneurial vision and its role in guiding business decisions and strategies.

■ **Navigating Uncertainty:** Learn how to navigate uncertainty and ambiguity as an entrepreneur, embracing challenges as opportunities for growth and innovation.

■ **Building Resilience:** Discover strategies for building resilience in the face of setbacks and obstacles commonly encountered in entrepreneurial endeavors. The psychology and systemology of the business entity.

■ **Mastering Adaptability:** Gain insights into the importance of adaptability in entrepreneurship and learn how to pivot effectively in response to changing market dynamics.

■ **Fostering Creativity and Innovation:** Explore techniques for fostering creativity and innovation within your entrepreneurial ventures, driving differentiation and competitive advantage.

■ **Strategic Decision-Making:** Learn how to make strategic decisions that align with your business objectives and drive sustainable growth and success.

■ **Balancing Risk and Reward:** Explore the delicate balance between risk-taking and risk mitigation in entrepreneurship, maximizing opportunities while minimizing potential pitfalls.

■ **Cultivating a Growth Mindset:** Cultivate a growth mindset that embraces challenges, seeks feedback, and views failures as valuable learning experiences.

■ **Creating Value for Stakeholders:** Understand the importance of creating value for all stakeholders, including customers, employees, investors, and the community, in building a successful and sustainable business. What is a system and what problem it solves?

Notes:

THE MINDSET: FOUNDER VS WORKER

Resilience required. If you watched any TV, a Super Bowl commercial, or listened to music in the first decade of the millennium, the chance that we played a part in it is relatively high. Dreaming creative ideas, executing the vision, and accounting for performance are all part of the executive's role regardless of industry, especially in showbiz. Resilience is the cornerstone of navigating the ever-changing landscape of entertainment and media. Through the highs and lows, the triumphs and setbacks, it is this unwavering resilience that enables us to persist, innovate, and ultimately succeed.

In the mindsets of business, the Founder is to the customer as the producer is to the audience—a symphony of roles and responsibilities, each playing a crucial part in the grand performance. Much like the elaborate production of a Super Bowl commercial or a mesmerizing action scene, the executive's role is multifaceted, involving the conception of creative ideas, meticulous execution of the *vision*, and rigorous performance analysis. In the world of showbiz, where every detail matters, the owner's role transcends industry boundaries, mirroring the intricacies of a blockbuster film.

Picture your favorite action scene, the car defying gravity, soaring over the Las Vegas Strip with explosive precision. What the audience witnesses is the result of exhaustive efforts—talented individuals, dedicated crews, and a meticulous arrangement of equipment—all working together to capture that one perfect cinematic shot. Beyond the surface glamour lies the reality of coordination and logistics, a complex dance that demands motivation and dedication from a unified team. It's not merely about "cracking the whip"; it's about fostering a culture of training, understanding, and collaboration, creating a harmonious chorus that brings the breathtaking scenes to life. The vivid spectacle that splashes across your screens is, indeed, far from the real picture behind the scenes. For starters, we do not shoot in the order of the film.

CHICKEN IS CHICKEN

When **little ol'** scary things get explained it's easier to analogize them to a simpler form. Understanding the **paradigms** of **blind men** is **nothing new**, regardless of changes in form or media, the fundamental function remains constant. A store remains a store, regardless of the external appearance, colors, or items it contains.

This metaphor and others like it serve as powerful tools for elucidating large and complex topics because they bridge the gap between the unfamiliar and the familiar, making abstract concepts more accessible and relatable. By drawing parallels between a complex idea and a more easily understandable analogy, metaphors provide a mental framework that aids comprehension. They simplify intricate subjects, offering a point of reference that taps into existing knowledge or experiences.[18] Metaphors engage the imagination, allowing individuals to visualize and conceptualize complex notions in a way that resonates with their existing understanding, fostering clearer communication and facilitating a deeper grasp of intricate topics. It also breaks some of the emotional attachment to the specific object. In essence, metaphors facilitate the translation of complexity into a language that is both comprehensible and possibly more memorable.

Amidst the discussions on poultry, a light-hearted joke emerged, echoing through the corridors of the **little ol'** business. "Where was the first turkey fried in? Grease." Laughter, a universal language, resonated as the team embraced the humor in their collective pursuit of success. It became a reminder that even in the serious lunchrooms of business, a good joke can be the seasoning that adds flavor to the daily grind.

Humans, by nature, are adept at categorizing and grouping things. This tendency extends from trivial jokes to the intricate workings of businesses. In your **little ol'** business, this skill was evident as team members effortlessly identified which element didn't quite belong, showcasing the innate ability to categorize and organize information. The power of grouping is not just a cognitive trait; it's a fundamental aspect of business operations, where streamlining processes and categorizing tasks contribute to efficiency.

Patterns weave through the fabric of human perception, and in the world of business, they emerge as the underlying structure that defines success. Every business, regardless of its nature, follows certain patterns. These patterns encompass the rhythm of operations, the flow of transactions, and the intricacies of decision-making. Recognizing these patterns allows **your little ol' register** to navigate the business landscape with a sense of familiarity and strategic insight.

In the bustling corridors of the **little ol' register**, a memorable story unfolded. It was a tale of a mischievous chicken who, in an attempt to avoid being fried, cleverly disguised itself among a group of turkeys. The team, drawing parallels with their own business challenges, found inspiration in the chicken's ability to adapt and integrate. The story became a metaphor for the importance of recognizing patterns, adapting to surroundings, and finding innovative solutions, leaving an indelible mark on the collective mindset of the **little ol' register.**

The metaphor "**chicken is chicken**" serves as a simplifying concept, emphasizing that, fundamentally, many things share common traits despite surface-level distinctions. In the context of products and services, this metaphor highlights the idea that, beneath specific details or variations, there exists a shared essence. Similarly, it reflects the cyclical nature of history, illustrating how patterns, ideas, and themes tend to reoccur across time. This notion suggests that, despite the ongoing evolution of technology and society, the core aspects of human nature, relationships, and struggles persist.

To enhance your learning experience, don't hesitate to fully immerse yourself in your metaphors. Act them out, sketch them, and even vocalize sounds to engage multiple senses. Research suggests that the more senses involved in learning, the more effectively information is retained. So, by embracing a multisensory approach, you can optimize your learning and deepen your understanding of the subject matter.[19] Regardless of your learning style, you'll learn it even better if you see it, hear it, and do it, than if you only receive it in one style.[18] We use metaphors and allegories to break things down. Even if you must take it out of the current situation, not only abstract it away, but mirror it so the most bizarre scenarios allow you to check your logic.

We can look at our hunger for some clarification. We all know the fastest way to a film cast and crew's hearts is through their stomachs. And if you haven't learned that already, you will if you ever incur meal penalties. Aside from being a production accountant's worst nightmare, meal penalties are a form of monetary compensation incurred when a production eats into a crew member's state-, federal-, and/or union-guaranteed workday meal period.

Like all elements of labor law, meal penalties exist in order to protect the rights of workers. The enforcement of meal penalties, in particular, is intended to discourage a business of any kind from forcing its employees to work for unreasonable lengths of time without eating. In film production unions, a meal is defined as a timely sit-down meal provided to employees. The IATSE union rules concerning meal breaks and penalties for violations are designed to financially motivate productions to provide employees with timely sit-down meals. Meal penalties are calculated per crew member for every 30 minutes of elapsed break time without a sit-down lunch or dinner.[20] These penalties can quickly add up to thousands of dollars in a given week for a film or TV crew.

Nourishing your cast and crew is a crucial aspect of film production, and understanding the intricacies of meal penalties is vital for a smooth production process. Meal penalties serve as a form of compensation when a production encroaches upon a crew member's guaranteed workday meal period, ensuring that workers are not forced to endure extended periods without sustenance. California labor law, in particular, emphasizes the importance of providing employees with adequate meal breaks.[21] In the fast-paced world of film production, where schedules are tight, the cost of meal penalties can quickly accumulate, underscoring the importance of meticulous planning and scheduling.

On the bustling film set, other than the possible looming penalties, the provision of sustenance isn't just a mere formality—it's a crucial component in maintaining the morale and productivity of the crew. There are four main factors at play. In the grand production of film catering, attention to detail is paramount. By recognizing and addressing the nuances of taste, dietary needs, and nutritional balance, a harmonious balance is struck, fostering an environment where everyone feels valued and supported. Just as a well-fed crew is essential for the success of a film shoot, so too is the satisfaction of customers in any other industry. In the end, whether on the silver screen or in the corporate boardroom, the principles of variety, quality, and inclusivity remain steadfast pillars of success.

■ **Variety**: Just as with any product, even the most delightful food becomes tiresome over time. Much like in any other business, variety reigns supreme, with an array of snacks and meals ensuring that everyone's tastes and preferences are catered to. To keep the crew engaged and content, it's crucial to offer a diverse selection of snacks and meals, rotating options daily and representing a wide range of tastes and food groups in both your meals and craft services.

■ **Quality**: Despite the fact that it might appear to be an easy budget cut, think long and hard before minimizing your meal allotment. Pizza is seldom acceptable. When it comes to food, quality is non-negotiable. While it may seem like a quick fix to cut corners, thoughtful consideration of meal options is essential. Again pizza, though convenient, is rarely sufficient as a sole meal option. It's imperative to prioritize high-quality ingredients and preparation methods to provide satisfying and nourishing meals that meet the crew's needs.

■ **Value**, Caloric but healthy: Meals should be healthy enough to sustain energy over prolonged periods of time, versus causing a brief high before the inevitable sugar or sodium crash. However, a crew cannot survive on lettuce alone. The physical work on set is extremely demanding and you will need to meet that demand with hearty and energizing meals. Consider lean proteins, plain starches, superfoods, and energy bars for the crafty table.

■ **Influence**, Dietary restrictions: But it's not just about filling stomachs; it's about catering to the individual needs and dietary restrictions of each crew member. By ignoring or under-serving these restrictions, you are at the very worst putting someone in life-threatening danger, and at the very least pissing someone off. As the person in charge of food, it's their job to ensure that every single crew member is adequately fed. That does not mean telling the vegetarian to just eat salad or satisfying a gluten-free request by just removing the breaded part, or simply telling the one PA with a nut allergy to avoid the crafty table altogether. As the individual responsible for food provision, it's essential to cater to each crew member's dietary needs, making chicken—a universally safe option—an integral part of the menu every day.[22]

In the world of film catering, as in any other business venture, the principles of variety, quality, value, and influence reign supreme. Just as a diverse menu keeps crew members on a film set satisfied and energized, offering a range of options for any product or service ensures that customers are engaged and satisfied. Quality is paramount in both realms, with attention to detail and craftsmanship elevating the overall experience. Value, too, plays a crucial role—whether it's delivering bang for the buck in a meal plan or providing cost-effective solutions in a corporate setting, customers expect to get their money's worth.

Finally, influence permeates every aspect, from the choice of ingredients to the presentation of the final product. Just as a well-prepared meal can leave a lasting impression on a film crew, the impact of a company's offerings resonates with its clientele, shaping perceptions and driving loyalty. Ultimately, whether it's serving up chicken on a film set or delivering a service in the corporate world, the key to success lies in understanding and embodying these fundamental principles.

Just like any meal from any establishment or even at home it truly is a product. By addressing these key factors—variety, quality, value, and influence—caterers can effectively meet the diverse needs of the crew, fostering a positive and productive working environment on set. Just as consumers weigh various considerations before making a purchase, catering decisions must align with the crew's preferences and requirements to ensure their well-being and satisfaction.

Now take your mind back to Forest Gump when Forrest (Tom Hanks) meets Bubba (Mykelti Williamson) who has a passion for shrimp. "You can barbecue it, boil it, brawl It, bake It, sauté it, lays on shrimp kebabs, shrimp creole, shrimp gumbo, pan-fried, deep fried, stir-fried."[23] Just as fried chicken, roasted chicken, orange chicken, grilled chicken, chicken fingers, and Italian chicken are all fundamentally dishes of chicken, products, and services, no matter how diverse, can be viewed as variations of the same fundamental concept—something designed to fulfill a need or desire. This **"chicken is chicken"** perspective challenges us to recognize the universal elements that underlie diverse offerings.

In the business world, it encourages a focus on the essential qualities that make a product or service successful, such as meeting customer needs, delivering value, and ensuring quality, irrespective of the specific form it takes. From sales orders to purchase orders, everything within the business **system** can be metaphorically viewed as different variations of the same fundamental concept—comparable to different dishes made from chicken. Embracing the idea that **"chicken is chicken"** fosters a deeper understanding of the interconnected elements within your **little ol' register's** products, services, and experiences.

Embracing the notion that **"chicken is chicken"** allows for a more profound understanding of the common threads that connect seemingly disparate elements in the complex hodgepodge of things in the world around us.

WANTS-NEEDS

Many people are familiar with Maslow's Hierarchy of Needs, a well-known psychological framework, which categorizes human needs into five overarching levels. It commences with fundamental physiological needs, progresses to safety and security, extends to the pursuit of love and belonging, ascends to the need for esteem, and culminates in aspirational, self-actualizing needs.[24] Abraham arranges these **needs** in ascending order, suggesting a natural progression. Once basic needs find fulfillment, individuals tend to gravitate towards more sophisticated **wants-needs**—yet do these evolving desires truly align with genuine needs, or do we sometimes cloak our wants in the guise of necessity?

Ultimately, the essence of choice lies in its purity, unaffected by fleeting impulses, emotions, or beliefs. A choice may be born from justification and logic, grounded in personal autonomy. For instance, when faced with the question of chocolate or vanilla ice cream, the reasons that cascade from one's lips—whether it tastes better, is smoother, or stains less—are merely ancillary. The crux lies in the fact that you choose vanilla not due to external factors or influences but simply because it is your choice, a manifestation of your unadulterated will.[25]

So **why** do people choose to spend as much as they make, irrespective of their profession? Well, several factors contribute to this phenomenon. One noteworthy influence is lifestyle inflation, the **wants-needs** get bigger. As individuals experience an increase in income, they may succumb to the temptation to elevate their standard of living by acquiring more expensive possessions or indulging in some of the more luxurious experiences. This desire to keep up with a certain lifestyle, keeping up with the Jones', can lead to increased spending, preventing individuals from saving or investing the surplus income.

Maybe we just needed to be taken by the ear as in the quaint neighborhood where young Jake spent his summers cutting lawns, a budding investor emerged. At the tender age of thirteen, armed with a rusty lawnmower and sheer determination, Jake began mowing lawns for the neighbors. While other kids might have squandered their earnings on fleeting delights, Jake's mother, a wise and financially savvy woman, imparted lessons that transcended the immediacy of youthful desires.

Jake's mother, a woman of foresight, instilled in him the value of delayed gratification and the power of long-term investment. Every week, without fail, Jake would diligently set aside 13% of his earnings and invest them in EE savings bonds. As the bonds accumulated over the years, so did Jake's understanding of the financial landscape. This mother-son duo, through the simple act of mowing lawns and making prudent investments, wove a tale of financial literacy and foresight that would undoubtedly shape Jake's future.

Jake's mother didn't just stop at teaching him the virtues of saving and investing; she also introduced him to this rule of thumb, subtlety preached each week, that would guide his asset allocation strategy. The formula was simple yet powerful: subtract your age from 100 to determine the percentage of high-risk assets versus low-risk assets. For a vibrant 13-year-old like Jake, this meant a portfolio consisting of 87% in high-risk ventures, embracing the potential for growth and higher returns, and 13% in more stable, stone-cold hard investments, like savings bonds.

This rule underscored the importance of aligning investment choices with one's risk tolerance and the time horizon for recovery. Aversion to risk, Jake learned, could impede the ability to recoup losses, and the link between time and recovery became a critical factor. This financial wisdom, imparted by his mother, became Jake's compass as he navigated the tumultuous seas of the investment world. Maybe this is **why** Jake added fertilizer sales to his mowing business—diversification.

Even with saving, the phenomenon of conflating **wants** and **needs** extends beyond personal finance into the realm of higher business, where the distinction between the two is often blurred by the allure of luxury items and symbols. The

pursuit of a certain class status becomes a barrier to entry, creating a narrative where the possession of prestigious symbols is perceived not just as a **want** but as a **need** within the competitive landscape. This dynamic adds a layer of complexity to decision-making, as businesses navigate the fine line between genuine necessities and the symbolic markers that confer a particular status. In the world of commerce, where perception can be as influential as substance, understanding and managing these dynamics becomes crucial for sustainable success.

In certain personal instances, unexpected financial gains or salary hikes might be viewed as a chance for indulgence rather than an opportunity for saving or investing. Indeed, 44% of those who have ever won large lottery prizes were broke within five years, according to a 2015 Camelot Group study.[26] The inclination towards immediate gratification can often overshadow the significance of financial planning and the rewards that come with delayed gratification. The Hierarchy of Needs serves as a useful reference point to prompt contemplation on discerning between our desires and genuine needs. Interestingly, individuals across various income brackets, from teachers to lawyers or doctors, often find themselves in a similar financial predicament—trapped in the cycle of being "Just Over Broke" a (J.O.B.)

In the perpetual dance between **wants** and **needs**, many find themselves caught in the delicate balance of spending what they earn. To fulfill an increasing array of desires, individuals are left with essentially two avenues: minimizing their **wants-needs** or amplifying their income. However, the latter faces an inherent constraint—the finite nature of time. The active hours devoted to fulfilling professional obligations impose an upper limit on the extent to which one can generate revenue.

Hence, the pursuit of financial equilibrium often entails a strategic tango, where finding harmony involves both optimizing income streams and carefully curating needs, all while recognizing the constraints of time and resources. It is a delicate symphony where financial prudence plays the leading role, guiding individuals towards a sustainable and fulfilling financial journey.

Ultimately, the tendency to spend all of one's income is a complex interplay of psychological, cultural, and financial factors. Most say that overcoming this pattern often requires a conscious effort to prioritize saving, investing, and cultivating financial literacy. Which are valid, yet is there a fundamental fault in this **paradigm** itself?

RICH THINKING

Are you ready to break free from the 9-to-5 grind and build a business that not only thrives but inspires? You're not alone. Millions of people share your aspiration. But the path to entrepreneurial success is fraught with challenges. One of the biggest challenges is overcoming limiting beliefs and adopting a rich mindset. What separates the successful entrepreneurs from the rest? Is it luck? Is it talent? Or is it something else? The answer lies in mindset. As the famous saying goes, "The mind is everything. What you think you become."

Once upon a time in the bustling town of Financialville, there were two fathers who lived side by side. One was known far and wide as Rich Dad, while the other was affectionately called Poor Dad. While both lived side by side, their approaches to money and life were vastly different.

Rich Dad, a savvy businessperson, always had a twinkle in his eye and a pocket full of financial wisdom. He believed in the power of investing and creating assets that would work tirelessly to build wealth. His children, Timmy and Sally, grew up listening to bedtime stories about the magic of compound interest and the importance of financial education.

On the other side of the picket fence lived Poor Dad, a hardworking soul who dedicated his days to a traditional job. While he loved his family dearly, he often found himself caught in the hamster wheel of bills and expenses. He taught his children, Johnny and Lisa, the value of hard work but seldom delved into the mysteries of money beyond the necessity of making ends meet.

One day, the two families decided to have a neighborhood barbecue. Rich Dad, with a gleam in his eye, brought out a board game called "Cashflow" to tutor the kids about financial strategies. The children were enthralled as they learned about assets, liabilities, and the importance of making money work for them.

Meanwhile, Poor Dad, sensing the joyous commotion next door, decided to join the festivities. Rich Dad welcomed him with open arms, and they all sat down to share stories and laughter. Rich Dad gently shared his financial philosophies, emphasizing the need to create wealth, while Poor Dad spoke about the dignity of hard work and the security of a steady job.

As the evening sun painted the sky with hues of orange and pink, both families realized the beauty in embracing the strengths of each approach. Rich

Dad learned the warmth of a close-knit family, and Poor Dad saw the potential in expanding his financial horizons.

In Financialville, the tale of Rich Dad and Poor Dad became a cherished parable, reminding everyone that wealth is not just measured in dollars but in the richness of relationships and the blend of financial wisdom and hard work. And so, the two families continued to learn from each other, creating a harmonious symphony of financial prudence and family values in their little corner of the world.

In Robert's world, the author of Rich Dad Poor Dad, tells his story of growing up with two dads—his real father and the father of his best friend, his rich dad—and the ways in which both men shaped his thoughts about money and investing. Robert's rich dad, who is not his biological father but a mentor, emphasizes the importance of financial education, investment, and entrepreneurship. He advocates for building assets that generate passive income rather than solely relying on earned income through traditional employment. Rich dad encourages you to think beyond the conventional path of working for money and to instead make money work for them by investing wisely and creating multiple streams of income.[27]

In contrast, the more common way of thought, Robert's Poor Dad embodies the conventional ideology of working hard, saving money, and relying on job security. Children from lower and middle-class backgrounds are often indoctrinated with the belief that the key to life's productivity lies in a prescribed sequence: excel in school to secure admission into a reputable college, graduate with honors to secure a lucrative job, and embark on the journey of raising a family, destined to repeat the same cycle of aspirations and necessities—an endless loop in the cul-de-sac of **wants** and **needs**.

We must evaluate **why** this contemporary philosophy has even perfused and engrained itself in today's education **system**. A cursory examination reveals the origins and the transition from an agrarian, farming society to a modern industrialized manufacturing one.[28] The structure of the education **system**, from the regimented school bells to the desk arrangement of stations, classroom size, lunch breaks with your lunch box, and the very concept of time, all echo the influence of Prussia's military model.[29] This design was intended to shape a conformist workforce rather than fostering independent thinkers, drawing a parallel between the regimented Prussian military training and the structured environment of factory workers within the educational **system**.

What about secondary education? Does it truly cultivate critical thinkers and diverse viewpoints? [30] While some individuals pursue knowledge through universities, which can be beneficial and aligned with their quest, others may have very different goals or learning styles and prefer hands-on experience, on-the-job training, or technical schools. Obtaining a degree from college signals to employers that you can consistently meet deadlines and fulfill assignments within a fixed timeframe. However, it's essential to recognize that diverse paths and methodologies exist for acquiring valuable skills and knowledge.

Why is this important? Paraphrasing the advice of Emilia Clarke's father, never argue with one whose TV is bigger than their bookshelf. With this in mind, we need to challenge the conventional beliefs taught to the masses about money, we need to start looking at assets and liabilities differently, and encouraging the adoption of a mindset that focuses on financial independence and wealth-building strategies, achieving all our desired **wants-needs**, rather than the traditional course of action.[31]

In turn, we need to upgrade our thinking in order to upgrade our lives. Before we can achieve BIG things, we must think BIG things. Success has truly little to do with intelligence, having rich parents, being lucky, or whatever. SUCCESS is determined not so much by the size of one's brain as it is by the size of one's thinking.[32] A simple **paradigm** shift can ignite the neurons firing one's achievement to success.

One simple enduring game, that highlights a change of thought, and has been cherished through generations, passed down, from a **Rich Thinking** father to son, is the whimsical "Who Paid Less" game. It's not merely a game of purchases; it's a journey through negotiation prowess, a quest for the most cost-effective vendor, and good old-fashioned bargain hunting. In the midst of it, a **paradigm** unfolds—the realization that when what one wearing is identical to another, yet one has only invested a mere 10%, this leaves the **wants-needs** pocketbook with a generous 90% to splurge on other delights. Just because one pays more doesn't mean it's worth more. It's a lighthearted dance with frugality, where laughter echoes through the aisles, proving that sometimes the best deal isn't just about the price tag but also the joy of the hunt. Unfortunately, this only gets us halfway.

Most would consider their homes an asset, not within this financial philosophy.[27] They are often classified as liabilities rather than assets because they typically do not generate income and, in fact, often incur ongoing expenses. According to these **paradigms**, an asset is something that puts money in your pocket, while a liability takes money out of your pocket. While homes may appreciate over time, they come with significant costs such as mortgage payments, property taxes, insurance, and maintenance. In the case of a personal residence, although it may appreciate, it doesn't contribute to ongoing cash flow unless it's being rented out. These are non-producing assets.[27]

Your **shiny** new car, despite how it might appear on your accounting balance sheet, does not qualify as an asset. Cars are infamous for draining finances, a fact acknowledged by businesses that often prefer leasing them. While transportation might be a necessity, the accompanying costs of depreciation, fuel, maintenance, and insurance can quickly accumulate. Following the principles of the **Rich Thinking** philosophy, it is recommended to prioritize income-generating assets that not only cover these expenses but also contribute to wealth accumulation. Robert's emphasis on distinguishing between assets generating cash flow and liabilities consuming it underscores the importance of building a portfolio centered around income-producing assets.[27] This approach aligns with the goal of achieving financial independence and freedom.

The financial independence **paradigm** beckons a transformative shift in mindset, liberating us from the monotonous cycle of living paycheck to paycheck. It encourages the embrace of a strategic and entrepreneurial approach, laying the foundation for financial success. Yet, to achieve this pervasive belief, it often centers on "you can," fostering a positive and proactive outlook, rather than succumbing to the limiting notion of "you can't."[33] It's a rallying call to reshape our financial narratives and carve pathways towards prosperity through innovation, perception, and resilience.

In the wardrobe of life, the threads of **Rich Thinking** weave a pattern of abundance, wisdom, and empowerment. As we navigate the complexities of finance and forge our paths towards prosperity, let us remember the lessons of Rich Dad and Poor Dad, embracing the power of financial education, strategic investment, and entrepreneurial spirit. With each step forward, may we expand our minds, enrich our lives, and inspire others to join us on the journey to financial freedom. For in the world of **Rich Thinking**, every dream is attainable, and every aspiration is within reach.

THE STOREFRONT: DEFINING YOUR BUSINESS

Illuminate the path and welcome aboard the exhilarating voyage of defining your business! Much like the buildup before the climax of a thrilling story, this journey is filled with anticipation, creativity, and a hint of unpredictability. So, what's the big reveal? It's not just about what you're selling; it's about shaping an identity and creating an experience that strikes a chord with your customers. This chapter serves as your compass for navigating the process of defining your business—from conceptualizing the *vision* to understanding the *purpose* to support it—making the dream.

RIVER FOR WATER

To embark on the journey of building a business, let's transport ourselves several centuries back, well before the Industrial Revolution and the marvels of Rome's aqueducts. Picture awakening each morning, greeted by the radiant sun, stretching in anticipation of the day ahead. Wrapping the comforting warmth of fur around your feet, shielding them from the harsh cold ground, you rise, eager for the new day. Swiftly grabbing your trusty bucket, you set out on the familiar path towards the river.

As you walk, the gentle murmur of the brook grows audible, the water flowing through pebbles in the distance. The sun's warmth filters through the trees, illuminating your favorite watering hole. Filling your bucket, you lift the weight into your hands and trace back the path you traversed. Approaching home, you anticipate the joy of starting your day, beginning with the ritual of kindling a fire to brew your first cup of coffee.

Day after day, week after week, year after year, this routine defines your mornings—a shared norm among villagers, a tradition and knowledge passed from father to son. Yet, what if there existed a better way? What if, with a modest investment, a bit of extra time, and unwavering dedication, you could reclaim this time lost to routine?

Your voyage begins anew, this time with a twist. Each day, you dig a little hole, extend it a bit further, and gradually commit a few extra minutes trenching towards the river. Small, consistent efforts accumulate and compounds make a substantial difference in the end. This is no quick fix; every step adds up. Until one day, in a shorter time than one might believe, you have reached your goal. It's a journey that demands perseverance, but quitting ensures never reaching the goal.

Part 1: Defining the Register

In the quaint village, deeply entrenched in its traditional ways, the sight of, you, one villager diligently digging a trench to the river stirred a ripple of bemusement and mockery among the community. The established social norms, rooted in generations of routine, couldn't fathom the purpose behind such an unconventional endeavor. Whispers echoed through the cobbled streets as the villagers, bound by shared expectations, exchanged curious glances, and suppressed laughter.

The act of trenching, a departure from the familiar routine of fetching water from the river, became the subject of gentle jests and raised eyebrows. Unaccustomed to this novel approach, the villagers struggled to comprehend the *vision* of a different, more efficient way. Little did they know that within the persistent rhythm of those digging strokes lay the seeds of transformation, challenging the village's ingrained norms and paving the way for a **paradigm** shift.

As rain falls the next day, threatening to stall your progress, you stand resilient against the whispers of doubt. You remind yourself that you're laying the foundation not just for your goal but for personal growth. Rain or shine, success belongs to you. In the face of obstacles and naysayers, you declare, "Success is mine." You shout back at those whispers "Success is mine." Feel like, don't feel like it; "Success is mine." Failure, setbacks, or the doubters; "Success is mine."

Your persistence yields visible results, inspiring bursts of dedication and courage. As you near completion, the work becomes not only easier but also more enjoyable. The *vision* of achievement eclipses any internal doubts. With the final pieces laid, a profound sense of pride and glory washes over you—you've conquered yourself; "Success is mine."

The next morning, your feet meet the same ground, but now, there's no lengthy journey ahead, only a short stroll to the kitchen. Turning on the faucet, freshwater sparkles into the kettle. You have triumphed. A broad smile graces your face as you sit back, warming your feet by the open flame, glaring at the crackling wood; "Fire, you are next!"

Stepping back for a moment in the midst of the village's whispers and raised eyebrows regarding the unconventional trench-digging endeavor, what if a transformative idea took root? What if, instead of embarking on this journey solo, you could recruit the assistance of fellow villagers? The prospect of communal involvement became a catalyst for change. As the first few curious souls joined in, a sense of collective purpose emerged, and the community began to appreciate the power of shared effort. The communal spirit ignited, and soon, a small team formed, each member contributing their share of effort to the daily excavation. Together, these villagers, each contributing a portion of their time during the workday, formed a dedicated team.

The impact was staggering—a realization unfolded that the combined strength of many, even if only for a few hours daily, equaled the productivity of a single person working full-time. The notion that individual efforts, when united, could achieve as much as a singularly dedicated endeavor permeated the community. The act of each villager contributing a fraction of their time demonstrated the profound impact of teamwork, challenging the traditional belief that a single individual should bear the burden alone.

This collaborative effort not only accelerated the trench-digging progress but also exemplified the potential of shared endeavors to challenge ingrained norms and amplify the efficiency of the entire community.

Maybe people will make fun of you for digging a hole in your yard, or maybe they already think something is wrong with you, but just wait, be diligent, and "watch your enemies float down the river."

Here, a journey filled with *purpose* took us from active to passive work (**rich thinking**), and the beginning of building the **system**, unfolds. Then, in time, we'll infuse your *vision* with structure and understand—it's not just about you.

SYSTEM

As we venture into the exploration of the **system**, let's transport ourselves back to the contemporary era, recalling the days of adolescence when some of us rode the short bus to school. The crux of the matter lies in the juxtaposition between "I want to be" and "I want to start." The former implies a desire for a particular identity or state, often associated with achieving a specific goal or outcome. On the other hand, the latter emphasizes the initiation of a process or journey, signaling the beginning of a proactive effort to bring aspirations to fruition.

While "I want to be" reflects a destination, "I want to start" underscores the crucial step of commencing the transformative journey towards that desired state. The choice between the two phrases carries implications for mindset, action, and the commitment needed to translate ambitions into reality.

In visioning young Emma, fueled by the dream of becoming a doctor. Even at her tender age, she was aware of the arduous journey ahead—a path marked by sleepless nights, grueling 20-hour days during residency, and the eventual crossroads of choosing between employment within a hospital **system** or embarking on the entrepreneurial path of <u>starting her own practice</u>.

As Emma grew older, her determination crystallized into a fervent ambition: she wanted to become a doctor and have her own practice. However, she soon discovered that the road to achieving her dreams was paved with trials that tested not only her intellect but also her resilience and dedication. those years sacrificing her college nightlife studying just to get admitted into medical school.

In the surrender of a traditional college experience, Emma was accepted and embarked on her journey into the world of medical education. Days turned into nights, and nights into early mornings, as she poured over textbooks, dissected cadavers, and navigated the labyrinth of medical knowledge. Time became an even scarcer commodity, and each moment was more precious. While her peers reveled in the fleeting pleasures of youth, Emma sacrificed social events, outings, and even family gatherings to stay immersed in the vast sea of medical literature.

Her pursuit of becoming a doctor demanded sacrifices beyond the confines of time. Sleep became a luxury and fatigue an unwelcome companion. Emma's dedication became her compass, steering her through the challenges that littered her path. The demands of medical school were not just academic; they were emotional and physical. Yet, through the sleepless nights and stressful exams, Emma persisted.

As the years unfolded, Emma's dedication deepened. She witnessed the fragility of life and the profound impact that a caring, skilled physician could have on a patient's journey. Her journey was marked by triumphs and setbacks, but with each obstacle, she emerged stronger, more resilient, and more committed to her calling.

Emma's journey was not just about acquiring knowledge; it was a transformation of the soul. She learned to balance empathy with clinical detachment, to navigate the corridors of the hospital with grace, and to communicate not just with words but with the profound language of compassion. The sacrifices she made were not in vain, for they forged her into a beacon of hope for those in need and an example on her path.

On the day Emma donned her white coat and recited the Hippocratic Oath, she carried with her not just the weight of medical knowledge but the wisdom that comes from sacrifice and dedication.

The Storefront: Defining Your Business

Driven by a deep-seated passion for healing, white coat in hand, and a profound commitment to making a difference, Emma, a skilled and empathetic medical professional, decided to embark on the next chapter in her career by starting her own medical practice. After years of rigorous education, countless hours of clinical experience, and a dedication that surpassed the challenges of medical school, Emma felt a calling to create a space where she could provide personalized and compassionate care.

Drawing inspiration from her diverse background and fueled by the desire to shape healthcare with a patient-centric approach, Emma meticulously planned the launch of her practice investing her last savings and piled with more than her student debt. With a clear and specific vision, a commitment to excellence, and a genuine connection to her community, Emma's journey into entrepreneurship became a testament to her unwavering dedication to the well-being of those she served. As the doors to her practice opened, Emma's dream of blending medical expertise with a human touch came to fruition, marking the beginning of a transformative and patient-focused healthcare experience.

Yet this does not tell the whole story. What transpires if Emma falls ill? How do her patients stay informed or become her patients to begin with? How many staff did she painstakingly sift through to assemble the right team, now obligated to sustain employment and care of that family unit week after week? Emma's practice encompasses every aspect of a typical business: marketing, payroll, overhead, and more. However, a fundamental distinction exists—Emma is compelled to show up daily to attend to her patients. Can she receive payment, or does the practice generate revenue if appointments must be rescheduled? The equipment remains idle without a patient, yet the monthly bills persist, demanding payment.

This same **paradigm** can be used for others from lawyers to hairdressers. What they have all done is buy their **J.O.B.** If they don't physically show up to work, if they don't actively do the work, there is no revenue, there is no money. Compounded on Emma's hard work and dedication her **wants-needs** are still imbalanced. The introspection of Emma's ultimate aim was solely to assist people without concerning herself with anything beyond that, it would be one scenario. However, her passion and aspiration extend far beyond such a safe straightforward goal. To balance the **want-needs** with **rich thinking**, the **paradigm** at hand, is freedom from time, the paramount difference between active and passive income.

Utilizing Rich Dad's Cashflow Quadrant, Robert conveys that employees and self-employed individuals operate within the world of active income, requiring ongoing effort to generate earnings.[34] In contrast, a business **system** and investors fall into the category of passive income, allowing for continuous wealth accumulation without constant active involvement. Those who work less, earn more, pay fewer taxes, and achieve financial freedom often do so by skillfully leveraging various foundational resources. It's not all about how much money you make, it's about how much money you keep.[35]

Robert explains through his examination of each quadrant in terms of unique advantages: employees leverage time for money, self-employed individuals leverage their services for income, businesses (B-type) leverage **systems**, and investors leverage money. The true purpose of a business.

Those in the investor and business quadrants of the passive world, comprising only 5% of the population, divide 95% of today's income with minimal ongoing effort. In contrast, the majority, 95% of individuals, the employee and self-employed quadrants, heavily depend on active work to earn income, viciously contending for the remaining 5%.[34] Now we can see, that a business without a **system** to leverage is not, in the essence of passive income, a true business.

True businesses, those emphasizing scalability and efficiency, leverage **systems** as a fundamental strategy for generating income—just as getting water from the river. Instead of relying solely on individual efforts or ad-hoc methods, true businesses focus on developing robust **systems** that can operate consistently and predictably.

Dave knew this, owning many other fast-food franchises, but he desired to develop something unique in the adolescent fast-food realm. He initiated a burger establishment and named it after his own daughter, Wendy. In a moment of inspiration at home, he even advised Wendy to tie her hair in pigtails and captured the iconic images. Adorned in a blue-and-white-striped dress crafted by her mother, these photos transformed Wendy's into a globally recognized fast-food mascot.

However, Dave is not seen daily opening doors, igniting fryers, or adjusting signs; one would hope not, he's deceased. Nor is he flipping burgers on his stove at home. Nonetheless, every day worldwide, Wendy's doors swing open, ready to serve customers. This illustrates the significance of a franchise as a crucial **system**, prompting individuals to invest money to access a pre-built structure that ensures operational continuity and passive income.

By establishing and fine-tuning these **systems**, true businesses create a foundation for <u>scalable and repeatable income generation</u>. The goal is to minimize reliance on individual efforts and create a more predictable and efficient operation. This approach allows the business to adapt to growth, changes in demand, and market fluctuations while maintaining a focus on delivering value and driving sustainable income streams.

Yet, consider Emma's desire to make a difference in helping people. Is it possible to own a practice or hospital **system** without undergoing years of medical school and practicing as a doctor beforehand? Absolutely! Constructing a **system** is tailored for those exact broader perspectives, one where your direct involvement is not a prerequisite but a choice.

One may want to argue that certain small enterprises are financially successful. Many of these "mom-and-pop" businesses excel in their operations, efficiently completing necessary tasks and generating commendable income for the owners and their families. However, when evaluating them as genuine businesses, the crucial aspect of constructing a **system** capable of functioning independently is often overlooked. A true business is characterized by the ability to operate seamlessly even in the absence of its owner, to have replaced themselves completely. If the business comes to a halt when you take a vacation or become ill, it doesn't fulfill the criteria of a genuine **rich thinking system**.

Systems serve as the cornerstone of any successful enterprise, functioning as the intricate gears that propel the entire machinery forward, all neatly encapsulated within the metaphorical **little ol'** black box. This box is the repository of your business's secret sauce—a precious concoction of processes and methods that define your unique identity, culminating in the creation of your distinctive product or service.

In the world of business, it's analogous to a straightforward transaction: input a dollar, and out comes a cookie. This fundamental black box is the blueprint, the treasure map guiding your journey through the complex landscape of entrepreneurship and the realization of a true business.

Constructing a **system** demands thoughtful consideration and strategic planning. Picture it as a challenging puzzle where every piece, when perfectly placed, contributes to the seamless functioning of the entire mechanism. Yet, this isn't a one-size-fits-all endeavor; it's an evolving process. The blueprint may undergo modifications—the rooms may expand or contract, and the product itself may undergo a metamorphosis.

Nevertheless, the essence remains unchanged, reminding us that **chicken is** still **chicken**, regardless of the variations of flavor. So now, we embark on the journey of tweaking, observing, and refining, ensuring that our **system** not only runs but thrives in the dynamic ecosystem of a passive-income business.

Part 1: Defining the Register

END IN MIND

In designing one's goals and your system with *purpose* and *vision*, always start with "beginning with the **end in mind**." These wise words are from the 2nd habit of The 7 Habits of Highly Effective People by Covey. The 2nd habit encourages individuals to define their long-term goals and ultimate purpose before engaging in any endeavor.[7] It invites people to consider their values, principles, and aspirations as they navigate the journey of life. In the heavenly realm of manifestation as a religious concept, this habit aligns with the idea of setting intentions in accordance with one's faith or belief **system**.

This religious or spiritual contexts that emphasize manifestation, individuals may believe in the power of thought, prayer, or intention to influence the course of their lives. They might envision their desired outcomes, aligning their actions and decisions with the principles and values rooted in their faith. This practice is akin to "beginning with the **end in mind**" by focusing on a future state that is in harmony with one's spiritual or religious beliefs.

For example, in certain New Thought or metaphysical belief **systems**, there's a notion that one can shape their reality through the power of positive thinking, visualization, and alignment with divine principles. This process involves setting clear intentions and affirming the desired outcomes in faith and belief that these intentions will manifest in reality. Biblically stated "Ask, and it will be given to you; seek, and you will find; knock, and it will be opened to you. For everyone who asks receives, and the one who seeks finds, and to the one who knocks it will be opened."[36]

Whatever path you take on your journey, know the consequences and never lose sight of your end goal. "Midway upon the journey of our life I found myself within a forest dark, For the straightforward pathway had been lost" uttered Dante. Beginning with the **"End in Mind"** is based on imagination—the ability to envision in your mind what you cannot at present see with your eyes. It is based on the principle that all things are created twice. There is a mental (first) creation and a physical (second) creation. The physical creation follows the mental, just as a building follows a blueprint.

If you don't make a conscious effort to visualize who you are and what you want in life, then you empower other people and circumstances to shape you and your life by default. It's about connecting again with your uniqueness and then defining the personal, moral, and ethical guidelines within which you can most happily express and fulfill yourself. Having the **end in mind** is the same within your business as well.

The Storefront: Defining Your Business

To achieve success, mastery in planning is paramount, transcending the aesthetics of the workspace, whether adorned with glass or wood desks, cozy sheep rugs, or branded elements. The critical factor of the **end in mind** lies in the meticulous design of the flow, the workspace, and the **system** in place. The success of your endeavors hinges on the strategic orchestration of these elements, irrespective of the external trappings. This mastery sets the foundation for efficient operations and paves the way for the comprehensive assessment detailed in the upcoming "**Count Your Steps**" section.

We can see and will explore even more throughout this book, on how incredibly powerful thoughts are, how they are completely intertwined with our actions and emotions, and those of others. This begs the question does actions influence our thought or does our thought influence our actions?

Consider the future implications of your decisions for your **little ol'** business, much like a child contemplating a college major. Instead of focusing solely on immediate **wants-needs**, envision the long-term impact and align your choices with your ultimate goals. This forward-thinking approach ensures that your decisions today contribute to the realization of your broader aspirations.

Conversely, a true business is a broader and more encompassing entity. It constitutes the entire framework or **system** involved in economic, commercial, or industrial pursuits, offering a product or service to customers. A business comprises diverse components, including management, operations, marketing, finance, and strategy, all collaboratively functioning together harmoniously to generate value and provide products or services to customers.

Businesses that have **rich thinking** are fundamentally centered around long-term sustainability and expansion. The objective is to construct something that transcends individual endeavors, aiming for a legacy that extends beyond even the lifetimes of your children's children. The pursuit is to leave behind a lasting and meaningful legacy, contributing to a legacy that will endure for generations to come.

This requires us to take a more analytical approach on what your business is. Do you have an idea? Is it a **system** or just a product? Does it entail your **end in mind**? When looking at traditional products, tangible or intangible items that are created mainly through a manufacturing or creative process and offered for sale or use, these can be a starting point.

Part 1: Defining the Register

Now let's take it a little further. How many variations does it have? How are you going to get it to your customers? Yes, you can have a great product, anything from a physical object like a smartphone or a piece of software to a service like consulting or education, but **chicken is chicken** and are only the offerings that businesses provide to meet today's customers' desire, the **wants-needs** of your target market, which all have a proverbial shelf life.[37]

Although a product holds significance in the business landscape, the triumph of a business extends beyond the confines of a specific product—it rests on the foundation of purpose. When constructing this **little ol' register**, it's imperative to delve into the "what for" question. The response may manifest in simplicity, such as "The purpose is engaging in any activities or business permitted under the laws of the jurisdiction and authority where these activities are performed" yet a purpose can be much more intricate and meaningful.

A business **system** has such facets to help it engage in any activities it should desire as well as effective management, marketing and customer relations, financial stewardship, and adaptation to market changes. Each section must be thought out and planned. A business often involves a range of products or services, and it may diversify its offerings to mitigate risks and tap into different markets. A single product, on the other hand, does not constitute an entire business, it is not your **register**, but it is what it rings up. A product is not a business, but can it be developed into one?

Let's delve into an anecdotal rendition of one of America's beloved beverages, cola. In 1893, Caleb Bradham introduced "Brad's Drink" at his drugstore in New Bern, North Carolina. During this era, predating the dominance of modern Coca-Cola and Pepsi corporations, Brad's Drink could be purchased directly from his little drugstore. The brand gradually became popular amount the town and its reach as popularity surged.

On the winding and tortuous path of Caleb's journey with his beloved drink, an unforeseen chapter unfolded during the tumultuous era of World War I. As the war cast its shadows, hardships descended upon Caleb, a humble worker in the land of business, not a visionary founder. The winds of adversity blew fiercely, and the storm of challenges battered the foundation of his once-thriving product. The scarcity and exorbitant prices of sugar, a crucial ingredient for his concoction, cast a shadow over Caleb's aspirations. Rationing, like a heavy anchor, restrained his *vision*, limiting the scope of his ambitions to the immediate concerns of survival. Amid the chaos, Caleb's unwavering focus remained fixated on his cherished drink, a beacon of hope in the darkened landscape of war-torn challenges.

The hardships didn't just stop at the scarcity of ingredients; they extended to the very core of Caleb's *vision*. His acute foresight, usually guided by the clarity of *purpose*, now found itself navigating treacherous waters. The challenges became a formidable adversary, hindering Caleb from producing an adequate supply of syrup, subjecting him to the capricious whims of fluctuating sugar prices, and wrestling with the Herculean task of meeting the relentless demands of consumers. In the crucible of wartime tribulations, Caleb's journey transformed into a poignant saga, a tale of resilience amid adversity, and a testament to the indomitable spirit that thrives even in the darkest corners of history.

Within the hushed corridors of corporate intrigue, whispers of Caleb's intentions reached the ears of his chief rival, sparking an unexpected turn of events. A clandestine proposition lingered in the air, catching the attention of Caleb's top competitor. The clandestine boardroom, perched high above the city, became the stage for a covert dance of negotiations. Caleb's desire to exit gracefully from the battlefield was no longer a mere rumor but a tangible opportunity, a chance for his adversary to acquire the remnants of Brad's Drink and, perhaps, put an end to the longstanding rivalry.

In the shadows of secret meetings, the details of the potential buyout were meticulously crafted, shrouded in an air of confidence. Caleb, the underdog in this high-stakes game, brought forth his two Ford Model T wagons, symbolic chariots of his entrepreneurial journey, and the last few precious cases of Brad's Drink. The proposal, a delicate dance of words and numbers, unfolded with the promise of a smooth exit for Caleb, leaving behind a legacy encapsulated in those final cases. The clandestine negotiations, fueled by both pragmatism and a touch of nostalgia, held the potential to reshape the landscape of the beverage industry, leaving analysts in anticipation of the outcome that loomed in the near future.

In the face of Caleb's unexpected proposition, Brand-X found themselves at a crossroads that defied the traditional playbook of business strategy. Rather than entertaining the prospect of Caleb's buyout, Brand-X boldly declared, "We won't buy you; we'll put you out of business." This audacious decision wasn't merely a strategic move; it was a testament to Brand-X's identity and pride. The company, deeply woven into the fabric of history, chose to safeguard its legacy rather than succumb to the allure of a monumental alliance. The resounding rejection reverberated through industry headlines, sparking a wave of speculation and leaving analysts grappling with the unconventional path taken by Brand-X.

For Caleb, the rejection wasn't a signal to surrender; it became a catalyst for transformation. He did not let his **mind-killer** dictate his next moves. Fu-

Part 1: Defining the Register

eled by the frustration of the moment, he harnessed it into motivation and perseverance, solidifying his *vision* for a genuine business with a robust **system** at its core. The rejection marked a pivotal moment in the ongoing "cola wars," a narrative of a company steadfastly upholding its unique identity amidst the fierce competition for market dominance. As the wars raged on, Caleb stood resolute, unwavering in his commitment to building a business that would stand the test of time.

Today, as of 2023, Pepsi remains the second most valuable soft drink brand worldwide behind Coca-Cola, locked in this long-standing rivalry infamously known as the "cola wars."[38] Both companies, guarding their secret recipes zealously, engage in fierce competition that captures the hearts and taste buds of millions. Ultimately, Coca-Cola's red and white emblem endured as a symbol of resilience and unwavering commitment to its singular, effervescent *vision*.

Yet, PepsiCo has evolved into an American multinational food, snack, and beverage corporation, far surpassing its humble beginnings as a single drink on a drugstore shelf. Its extensive business spans the food and beverage market, boasting 23 brands with over US$1 billion in annual sales each. Operating globally, PepsiCo's numerous products reach over 200 countries, generating annual net revenues exceeding US$70 billion.[39] With brands like Frito-Lay, Quaker Oats, Gatorade, Tropicana, and more, PepsiCo has become an industry juggernaut.

Starting with a simple drugstore creation and culminating in a corporate behemoth, Caleb confronted the ultimate objective of longevity. Undeterred by challenges, he dug deeper into the depths of determination, refusing to abandon his dream. Unearthing untapped reservoirs of resilience within, he mustered the courage for one more truck, one more product, one more store—each step a progression towards his **end goal**, each addition a vital piece of his growing **system**.

Caleb's unwavering commitment to his *vision* in the face of rejection poses a poignant question to us all: What would you do if you knew you couldn't fail? The tale of Brad's Drink, Pepsi Cola, and the subsequent "cola wars" prompts introspection, challenging each entrepreneur to define the purpose of their own **little ol' register**. In the ever-evolving world of business, where giants clash and underdogs rise, Caleb's journey becomes a source of inspiration to all founders and entrepreneurs. It urges us to reflect on the driving force behind our endeavors, the resilience needed to navigate setbacks, and the determination required to build something enduring.

As we embark on our entrepreneurial quests, Pepsi's story serves as a beacon, inviting us to envision the purpose, finding the **end in mind**, that will shape the destiny of your **little ol' register**.

Part 1: Defining the Register

THE CASH REGISTER: YOUR BUSINESS'S HEARTBEAT

The biggest welcome to "The Cash Register: Your Business's Heartbeat," where we dive into the melodramatic world of your business's central nervous **system**. Picture this: your **register**, like a moody teenager, throws tantrums, monopolizes your time, and occasionally makes you question your life choices. But fear not! In this section, we'll explore the highs and lows of nurturing your **register** from infancy to independence, all while dodging its dramatic outbursts and mind-boggling conundrums. Get ready to laugh, cry, and maybe even pull your hair out as we navigate the wild ride of entrepreneurship together. So, grab your tissues and your sense of humor, because the saga of **Solving the Solution, Register, Mind-Killer** is about to unfold.

We start with classifying your business and the essence that goes beyond labels; it's about clarity and focus. In the upcoming discussions, we'll delve into the nuances of classification, helping you choose the right path for your venture. From deciphering the IRS codes to providing hints for effective business definitions, we're here to set the stage for your journey to a well-defined and successful storefront. Let's turn the key and open the door to a world of possibilities for your business. Whether you're a sole proprietorship, a partnership, a corporation, or something in between, understanding your business's classification is the first step toward strategic growth and sustainable success we're here to set the stage for your journey to a well-defined and successful storefront. Let's turn the key and open the door to a world of possibilities for your business.

SOLVING THE SOLUTION

Is the glass half empty or half full? Well, an optimist would say it's half full, a pessimist would grumble it's half empty, but leave it to an engineer to pipe up and say, "Hey, that glass is clearly the wrong size for the amount of liquid!" And there you have it, folks—a classic case of overthinking brought to you by the brilliant minds of engineers. They'll find a problem even when there isn't one, just for the thrill of solving it!

With the distractions of today's socially challenged attention spans, we have an unprecedented task before us. Understanding, that we should not be clouded by the unknowns on the path of progress, we must provide a solution to the problems at hand. Sound simple enough. The trick may lie in solving how we get to that solution, which solves the problem at hand: **Solving the solutions**.

A straightforward query loomed before the producers: where to shoot the upcoming scene? The answer seemed simple—the pristine, white-sand beaches of Fiji. The solution in hand. Yet, the subsequent question posed a more intricate challenge than the solution itself: how to transport the entire crew to this idyllic location? Enter the answer to the solution as ingenious as it was straightforward—overnight delivery. The entire production equipment and crew gear embarked on a guaranteed journey to Fiji, courtesy of FedEx. Voila! Problem solved, courtesy of the magic of speedy delivery and a hefty checkbook.

In the domain of business solutions, the perennial debate between quick fixes and strategies that are repeatable and scalable stands at a pivotal crossroads. Quick fixes often provide immediate relief, addressing the symptoms rather than the root cause. While they might offer a momentary reprieve, relying solely on quick fixes can lead to a cycle of recurring problems, hindering long-term sustainability. On the contrary, an emphasis on solutions that are repeatable and scalable fosters a proactive approach, identifying underlying issues and creating lasting remedies. It's equivalent to building a robust foundation that can withstand the test of time, allowing for adaptability and growth.

During the filming of a national home makeover show dedicated to helping impoverished families, the production team faced a Herculean task. With only a three-day window for the home, they had to demolish the old structure, frame a new one, and complete the entire rebuilding process. Imagine a swarm of 500 construction workers, a bustling colony of fire ants, operating in continuous eight-hour shifts, all the while strategically avoiding the camera's lens. It was movie magic at its finest.

Now, enter the unexpected plot twist: taxes. To circumvent the looming burden of capital gains tax on the substantial property upgrade, the production team capitalized on a simple tax rule. Improvements made by a renter were exempt from tax, providing a compelling reason for the production to lease the property from the family for those three days.[40] Furthermore, the production's **little ol' register** cleverly exploited the very same transactions as tax deductions, categorizing everything as an expense for a clean write-off.

Knowing your business inside out is fundamental in crafting effective solutions. A deep understanding of operations, customer needs, and market dynamics equips businesses to tailor solutions that align seamlessly with their unique contexts. This knowledge acts as a compass, guiding decision-making and ensuring that solutions are not only relevant but also strategically aligned with the broader business objectives.

The Cash Register: Your Business's Heartbeat

Navigating solutions can be like finding a needle in a haystack, or in our case, a grain of sand in the vast desert. Picture this: it's 3 am, and we're on a quest to locate that exact spot, we scouted during the day and marked with stone. Armed with flashlights and a determination bordering on desperation, the entire crew embarks on a comedic odyssey, trying to set up everything before the client arrives. It's like a circus in the desert, with trailers, generators, and gear coming to life. To all approaching, they are greeted by the faint echoes of "Entry of the Gladiators," a circus melody begins to crescendo in their minds. In the hand of the tallest clown, the GPS on their phones tries its best, but in the middle of the valley of death, it's as accurate as reading the stars. As the chaos unfolds, coffee starts brewing, and just as the client shows; whispers, "Shouldn't you be more resourceful?"—cue the laughter.

Thinking freely and outside the box becomes a mantra for businesses seeking innovative solutions. When faced with challenges, the conventional may not always suffice. Creativity and a willingness to explore uncharted territories can unveil unconventional yet effective solutions. This approach encourages a culture of continuous improvement, propelling the business beyond its comfort zone to discover novel and resourceful paths.

Nevertheless, consider the simplicity of some solutions, like infusing a burst of color into your workspace. Perhaps it involves letting loose the crayons on your desk and adopting the quirky habit of coloring folders. As playfully hinted at in the opening of this book, assigning distinct hues to folders serves more than an aesthetic purpose—it creates a vivid language for your **little ol' register**. Picture the purple folder for employees, playfully leaving them, or you, black and blue (but in a good way). The green folder evokes the essence of money flowing in from customers, while the blue folder signifies the sad cycle of paying vendors. Red folders stand tall for assets, embodying bank accounts, and yellow ones glow with critical importance, maybe housing those sacred **little ol'** tax returns.

Now, envision your desk adorned with an array of green folders nestled aside your **Sim** corporate binder. Beyond the visual appeal, this simple act becomes a multisensory engagement, offering a line of defense for your **little ol' register**—one that communicates across the spectrum to any **hats** worn up and down the organizational hierarchy.

The ability to improvise, adapt, and overcome encapsulates the resilience required in the face of evolving challenges.[41] Markets fluctuate, technologies advance, and unforeseen obstacles emerge. Businesses that embrace flexibility and agility can pivot swiftly, turning challenges into opportunities. The ethos of improvisation allows for on-the-fly adjustments, adaptation ensures alignment with the changing landscape, and overcoming challenges becomes a testament to a business's enduring strength. In essence, solving solutions is not just a task; it's a dynamic process intertwined with the very fabric of a business's journey.

Alright, now that we've established our thirst for knowledge, our desire for a purpose-driven **system**, and our fondness for the humble "**little ol'**," we're ready to embark on our journey. Remember, in the grand scheme of things, there's nothing entirely novel—everything has its roots, just like the universal presence of **chicken** in various forms. With these foundational principles in mind, we're off to a promising beginning, echoing the timeless wisdom of the proverbial **blind man's** perspective.

To effectively navigate this process, it's essential to make each action clear and intentional. Just as you wouldn't hide the books you need to read or the healthy snacks you want to eat, don't obscure the actions necessary for business decisions or needs.[42] By keeping your objectives visible and your intentions transparent, you can stay focused and motivated to form new habits and make progress towards your goals.[7]

Small, incremental improvements are key to long-term success. As James advises, focusing on just "1% improvement" each day can lead to significant results over time. [42] By consistently making small changes and building positive habits, you can harness the power of time as your ally. Remember, challenges are opportunities for growth, and how you approach each moment defines not only your present but also your future. Embrace the journey, stay committed to your *vision*, and let each decision bring you closer to your desired outcome.

Therefore, in the journey of solving problems and achieving goals, it's crucial to start with the **end in mind**. By envisioning the desired outcome and working backwards, you can identify the steps needed to reach your destination. Every decision made along the way becomes a strategic move towards **solving the solution**. Just as in the **paradigm** of the **blind men**, where each individual's perception contributes to a greater understanding, every action taken is a piece of the puzzle leading to success.

This is not a problem! This is a challenge! You decide on how this moment defines your life. You decide on how this moment defines your future.

REGISTER

Whether you're running a church, a bakery, or a construction business, the universal thread that ties them together is the register. In each scenario, the cash **register** becomes the epicenter of revenue generation and transactions. Its humble presence signifies not just the financial heartbeat of the enterprise, but also the pulse of customer interactions and business operations.

Consider the bustling bakery, where the sweet aroma of freshly baked goods fills the air. Behind the counter, the cash **register** diligently records each sale. It becomes the nexus where the exchange of delicious treats for currency takes place. In this setting, the **register** is not just a tool for financial accounting; it's the facilitator of customer satisfaction, ensuring that every pastry or loaf of bread contributes to the revenue stream.

Now, shift the scene to a construction site. The heavy machinery hums in the background as contractors and builders move about their tasks. Amidst the organized chaos, the **register** at the site office becomes the focal point for tracking expenses, billing clients, and managing project finances. Each transaction recorded echoes the intricate dance of resources and revenue that propels the construction business forward.

Even in the serene setting of a church, where spirituality takes precedence, the **register** plays a vital role. Donations, tithes, and other contributions find their way into the **register**, not just as financial entries but as expressions of faith and support. The **register** becomes a conduit for the congregation to actively participate in the sustenance of the church community.

In essence, the cash **register** transcends its role as a mere accounting tool. It becomes a narrative of the business, chronicling every interaction, transaction, and contribution. It symbolizes the bridge between service and sustainability, reminding entrepreneurs of the interconnectedness of revenue, customer engagement, and the systematic operations that keep the business thriving.

In the realm of business and entrepreneurship, the **little ol' register** stands as a symbol of more than just financial transactions; it encapsulates the core idea, the systematic approach, and the ultimate solution. Imagine it as your entrepreneurial twin, a clone of yourself that embodies the essence of your business strategy and is infused with the soul of the *vision* and *purpose*. Your **little ol' register** becomes a faithful sidekick, a cookie-cutter companion that mirrors your methods and reflects the **system** you've meticulously crafted.

Cloning yourself in the form of a systematic approach is the secret sauce to scalability and consistency. It's about preserving the successful elements, replicating the effective processes, and ensuring that the essence of your business remains intact. Your **little ol' register** becomes the tangible manifestation of your entrepreneurial DNA, a reliable tool to **register** not just transactions but the very essence of your business.

In the journey of entrepreneurship, the **system** is your ally in navigating challenges and seizing opportunities. Your **little ol' register**, with its simplicity, becomes a powerful instrument for keeping the **end in mind**. It's a constant reminder of the overarching goals and the systematic steps needed to achieve them. As you clone your processes, you establish a foundation for growth, expansion, and sustained success, all neatly recorded in the unassuming pages of your **little ol' register**.

When you infuse the **little ol'** principle into the heartbeat of the **register system**, something magical happens—it gains a personality, a character, a distinct identity. Picture it one day donning a political party badge, undergoing a wardrobe makeover, and perhaps even having to shell out the necessary coins to enjoy a ride it's finally tall enough to experience. Your **little ol' register**, now more than a mere transaction recorder, steps into the realm of responsibilities that come with growth.

Just like a student in school, your **little ol' register** embarks on a journey of learning. It faces tests in the form of transactions, fills out financial forms, and, in a world of regulations, hopefully, learns not to talk back to the authorities. Your **little ol' register** serves as the guiding force, instilling a sense of discipline and responsibility in the business' actions. It's not just about recording sales; it's about navigating the complexities of business life.

Much like a young individual navigating the challenges of adolescence, the **register**, under the influence of the **little ol'** principle, begins to comprehend the intricacies of financial maturity. It learns to balance its books, understand the language of receipts and ledgers, and adapt to the evolving surroundings of business regulations. This education becomes a pivotal chapter in your **little ol' register's** existence.

So, as your **little ol' register** grows and evolves, it becomes more than a mechanical device for financial transactions. It becomes a symbol of resilience, adaptability, and responsible engagement with the business world. Your **little ol' register** as a mentoring **system**, guides this growth, ensuring that the **register** not only rings up sales but also rings in a harmonious harmony between operational efficiency and ethical financial practices.

As we wrap up the **register** section, take a moment to delve into the emotional core of your business **system**—a living entity with its own profound narrative, a journey marked by triumphs and trials.

- **Craft a compelling story:** Your **register** carries a story, a saga that unfolds from its birth, navigating through growth, and aspiring towards an unwritten future. Illuminate those pivotal moments that etched its identity into the fabric of your business.

- **Define the problem:** Understand how people will interact with your **system**. Envision its appearance and identify those responsible for its functionality. Clearly articulate the challenges it addresses—solution.

- **Practice as much as you can:** Rehearse the workings of your **system**, measuring progress and improve each iteration. Familiarize yourself with its intricacies, ensuring smooth operation and adaptability to evolving needs.

- **Be realistic:** Ground your expectations in reality. Acknowledge the strengths and limitations of your **system**, setting specific achievable goals that align with your business *vision*.

In essence, your **system** and *vision* serve as the pulse, the very soul residing at the center of your **little ol' register**. They embody the core principles that propel your business forward.

MIND-KILLER

As we grow up, we gradually become aware of the many things in the external world that are largely beyond our ability to control. These include other people in general and most events in our lives. Being able to recognize what we can and can't control will be the wisdom that is needed to move forward.[43] The knowledge of how to break the chains that enslave our minds.[44] Initially, this is difficult to accept, but a more shocking realization is that there are many things about ourselves that we may seem powerless to control.

We all grapple with moments of uncertainty, fears, and instances of shame and disappointment, yet within each of us lies a resilient **warrior**. One prevalent fear, particularly noticeable after achieving a promotion or starting a new job, is known as "Imposter Syndrome." It manifests itself as a pervasive feeling of anxiety and an internal reluctance to acknowledge one's success, despite external evidence of high performance. Individuals grappling with Imposter Syndrome struggle to view themselves objectively, often downplaying or dismissing the merit of their accomplishments and skills.

This condition leads to an unsettling sense of being a "fraud" or "phony," fostering self-doubt and undermining confidence. It's essential to recognize that the fear we build up in our minds is often more daunting than the actual situation we face, and acknowledging our accomplishments with merit can help dispel the shadows of doubt. [45] What you are afraid of is never as bad as what you imagine. Fear not, **nothing is new**: it has all been done before.

Most of us are well adept at justifying almost anything, often even convincing ourselves of the righteous logic or factors in that decision-making process.[33] Could this be the thread woven in the fabric of "Excusitis," a condition where every circumstance is met with an excuse? Frequently, these excuses originate within our own thoughts, emotions, and actions, becoming internal sources of distress.[46] These thoughts might manifest as "I can't overcome my resentment towards my boss for overlooking me for a promotion" or "It's already been done by someone else." Emotions can also play a significant role, like grappling with the sadness, loneliness, and feelings of being unloved after a breakup, or the belief that no one will appreciate or purchase a creation. Behaviors, too, can fall prey to "Excusitis," whether it's an inability to resist sweet desserts or constant snacking, or the reluctance to knock on a door, fearing a potential "no" that could impede a potential "yes." The self-fulfilling prophecy of self-oppression unfolds—Marxism's cyclic consumption, where the self, devours itself in an endless loop—the oppressed and oppressor.

But are we really truly powerless to control our own maladaptive thoughts, overcharged feelings, and self-justified actions? Maybe an old Cherokee Indian story passed down from generation to generation can help us see our way.

One evening an old Cherokee told his grandson about a battle that goes on inside people as he was so filled with anger at another boy who had done him injustice. The grandfather touches the grandson's heart saying "I too, at times, have felt a great hate for those that have taken so much, with no sorrow for what they do. But hate wears you down, and hate does not hurt your enemy. Hate is like taking poison and wishing your enemy would die. I have struggled with these feelings many times."

He shared, "My son, within each of us rages a fierce battle between two wolves. One embodies malevolence, harboring envy, sorrow, regret, greed, arrogance, self-pity, guilt, resentment, inferiority, lies, false pride, superiority, and an ego steeped in anger. The slightest provocation can ignite his wrath, prompting him to engage in incessant conflicts, driven solely by fear. Blanketed in sadness, his anger and hate overpower reason. It's a paralyzing fear, as the release of doubt and anger changes nothing."

He went on to say, "On the other side, goodness prevails—embodying joy, peace, love, hope, serenity, humility, kindness, benevolence, empathy, generosity, truth, compassion, and faith. This wolf exists in harmony with the world, refusing to take offense when none was intended. He engages in battles only when it is right and in the right manner."

"The same fight is going on inside you - and inside every other person, as well. Its strength grows within the soul. Its capacity is limitless and is only controlled by the Master, you." The grandson thought about it for a minute and then asked his grandfather, "Which wolf will win?" The old Cherokee simply replied, "The one you feed."[47]

We all have this wolf inside of us, this same **warrior** who has the determination to take on any challenge that may lie in our way. Every action initiates a chain of events. The White Wolf, once fed, continues to grow in strength and can combat the Black Wolf; the Black Wolf, once fed, can battle the White Wolf easily. One can find the reflection of themselves within this battle as he or she is the Master; the one who controls it.[48]

This fable inspires a shift in your mindset, empowering, and encouraging you to embrace a more positive outlook on life, a perspective that holds immense power. To ignite the burning desire to win, to spark a passionate desire to triumph, an honorable commitment to stand for what is right, and the determination to achieve what one truly believes in.

Unfortunately, most people live their lives in a cowardly way. They hide their **warrior** spirit in fear of the judgment of others feeding the black wolf. They hide the **warrior** in fear of defeat. They don't stand, they back down, cowering from every challenge that life throws their way all in the name of fear. The cowards don't believe in themselves or have the ability to defeat the evil forces, so they don't even try and therefore they lose every time. They are uninspired, unmotivated, and lack the drive and ambition to conquer themselves; conquering fear itself.

Fear is an inherent aspect of human existence, not a manifestation of weak willpower but a testament to the mind's protective nature. It serves as a vital mechanism, alerting us to potential threats—a universal tool shared with most creatures. However, living in a perpetual state of fear is untenable. While the experience of fear itself is not inherently harmful, allowing it to dictate our actions can lead to self-imposed limitations. True empowerment comes from acknowledging and facing our fears, not attempting to eradicate them entirely. In the journey of life, fear becomes a companion, growing alongside us and reinforcing our resilience. It resembles the two sides of a coin, where strength and doubt coexist. Delving deeper into this concept is the **True Power** section of Part 4: Working at the Counter

Understanding the intricate connection between madness and sadness, strength and doubt, as well as perception and emotion, leads to the realization that building strength and courage necessitates a direct confrontation with fear, as it never truly disappears only subsided by its adversary—confidence. As Eleanor Roosevelt wisely stated, true growth emerges when we confront our fears head-on, gaining the strength, courage, and confidence needed to navigate life's challenges.

Warriors are certain in the direction they are going, certain in the inspiration of others, and do not fear failure. They do not look around at others to make sure they are on the right path. They know they are on the right path. They are on the path less traveled. "I Can! I Will! I Must!" Reprogram your mind, control your thoughts, always move forward and out of the fear.

There is zero hesitation deep in the soul of the **warrior**. The white wolf says: "It is all or nothing. I have a clear goal. I have a clear mission. I have a meaningful purpose. I believe in myself. I will give all that I have for this goal for this *vision*. This is my purpose and will not back down. I got this." The **warrior** says: "I am ready. I will act now. I will fight. I will fight with everything I have inside me. I will not be defeated."

Navigating the intricate web of the mind, we encounter the powerful interplay between emotion and logic—a dichotomy that can either propel us forward or act as a formidable obstacle for your **little ol' register**. Zig argues that a positive attitude is crucial to success in any area of life, whether personal or professional. [49] The emphasis that our attitudes are under our control and that we can choose to have a positive outlook on life, regardless of the circumstances. We must cultivate a "can-do" attitude and focus on **solving the solutions** rather than problems.[33, 49] You have this **warrior** inside you, it's the mindset, a **paradigm** of action or inaction.

Drawing inspiration from the mindset **paradigm** in Frank Herbert's Dune, we confront fear as the ultimate **mind-killer**—a force that can obliterate rational decision-making. "I must not fear. Fear is the **mind-killer**. Fear is the little-death that brings total obliteration. I will face my fear. I will permit it to pass over me and through me. And when it has gone past, I will turn the inner eye to see its path. Where the fear has gone there will be nothing. Only I will remain."[50]

The power to choose a positive attitude in the face of challenges becomes a fundamental tool in the entrepreneur's arsenal.

In the battlefield of the mind, the entrepreneur is not a servant but a commander, choosing which wolf to feed. The directive is clear: direct the mind with clarity and focus, allowing fear to pass while remaining committed to goals. In the face of life's uncertainties, the entrepreneur **warrior** declares, "I can handle this. I am ready." This resolute mindset becomes the guiding force, ensuring that emotion, whether good or bad, serves as a tool for success rather than a hindrance to your **little ol' register's** decisions and actions.

Be defiant and confident in your being, pursue your desires with vigor and dignify, pursue your independent beliefs unapologetically, deviate from the collective exhibiting strategic selfishness, and act with aggressiveness and grandiose - be ruthlessly pragmatic.[3, 51] As Nietzsche once said, "Become who you are."

Yet, as we dive headfirst into the deep end of emotions, we find that while positivity can be a driving force, unchecked emotions—be they excitement, dedication, or any extreme—can cloud the waters of logic. It's a delicate balance between embracing the can-do spirit and preventing emotions from becoming a **mind-killer**. The essence lies in cultivating emotional intelligence, the ability to identify and harness emotions to our advantage without succumbing to their potential pitfalls—**true power**.

In the face of daunting challenges, many individuals perceive certain tasks as insurmountable. Imagine the seemingly impossible feat of you selling 100 vacuums in a single day door to door. While this notion may appear absurd to the average person, let's consider a shift in perspective. Picture the scenario where the challenge of personal life or death, involving your prodigy or a loved one, is now at risk if you lose the challenge.

Suddenly, the motivation becomes palpable, demonstrating that the perceived impossibility is often a matter of mindset. It's not the size of the dog in the fight, it's the size of the fight in the dog. You're betting on yourself, adopting the ethos of a growth mindset, trusting in your capacity to evolve and conquer obstacles over time—the "not yet" mentality.[33] It's an empowering and transformative journey from "I will" to "I have," standing on the precipice of the full embodiment of "I am."

As you navigate the battlefield of the mind, summon the clarity and focus needed to navigate through fear. The path to success lies in decisive choices and unwavering commitment. Regardless of the obstacles that life hurls in your direction, cultivate the belief that you possess the strength to overcome them to unfold your full potential. Stay resolute in your pursuit of goals, refusing to

Part 1: Defining the Register

compromise or deviate from the chosen path. Ready yourself for the journey ahead, armed with determination and the unwavering conviction that you are prepared for whatever challenges may arise. Yell "I am Ready."

Part 2: Building the Register

"You don't need to be a genius or a visionary, or even a college graduate for that matter, to be successful. You just need framework and a dream."

– Michael Dell, CEO of Dell

LEARNING OBJECTIVES, THE GOVERNING BOARD MINDSET

In the Governing Board Mindset view, as the ground game becomes closer, the pivotal role of corporate governance in steering the course of organizations towards sustainable growth and success. Here we'll continue to free fall into the intricacies of company structures, governance best practices, and the critical decisions that shape the trajectory of businesses, placing them all in a plan. From understanding market trends to conducting risk analysis, each learning objective is tailored to empower board members with the knowledge and insights needed to drive strategic decision-making and ensure effective oversight.

■ **Understanding Company Structures and Protections:** Explore various forms of company structures, including sole proprietorships, partnerships, corporations, and limited liability companies (LLCs), and understand the legal protections and implications associated with each.

■ **Developing a Comprehensive Business Plan:** Learn how to develop a comprehensive business plan that outlines your vision, purpose, and mission, as well as your market analysis, competitive advantage, and growth strategies.

■ **Defining Vision, Purpose, and Mission:** Understand the importance of defining a clear *vision*, *purpose*, and *mission* for your business, and learn how to articulate these guiding principles effectively to stakeholders.

■ **Analyzing Market Trends:** Explore methods for analyzing market trends, identifying emerging opportunities and threats, and adapting your business strategy accordingly to stay ahead of the competition.

■ **Conducting Risk Analysis:** Develop strategies for identifying, assessing, and mitigating risks, and learn how to effectively respond to crises and disruptions to minimize their impact on your organization. Learn how to conduct a thorough risk analysis, identifying potential risks and developing mitigation strategies to safeguard your business against unforeseen challenges.

■ **Formation, Equity, and Tax Election:** Gain insights into the formation process of your business entity, including considerations for equity distribution, tax election, and compliance with regulatory requirements.

■ **Understanding Organizational Hierarchy:** Explore the concept of organizational hierarchy and the roles and responsibilities of key positions within your company, including the president, board members, and executive team.

■ **Competitor Analysis and Benchmarking:** Learn how to conduct a comprehensive competitor analysis, benchmarking your business against industry peers to identify strengths, weaknesses, opportunities, and threats.

■ **Ensuring Compliance and Governance:** Understand the importance of compliance with legal and regulatory requirements, as well as governance best practices, in ensuring the long-term success and sustainability of your business.

Notes:

GOING TO THE MARKET: KNOWING THE PEOPLE

Path of to "Going to the Market - Knowing the People," is where your **little ol' register** embarks on a journey to conquer the world, one customer at a time. While the dream of global domination may seem lofty, it's essential to begin with a solid foundation rooted in understanding your audience.

In this chapter, we explore the pivotal roles of **Think Customer**, **King of My Own Domain**, and **High Horse** in shaping your business's market strategy. From deciphering consumer preferences to asserting your brand's authority in the competitive landscape, we delve into the intricacies of customer-centric thinking, strategic positioning, and market dominance. So, let's chart a course to success by honing in on the people who hold the key to your **little ol' register's** triumph in the vast marketplace.

THINK CUSTOMER

On the grand stage of business, thinking like a customer involves more than mere empathy; it requires donning the clouded perspective that veils their eyes and uncovering the artistry behind the scenes.[52] Just like the masterful illusionist conceals the secrets behind a captivating performance, businesses craft a circus front for every storefront, meticulously hiding the intricate process of sausage-making from the discerning eyes of the customer. It's a dance of perception, a delicate balance between transparency and illusion.[53, 54]

To embark on this journey, the first step is defining your market—identifying the audience that will witness the show.[52] Some customers linger at the looking window, while others may choose to observe later, each requiring a tailored experience.

In swiping through the intricate web of demographics and psychographics, the aim is to unravel the multifaceted layers that compose the essence of your customer base. Demographics provide the foundational data, encompassing tangible attributes such as age, gender, income, and geographic location. However, to paint a more vivid portrait, psychographics step into the spotlight, focusing on the intangible aspects of consumer behavior, preferences, values, and lifestyles.

Understanding demographics may reveal the "who" of your audience, but psychographics illuminates the **"why"** and "how." What are their aspirations, fears, and motivations? How do they spend their leisure time, and what cultural or societal influences shape their choices? By answering these questions, you embark on a journey beyond mere statistical data, gaining insight into the nuanced intricacies that shape individual decision-making.

This deeper understanding fosters a more personalized and resonant connection with your audience. It allows you to tailor not only your products or services but also **your little ol' register's** messaging and marketing strategies to align seamlessly with the beliefs and desires of your customers. Whether they are driven by a sense of community, environmental consciousness, or a thirst for innovation, psychographics provides the emotional and psychological context that transforms transactions into meaningful relationships. Those who resonate closely with the core of the **wants-needs** circles is bound to form enduring connections, fostering a longer life for your enterprise.

In the intricate dance of business, resonating closely with the core of **wants-needs** circles signifies a profound alignment between your offerings and the essential desires of your target audience.[55] The **wants-needs** circles encapsulate the intersection of what customers truly need and what they ardently desire. Needs represent the practical essentials, the fundamental solutions your product or service provides. Wants, on the other hand, delve into the emotional and aspirational spheres, catering to the deeper yearnings and desires of your customers.

When your business not only addresses the practical necessities but also fulfills the emotional cravings and aspirations of your customers, it forms a connection that transcends the transactional. This resonance engenders a sense of loyalty, as customers find that your offerings not only meet their basic requirements but also speak to their desires and dreams.

As a result, your enterprise becomes more than just a provider of goods or services; it becomes a companion in the journey of fulfilling both the essential and the aspirational. These enduring connections, rooted in a profound understanding of your customers' core needs and wants, contribute to the longevity of your business. Customers are more likely to stay loyal when they feel seen, understood, and fulfilled on multiple levels, fostering a sustained and thriving relationship between your **little ol' register** and its audience.

In this intricate ballet, never underestimate the importance of gratitude. A heartfelt thank you extends not only to the dedicated crew orchestrating the spectacle behind the curtain but, most importantly, to the central figure in this captivating drama: you, the customer. In the intricate symphony of commerce, each patron isn't merely a passive observer but an integral player in shaping the narrative of success. Every touchpoint, every interaction becomes a note contributing to the emotional deposits of the customer.[7] It's in these moments of connection that the harmonious melody of a positive customer experience is composed, and each participant, whether customer or business, plays a crucial role in the grand orchestration of success.

Think customer, discover their desires, and construct your offerings around those **wants-needs**. When contemplating customers, it's essential to extend the scope beyond just individual consumers; the branch of business-to-business transactions must be considered. While business-to-business contracts might take a bit more time to secure, they generally involve less emotional turbulence than dealing with the general population. Much like determining the appropriate price point, defining your customer base and target is paramount.

To get to the correct answer, you must first start by asking the correct questions. Products and services tailored for the consumer market often require a higher volume of units due to the pricing constraints and financial capacities of the average individual. These concepts will be further fortified and grounded in factual exploration in the subsequent chapters.

KING OF MY OWN DOMAIN

Acquire extensive knowledge and expertise within your specific industry or field. Become transformative and intimately familiar with your domain.[56] If your ambition is to excel in sales, immerse yourself in mastering every closing technique, understanding the art of persuasion, and honing the ability to read people like an open book.[57] If your passion lies in neurobiology, examine the intricacies of the human mind, mapping and comprehending the intricate dance of firing neurons within each individual. Strive to be the best in your chosen field. Be the best at what you want. Be the **king (or queen) of your own domain**.

As your **little ol' register** navigates through different industries, it will encounter diverse problems, allowing it to flex various problem-solving muscles. However, **chicken is chicken,** at the core, whether you're selling something or being sold to, the essence remains the same. Even seemingly mundane tasks, such as obtaining insurance for a company **vehicle**, involve a sales process. The insurance agent sells the company the protection it needs, a crucial element for making sales to the company's customers.

When interacting with individuals from other businesses, they are typically oblivious to the intricate details of ownership or board members. Similarly, you should adopt this mindset. You're constructing roles and responsibilities that extend far beyond your tenure, embracing the notion that your **little ol' register** will thrive long after your departure.

Reflecting on the dynamic partnership between Steve Jobs and Steve Wozniak at Apple underscores the importance of recognizing individual domains. While Jobs was known for his marketing and visionary skills, Wozniak was the technical genius behind the early Apple computers. Together, Jobs and Wozniak laid the foundation for what would become one of the most successful and influential technology companies in the world. Yet how was this achieved?

Steve Wozniak's domain at Apple was primarily in the scope of technical and engineering aspects. As the co-founder and technical wizard, Wozniak was responsible for the design and development of Apple's early computers, including the Apple I and Apple II. His expertise was in hardware engineering, and he played a crucial role in creating the technological foundation for Apple's success.

On the other hand, Steve Jobs focused more on the business, marketing, and strategic aspects of Apple. While Jobs certainly had technical knowledge, his strengths lay in his ability to envision products, understand consumer needs, and market them effectively. Jobs was the face of Apple, known for his charismatic presentations and product launches.

We can clearly see the division of roles between Jobs and Wozniak were complementary. Wozniak's technical brilliance allowed Apple to create innovative and groundbreaking products, while Jobs' *vision* and marketing prowess helped bring those products to the masses. Jobs didn't delve deeply into Wozniak's technical domain because each co-founder excelled in their respective areas, and their collaboration was a key factor in Apple's early success. They have the **paradigm** of being the king of their domain.

In the kingdom of so-called "experts," one must acknowledge that everyone perceives themselves as the ruler of their own little kingdom. Some may genuinely possess expertise, while others merely think they do. Dealing with these so-called "experts" involves navigating through their territorial tendencies and occasionally uncovering lies or mistruths. Okay, purported mistruths, to cover their own lack of knowledge or even possibly more sinister actions.

Once upon a time in the quirky world of insurance, a bustling company named Acme Widgets found themselves on the verge of a peculiar adventure. The CEO, Mr. Whizbang, decided it was high time to secure a Missile Insurance Rider for their General Liability policy. **Why**? Well, they had just landed a big contract to supply widgets to a military base, and Mr. Whizbang was convinced that an airborne widget malfunction might just be a real threat. Better safe than sorry, right?

Enter Agent Ned, a well-meaning but somewhat befuddled insurance agent from the local brokerage, who prided himself on being the king of his tiny insur-

Going to the Market: Knowing the people

ance kingdom. He had a little plaque on his desk that read, "Ned, the Insurance Guru." When Mr. Whizbang called to request the Missile Insurance Rider, Agent Ned scratched his head, furrowed his brows, and thought, "Missile insurance? Is that even a thing?" Determined to keep his client happy, he enthusiastically replied, "Absolutely, we've got you covered!"

Little did Agent Ned know that the journey into the world of missile insurance was about to become a crash course in high-flying absurdity. Armed with a stack of insurance manuals and a bewildered expression, he began the quest to unravel the mysteries of missile coverage.

As Agent Ned dove into the fine print, he discovered terms like "trajectory indemnification" and "warhead liability." Bewildered, he wondered if he'd accidentally stumbled into a sci-fi novel. With each clause and subclause, Agent Ned felt like he was decoding a secret language.

The next step involved reaching out to his contacts in the insurance world. However, every conversation seemed to raise more questions than answers. He found himself explaining to fellow agents, "No, I'm not kidding. Missile insurance is a real thing— apparently."

Undeterred, Agent Ned decided to take matters into his own hands. Armed with a borrowed aerospace dictionary and a YouTube crash course on missile mechanics, he delved deep into the complexities of projectiles, guidance **systems**, and aerodynamics. His desk transformed into a makeshift war room, complete with toy rockets and a dartboard labeled "Widget-Seeking Missiles."

Days turned into weeks, and Agent Ned became the unlikely expert in missile insurance. He crafted the Missile Insurance Rider, complete with clauses that even NASA scientists might find impressive. Mr. Whizbang, pleasantly surprised by the newfound expertise of his insurance agent, nodded in approval.

As the final paperwork was signed and the Missile Insurance Rider secured, Acme Widgets was ready to take on the military base contract with confidence. Agent Ned, still recovering from his unexpected foray into rocket science, sighed in relief. He had conquered the bizarre world of missile insurance, and though he may not have grasped all the intricacies, he emerged victorious, slightly wiser, and with a newfound appreciation for the whimsical absurdities that can unfold in the world of insurance.

By the end of the meeting, Ned had not only secured a potential Missel insurance policy for Acme Widgets but had also gained a newfound appreciation for the peculiarities of insurance requests. As Mr. Whizbang was leaving, Ned couldn't help but shake his head and mutter, "Well, who knew missiles could be so complicated?" Mr. Whizbang replied, "You should ask our rocket scientists." And so, the tale of Ned, the Insurance Guru, continued, with each day bringing new surprises and opportunities to learn the intricacies of the insurance kingdom, one amusing encounter at a time.

This story involving an insurance agent's lack of knowledge, requiring guidance to understand their business, exemplifies the need to lead them towards your goals while allowing them to maintain the illusion of control.

In the ever-changing sandboxes at the playground of competitors and competitive analysis, navigating the intricate play of industry dynamics requires more than just a mere awareness of your own little kingdom. It's about recognizing that the chessboard is vast, and every **king (or queen) has their domain**, each with its own unique rules and strategies.

To succeed in this intricate game, it's imperative to understand the domains of other kings—the competitors, vendors, and even customers. The business realm is not a solitary venture; it's a complex ecosystem where interconnected relationships and power dynamics shape the course of success or failure. By comprehending the territories, strengths, and weaknesses of other players in the field, you gain a strategic advantage.[56]

Identifying key players in your industry is akin to recognizing the knights, bishops, and rooks on the chessboard. These are the entities that can influence the game, whether through market dominance, innovative practices, or sheer financial might. Studying their moves and anticipating their strategies become essential components of your competitive analysis.

Establishing strong networks is the equivalent of forging alliances on the chessboard. Networking is not merely about accumulating contacts; it's about creating mutually beneficial relationships that open doors to opportunities, collaborations, and valuable insights. Your **little ol' register** doesn't exist in isolation; it coexists with other kingdoms that may hold the keys to growth and sustainability.

Positioning your **little ol' register** for success involves not only understanding your own strengths and weaknesses but also anticipating the moves of others. In this intricate dance, knowledge is power. Keep your ear to the ground, stay informed about industry trends, and be aware of shifts in the competitive landscape.

Moreover, recognizing that the business terrain is ever-evolving is crucial. The chessboard is not static; it undergoes constant transformation. New players may enter, strategies may change, and market winds may shift. Being agile and adaptable, much like a seasoned **chess** player, allows your **little ol' register** to navigate the uncertainties and seize emerging opportunities.

In essence, understanding the domains of other kings is not just a defensive strategy; it's a proactive approach to thriving in the intricate game of business. It's about recognizing that the chessboard is vast, the pieces are in constant motion, and success lies not just in mastering your own moves but in anticipating and responding to the strategic plays of others. Keep in mind, even in the grandest of kingdoms, everyone believes they reign supreme in their own realms. After all, we're all the monarchs of our own little castles, ruling with flair and sovereignty over our domains, be they vast or modest—hail to the **Kings** (**and Queens**) **Of Their Own Domains**.

HIGH HORSE

To be on a "**high horse**" is to have an attitude of arrogance, of self-righteousness. When the expression originated: in the 1780s Being told you were on a high horse used to be a compliment: Then, as people lost respect for the high and mighty during the revolutions of the late 1700s, the high horse was seen as uppity.

The expression "**high horse**" originally conveyed a sense of elevated status and superiority, as riding a tall war charger symbolized authority and privilege, a high compliment. The physical height of being up on the horse is equated with being in a superior position. Only the custom of high-ranking officials, soldiers, and royalty traveling on horseback rode tall war chargers, while commoners walked.

However, as people lost respect for the high and mighty and societal attitudes shifted during the late 1700s revolutions, being on a **high horse** came to be associated with arrogance and self-righteousness. The sentiment changed from "Be careful of the high horse you're riding; it may eventually kick you off" to becoming more humble "get (down) off one's **high horse**" and to be less haughty. The admonition to "get down off one's high horse" evolved from a compliment to a reminder to be humble and recognize equality among individuals.

When blind men become righteous, individuals, adopt an attitude of self-righteousness, they metaphorically ascend onto a **high horse**. This phrase encapsulates the notion of arrogance and an unwarranted sense of superiority. The metaphor implies a lack of humility and an unyielding adherence to one's own viewpoint, even when it may be limited or misguided. The cautionary message is to avoid becoming entrenched in a self-righteous stance, recognizing the importance of humility and openness to different perspectives.

It's a fundamental truth that it's high time to step down from the pedestal and acknowledge the inherent equality among all individuals. No one stands above another; we are merely playing our respective roles in the grand game of life. This axiom is a poignant reminder that each person contributes uniquely to the intricate interwovenness of existence, and no role is inherently superior. It's a call to embrace humility and recognize that, despite our varied positions and responsibilities, we all share the common ground of humanity.

In the context of your **little ol' register**, this axiom takes on a practical and sometimes humorous twist. Picture the scenario where the first person to be held accountable for everything—the good, the bad, and everything in between—is none other than the El Jefe, the chief orchestrator of your **little ol' register**; You! In the journey of entrepreneurship, the leader often finds themselves at the forefront, facing both commendations and criticisms, just like the first parent who gets yelled at for every action of their little one. It's a nod to the inherent responsibility that comes with steering the ship, where the leader becomes the face and voice of the entire enterprise.

In the monarchy of ownership and titles, the caution against riding the **high horse** extends beyond a mere warning against adopting an arrogant attitude. The essence lies in maintaining a level of ambiguity, steering clear of the pitfalls associated with asserting authority and titles, particularly in the context of negotiations. Let's be honest; titles can be a double-edged sword, especially when the phrases "I'm the boss" or "I'm the owner" are casually tossed around. The real trouble arises when this acknowledgment becomes a focal point, potentially leading to challenges and emotional manipulation.

Consider the scenario where, as the person accountable, you find yourself not only exposed to liability concerns but also susceptible to tactics during negotiations. The moment someone recognizes your authoritative position, they might attempt to leverage it for their benefit. Phrases like "Com 'on man, you can do it; you're the boss, you have the power" or "You're the big man, can't you just help me out" can be thrown your way. This places you in a vulnerable position, subject to emotional appeals laden with guilt.

To counteract such situations, it's vital to protect yourself strategically. Instead of succumbing to emotional pressure, proactively shift the narrative at the start, then stating you can reply, "If I do that, my boss will fire me" or "You wouldn't want me to lose my job, would you?" This tactical move places the negotiation back into a more neutral and advantageous stance, deterring attempts to exploit emotional appeals. It establishes a boundary, making it clear that, just like anyone else, your decisions are bound by external constraints, regardless of your true position in the organizational hierarchy.

To navigate the delicate balance of authority and equal footing, maintaining an air of ambiguity becomes paramount. Leaders, from executives to presidents, are consistently cautioned against wielding titles in a manner that could invite challenges and emotional pressure.[58] This caution underscores the necessity of navigating authority with finesse and a keen awareness of the larger dynamics at play.

By staying ambiguous, leaders not only avoid projecting an air of superiority but also create an environment where interactions are based on merit and mutual respect rather than hierarchical positions. This approach fosters collaboration and open communication, allowing for more authentic relationships within the organizational structure.

In essence, the avoidance of riding the **high horse** is not a call for self-effacement or relinquishing authority. Instead, it's an acknowledgment of the nuanced dynamics of leadership and the impact that titles can have on interpersonal relationships. Leaders who recognize the potential pitfalls of overtly asserting their positions are better equipped to cultivate an inclusive and collaborative environment, where the focus remains on collective success rather than hierarchical posturing.

In the vast ocean of business, there is always a bigger fish than you are. Staying humble while remaining vigilant is not just a leadership strategy; it's a philosophy that safeguards against the tides of overconfidence and arrogance. Leaders who recognize the transient nature of success, acknowledging that they are part of a larger ecosystem, are better poised for sustained growth and adaptability.

A touch of charisma, coupled with the ability to quell an over-boastful pride, serves as a powerful tool in the leader's arsenal. Whether it's through relatability, an appearance of down-to-earth authenticity, or even the strategic advantage of being underestimated, humility becomes a strategic advantage. In the game of conquest, the leader who never mistakes kindness for weakness gains the upper hand, utilizing humility as a cloak for strategic maneuvering.

Ultimately, embracing humility is not a surrender of power but a mastery of it. It's an understanding that true strength lies in the ability to connect, adapt, and lead with authenticity. As the leader, you become the orchestrator of a symphony, recognizing that every instrument, regardless of its size, plays a vital role in creating harmonious success. So, step down from the **high horse**, join the ensemble, and let the music of humility resonate through the corridors of your **little ol' register**.

SETTING UP SHOP: CREATING A BUSINESS PLAN

To embark on the journey of starting your own business it is analogous to giving birth to a new entity—the birth of your **little ol' register**. Just as parents meticulously plan for the future of their children, it is crucial to establish a comprehensive and thoughtful business plan to guide your entrepreneurial venture. The initial plan of attack is your roadmap, outlining the life plan for your business progeny.

A well-crafted business plan serves as the foundation on which your **little ol' register** will stand. It's not merely a document; it's a dynamic tool that helps you envision the trajectory of your business, identify potential challenges, and strategize for success. This plan is your chance to articulate the core *purpose* of your business, define your target audience, and outline the products or services you'll offer.

Consider it as a blueprint that not only charts the path forward but also provides a solid framework for decision-making. From financial projections to marketing strategies, your business plan is a compass that guides you through the exciting and, at times, challenging terrain of entrepreneurship. So, as you set up shop for your **little ol' register**, invest the time and effort to create a robust business plan that will serve as your trusted companion on the road to success.

WHY

Why? Well, we need to upgrade our thinking in order to upgrade our life. Before we can achieve BIG things, we must think BIG things, remember. Now it is time to understand the size of one's thinking.[32] We must have a "**Why**," we must share the "**Why**." Not only "**Why**" with the **End in Mind**, not only **why** this **Hat** or that **Vehicle**, but **why** for every action in **The System**—going to the **River for Water**.

Have you ever wondered "**why**" children have numerous sometimes obnoxious questions? It's a fundamental part of their cognitive and social development. And so shall we at this age of development of your **little ol' register.** The constant questioning is driven by a natural curiosity about the world around them. Young minds without the blockage of pride or self-doubt are eager to explore, understand, and make sense of their environment, and questioning serves as a primary means of acquiring knowledge.

Neuroplasticity, the brain's remarkable ability to reorganize itself by forming new neural connections throughout life, offers profound insights into the importance of knowing the "**Why**" at various stages of development. In younger minds, especially during critical periods of growth and learning, neuroplasticity is at its peak, enabling rapid acquisition of knowledge and skills.[59] Children's brains are highly adaptable and malleable, constantly reshaping in response to experiences and stimuli. Understanding the "**Why**" behind their actions, lessons, and experiences is crucial during this formative stage, as it helps shape their neural networks and lays the foundation for future learning and development.[60]

Asking "**why**" helps children grasp cause-and-effect relationships, develop critical thinking skills, and form a deeper understanding of the most fundamental concepts.[61] Additionally, questioning fosters communication and social interaction, allowing children to engage with adults and peers, seek guidance, and build a foundation for effective communication.[8]

Through the incessant "**whys**," we not only gain knowledge but also establish a connection with the world and the people in it, setting the stage for our ongoing learning journey. We should never forget this simple word unbounded by any self-preservation of one's ego.

As individuals age, neuroplasticity gradually declines, and the brain becomes less malleable.[59] However, this doesn't diminish the significance of knowing the "**Why**." In fact, it becomes even more critical as older minds tend to rely more on established neural pathways and ingrained habits. Understanding the rationale behind decisions, tasks, and goals can stimulate cognitive engagement and activate dormant areas of the brain.[62] By connecting new information to existing knowledge and beliefs, individuals can reinforce neural connections and foster continued growth and adaptability.[63]

Moreover, knowing the "**Why**" provides a sense of purpose and meaning, which is essential for mental and emotional well-being, regardless of age. It fuels motivation, resilience, and perseverance, empowering individuals to overcome obstacles and pursue their aspirations. In older minds, where cognitive decline may be a concern, maintaining a sense of purpose can mitigate age-related changes and promote cognitive vitality—you can always teach an old dog new tricks.

In essence, while the mechanisms of neuroplasticity may vary between young and older minds, the importance of knowing the "**Why**" remains constant.[64] It serves as a guiding principle for learning, growth, and fulfillment, shaping the brain's architecture and fostering lifelong resilience and adaptability. Whether we're nurturing young minds or nurturing our own, understanding the "**Why**" is essential for unlocking our full potential and leading meaningful lives.

Understanding the "**Why**" behind a concept empowers us to recreate it without relying on mere memorization. It involves grasping the foundational principles that govern the concept. For instance, the multiplication fact 2 x 2 = 4 can be memorized through rote repetition or, alternatively, by understanding the underlying principle of multiplication as repeated addition. This comprehension allows for a more flexible and intuitive application of the knowledge, as opposed to relying solely on memorized facts.

Understanding the rationale behind a concept transcends the surface-level memorization of information, "regurgitation," fostering a deeper level of learning with profound implications for practical application in diverse contexts. When we delve into the **why** of a concept, we unravel the underlying principles and mechanisms that govern it. This comprehension extends beyond the rote, allowing us to connect the dots between different ideas and see the interplay within a broader framework.

By grasping the underlying rationale, learners develop a more robust mental model that accommodates variations and nuances. It's not just about knowing the answer; it's about understanding the processes, relationships, and implications associated with the concept. This deeper understanding paves the way for flexible thinking, enabling individuals to apply their knowledge creatively and adapt it to novel situations as **chicken is chicken**.

Moreover, understanding the rationale behind a concept enhances problem-solving skills. Instead of relying on predefined solutions, individuals equipped with a deeper understanding can analyze problems, identify patterns, and devise innovative solutions—**solving the solutions**. This adaptability is crucial in real-world scenarios where challenges rarely align neatly with memorized facts.

The emphasis on understanding the rationale behind a concept promotes a deeper level of learning and the ability to apply that knowledge in various contexts. In the space of education, emphasizing the **why** encourages a shift from passive absorption to active engagement. Learners become critical thinkers, asking questions, making connections, and exploring the intricacies of a subject. This approach fosters intellectual curiosity and a lifelong love of learning.

Whether facing complex challenges in the workplace or making informed decisions in everyday life, individuals armed with a deep understanding of the rationale behind concepts are better equipped to navigate the tumultuous and ever-changing universe of knowledge and application.

If you don't know ask. Seeking knowledge through inquiry is a demonstration of genuine strength, not weakness. True strength lies in the humility to acknowledge what one doesn't know rather than pretending omniscient. Those who admit their lack of knowledge and display a willingness to learn are regarded as authentic and earn higher respect. Consider the last instance you conversed with someone genuinely attentive to your words or valuing the authenticity of your response. Such interactions foster a sense of openness and sincerity, encouraging a reciprocal willingness to engage and share.

Regrettably, it's uncommon to encounter individuals genuinely interested in others beyond themselves, a reflection of human nature prioritizing self-concern. However, when we invest the effort to truly observe and understand another person, we often discover aspects of genuine interest and a deeper understanding of ourselves.[65] Demonstrating authentic interest in others is a key element in building connections, as people naturally appreciate those who take a sincere interest in them. Genuine curiosity forms a solid foundation for meaningful relationships, fostering a sense of connection and mutual understanding.[65]

You never know what knowledge may follow by understanding the "**Why**" someone has a certain view, the goal becomes more about what is right than about who is right.[65] Even though sometimes it requires digging out the real reasons because of the blindness experienced with being in emotion or just **blind men**. That is **why** one should deal with emotions before content.[8]

The "**Why**" leads us to "Chance favors the prepared mind," which resonated with Louis Pasteur's most renowned quote, spoken during his tenure as the dean of the new Faculty of Sciences at Lille.[66] This sentiment of humility finds an echo in the wisdom of the most esteemed Nobel laureates, shrouded in their profound understanding of the universe. The pursuit of knowledge, marked by humility, only begins with the opening of a door, leading invariably to more doors—an endless exploration. As we navigate these paths through the doorways of life, laureates acknowledge the integral role of failure in success, understanding that it often paves the way for triumph and understanding the "**Why**." Failure, in their eyes, is not a lost cause but a valuable source of learning, a principle that many Nobel laureates and the wisest minds have embraced throughout their journeys.

You must also learn from failure and be prepared when chances arrive. Thomas Alva Edison when asked," Mr. Edison you have failed 10,000 times." "I have not failed 10,000 times. I have not failed once. I have succeeded in proving that those 10,000 ways will not work. When I have eliminated the ways that will not work, I will find the way that will work."

How do we find the way that will work? Firstly, waste is worse than loss. The time is coming when every person who lays claim to ability will keep the question of waste before him constantly. Just as Thomas did not waste or fail, any individual should "Waste

Setting Up Shop: Creating a Business Plan

not, want not." Let's not waste, let us start planning the **system** of your **little ol' register**, with the **paradigm** of your **"why"** and the **end in mind**.

Now, at the center desk of planning, delving into the fundamental questions of **"why"** is paramount. Take the traditional business plan, as outlined by the Small Business Administration (SBA), which encompasses nine core sections: executive summary, company description, market analysis, organization and management, service or product line, marketing and sales, funding needs, and financial projections. Each of these sections serves as a critical component in understanding the underlying rationale behind various aspects of the business.

Why do we need these specific individuals in our organization? What is the purpose behind our company's existence? **Why** would potential customers choose to purchase our products or services over alternatives? What motivates certain demographics to seek out our offerings? **Why** is external funding necessary for our business operations? What are our expectations regarding revenue generation, and **why** do we anticipate achieving profitability? **Why** does each component of our business model function in the manner it does?

Throughout this book, we will embark on a journey to explore these **"whys"** in depth, unraveling the underlying motivations and strategic considerations that underpin the operations of your **little ol' register**. By gaining a comprehensive understanding of the **"Why"** behind every aspect of your business, you will be equipped to chart a course towards excellence, informed decision-making, and sustainable growth.

Winning is when your **"WHY"** is bigger than their **"why."** It only takes one moment to decide you're going to be a winner. One moment to separate yourself from the rest. Winning is reserved for the lucky, as the failed will tell you, but it is NOT! [57] Winning is what happens when your desire to win is greater than your fear of failure when your hunger is greater. Winning is simple—mindset. A mindset that is only developed when we utterly understand our **paradigm**, when we have fully internalized the **"why."** Know your **why!**

SIM

Welcome to the vibrant and vigorous open-world of business planning, where the strategic simulation game unfolds in intricate patterns, and successful triumph rests on the thoughtful orchestration of moves. In this territory, the health of your **little ol' register** is not a passive outcome but a deliberate result of a meticulously crafted plan. Join us as we delve into the nuances of mastering the simulation game, exploring how strategic foresight, adaptability, discovering how strategic foresight, adaptability, and a profound grasp of business intricacies can not only shield but nurture your **little ol' register**.

From maneuvering through challenges of the marketplace to anticipating industry shifts, each move in the simulation contributes to the life force of your financial backbone. Brace yourselves, as we set off on this voyage where the cash **register** transforms from a mere transaction receiver into a strategic player in the grand game of business.

Our trek begins with an empty binder—the "Corporate Binder," the sanctum where vital documents find their home. This binder isn't merely a repository; it's the heartbeat of corporate governance, capturing pivotal decisions and fostering transparency and accountability Traditionally, all essential documents of a company find their home in this binder, ranging from Articles of Incorporation and bylaws to meeting minutes and stock-related papers, come together. It serves as a sanctuary for the tangible essence of a company's existence.

The corporate book stands as a cornerstone of corporate governance, capturing key decisions made by the board of directors and shareholders. In doing so, it exemplifies transparency and accountability in the management of the company. Understanding the "hows" and "**whys**" behind pivotal choices offers invaluable lessons for both current and future leadership.

Imagine a HUD-like summary sheet embracing its exterior, offering a quick glimpse into the intricate game of **your little ol' register**. Here, one may indulge in a touch of whimsy, perhaps drawing parallels to a mini-**Sim**'s game. But can anyone find fault in this analogy? After all, isn't business, at its core, <u>a game of strategy and interlinked maneuvers</u>?

The idea of this binder-as-a-**sim**ulation phenomenon made its debut in the world of high school biology, courtesy of none other than Michael, an esteemed teacher.[67] Call it a stroke of luck or chalk it up to the teacher's pet status, but Michael bequeathed unto his pupil a binder that became a gateway to a dominion of endless possibilities. Within its confines, every minuscule **system** unfolded like a well-crafted simulation, revealing the intricate dance of cogs in a timepiece, each with its unique "**why**" on how it moves.

Much like the game **Sims** published by Electronic Arts in 2000, where virtual lives were created and controlled, this binder becomes a tool to assume distinct roles within the intricate **system** of a company. Inspired by Christopher Alexander's A Pattern Language, the binder becomes more than just a record-keeping vessel; it morphs into a living, breathing entity that allows anyone to pull strings, make changes, and see how each tweak affects the vast interconnected web of the business.[68] It's not just about documentation; it's about playing the game of improvement and evolution.

Over the years, this binder has taken to using more than a paper holder, a tool not only for record-keeping, but also to magically assume whatever **hat** (role) that may be in that **Sims** game. To pull off the shelf and bring to life all the interconnected strings interlaced through the entire company. Pulling, cutting, or making can affect vast amounts of attachment points. Every time to critique and make slight changes to improve the **system**.

In essence, the corporate book is a living document that encapsulates the corporate journey. Reading the decisions of the past is not just an administrative task but a strategic initiative to leverage the wisdom embedded in the company's history for ongoing success and sustainability. Recognizing what has worked well and learning from challenges helps leadership make new informed decisions for the future and success of your **little ol' register**.

Conducting simulations repeatedly is no different than playing a new character, or assuming new roles and assembling diverse teams of **warriors**, all aimed at refining products and services to carve out a distinctive niche in the chosen market. The objective is not merely to outdo competitors but to transcend their successes.

Adopting a perspective championed by Sam Walton, the visionary behind Sam's Club and Walmart, involves scrutinizing competitors not for their missteps but for their triumphs. As Walton famously stated, "I probably have traveled and walked into more variety stores than anybody in America. I am just trying to get ideas, any kind of ideas that will help our company. Most of us don't invent ideas. We take the best ideas from someone else."

In this perpetual game of strategy, each industry serves as a variant map, and the fundamental principles of gameplay remain constant. Understanding the sandbox in which you're playing and pinpointing the specific playground you occupy are crucial. Repeatedly running the **sim**ulation equips you to anticipate every move, analogous to the strategic planning involved in a game of **chess**. So, define your **little ol' register's** essence in your corporate book—the **sim**ulation that guides your strategic journey.

As we conclude our exploration of the **sim**ulation game, we emerge with a newfound appreciation for the intricate dance of strategy and foresight that defines the business landscape. The journey through **sim**ulations has not only honed our ability to navigate challenges and anticipate industry shifts but has also instilled in us a deeper understanding of the vital role played by your **little ol' register**. Armed with insights gleaned from the corporate binder and the lessons learned from virtual experimentation, we stand poised to chart a course towards sustainable success and enduring growth. So, let us venture forth, emboldened by our strategic acumen and fortified by the wisdom acquired on this **sim**ulation-driven odyssey.

SH*T HAPPENS!

Once upon a time in the whimsical land of Entrepreneurville, a group of eager startup enthusiasts gathered to unveil their grand plan. Picture this: a room filled with whiteboards scribbled with brilliant ideas, flowcharts that looked like modern art, and a vibe so optimistic you could practically bottle it and sell it as "Startup Sunshine **Kool-Aid**."

Amidst the excitement, the fearless leader, let's call him Captain Venture, stood confidently at the front, outlining the grand strategy. "Nothing can go wrong!" he declared, his PowerPoint slides radiating confidence. Little did Captain Venture know that just around the corner, lurking in the shadows of overconfidence, was Murphy's Law in a mischievous disguise, ready to play its favorite game: messing with well-laid plans.

The startup journey kicked off with high hopes and dreams of unicorns. However, just as Captain Venture proudly declared, "Can you do this? Can you do that?" Fate chuckled and whispered, "Hold my coffee." Sure enough, **sh*t happens**! Unexpected twists, turns, and surprises appeared like mischievous imps in a Shakespearean comedy. Cory's words echoed in the air, "The first casualty of any battle is the plan of attack."[69] It seemed Murphy's Law had taken a page out of Cory's book, quite literally.

Murphy goes all out. Employees were poached, not by headhunters but by rival startups wielding metaphorical butterfly nets. The once harmonious team faced the heart-wrenching task of bidding farewell to friends who were no longer the perfect puzzle piece for the startup mosaic.

But fear not, dear reader, for in the midst of chaos emerged a guiding light—the wisdom from those past. A magical tome filled with the collective wisdom of battle-hardened entrepreneurs who had faced the dragons of bankruptcy, the ogres of employee poaching, and the occasional unicorn that turned out to be a donkey in disguise.

One such tale was amidst the hustle and bustle of shooting a high-stakes action sequence involving rappelling Marines off a helicopter over a notorious wise guy watering hole near the dazzling lights of the desert's most famous playground, the film crew found themselves inadvertently entangled in a comedic escapade.[70] As the adrenaline-pumping scene unfolded, the lead cinematographer, sporting a look of sheer horror, realized that a ridiculously expensive camera lens had taken an unplanned plunge into the depths of Lake Mead. Cue the collective gasps and frantic discussions about how to rescue the stranded lens from its newfound aquatic home.

In a bid to rectify the situation, the crew members, armed with makeshift flotation devices and a dash of desperation, embarked on a nautical rescue mission. Picture a comical ensemble of crew members and production assistants attempting to navigate the waters, resembling a scene straight out of a slapstick comedy. Alas, despite their valiant efforts, the elusive lens remained submerged, joining the ranks of Lake Mead's unconventional treasures and concrete shoes.

Undeterred by this aquatic misadventure, the crew shifted their focus to the next challenge: attempting to land a helicopter on the one-lane Hoover Dam; brilliant, right? The once grandiose *vision* of a seamless landing metamorphosed into a spectacle of airborne acrobatics and audacious maneuvers. The cinematic dreams of a picture-perfect landing on the dam were slightly thwarted as the helicopter found itself in a precarious position, not quite fitting the narrow landing space.

In the end, what started as a mission to capture thrilling movie magic turned into a blooper reel for the ages. The crew, now drenched from their aquatic endeavors and hovering precariously above the dam, had inadvertently created a storyline even more entertaining than the scripted action they had originally planned. And so, amidst the laughter and camaraderie, they learned that, indeed, in the unpredictable world of filmmaking, **sh*t happens**—and sometimes, it makes for the best stories.

These enchanted stories throughout this book should become your **little ol' register's** training wheels, offering advice on navigating the stormy seas of entrepreneurship. Some will whisper tales of firing friends with grace, stealing talents from competitors like a corporate Robin Hood, and surviving the looming specter of the black death—bankruptcy. No matter what fence needs whitewashing, it all has been done before, if not, it definitely rhymes.

And so, in Entrepreneurville, where whiteboards met reality and flowcharts faced the chaos of the startup jungle, the brave founders armed themselves with the resilience to exclaim, "**Sh*t happens**, but we've got this!" And so, the adventure continues, with laughter, tears, and a sprinkle of startup magic.

Startup life is hard. No matter how much planning or research you do, there will be unexpected surprises along the way. Unfortunately, there is no recipe or formula for dealing with the most difficult challenges that founders and owners face. Not to mention the emotional struggles that come along with them.

Indeed, we can apply the metaphorical "bubble wrap protection" method and shield a business from all potential risks and challenges. While protection and caution are essential, an overly cautious approach can stifle growth and innovation. Just like a delicate item wrapped in layers of bubble wrap may be shielded from external impacts but remains hidden and unable to fulfill its purpose, a business too sheltered from risks may miss out on opportunities for development.

Businesses, like individuals, need room to breathe, experiment, and adapt. The path to success often involves navigating uncertainties, learning from mistakes, and embracing the unexpected. The metaphor suggests that, much like fragile items need exposure to the world to serve their purpose, your **little ol' register** must venture beyond the safety of excessive protection to thrive.

In the dynamic model of commerce, adaptability, resilience, and a willingness to take calculated risks are often key ingredients for success. A business that is too encased in protective measures may find itself isolated from the market, innovation, and the valuable experiences that come with overcoming challenges. While protection is crucial, finding the right balance ensures that a business can navigate the unpredictable terrain of the business world and emerge stronger and more agile.

Navigating the unpredictable terrain of Entrepreneurville, one learns quickly that stepping in proverbial "**sh*t**" is an unavoidable occupational hazard. The temptation to take on tasks outside the established business scope is especially tempting. This additional revenue can be alluring, particularly when faced with the challenging questions of "Can you do this?" or "Can you do that?"

However, veering off the path of expertise can lead to unanticipated obstacles and setbacks. It's a cautionary tale to resist the allure of every opportunity that comes your way and to remain steadfast within the defined boundaries of your business expertise. In the whimsical dance of entrepreneurship, it's the mastery of one's own scope that keeps the journey less messy and more navigable.

■ **The Conundrum:** In the quiet expanse of a property owner's domain, a decision stirs—a new fence is needed. The old one, weather-worn and sagging, has whispered its final plea for replacement. And so, the property owner steps into the labyrinth of choices, each path leading to a different *vision* of enclosure.

■ **The Fence Contractor:** Clad in denim and measuring tape, the fence contractor strides forth. Their world revolves around cedar, wrought iron, and chain-link. They speak the language of pickets, posts, and gates. For them, a fence is a symphony of angles, a dance of materials. They envision privacy screens, dog-eared elegance, and the rhythmic beat of hammer on nail.

■ **The Landscape Contractor:** With soil-stained boots and a trowel in hand, the landscape contractor emerges. Their gaze extends beyond mere boundaries. To them, a fence is a canvas—an opportunity to blend form and function. They consider ivy-clad trellises, flowering borders, and how the fence harmonizes with the garden's whispers. For them, it's not just about enclosure; it's about the poetry of place.

■ **The Security Company:** In sleek suits and digital codes, the security company strides forth. Their eyes scan for vulnerabilities, their minds calculating risk. To them, a fence is a fortress—a line of defense against intruders. They envision motion sensors, electrified wires, and surveillance cameras. For them, the fence is binary: secure or breached.

But beware! As the property owner contemplates, a shadow looms—the handyman, the plumber, the ditch digger. They sidle into the bidding process, tools in hand, eager to contribute. Their skills are undeniable; they can wield hammers, fix leaks, and excavate earth. Yet, their inclusion risks muddying the waters.

Why? Because their core competencies lie elsewhere; their blind men perspectives are more diverse than even the experts. The handyman, adept at patching roofs, may fumble with fence posts. The plumber, a maestro of pipes, might misjudge the alignment of rails. And the ditch digger, well-versed in earth's secrets, could inadvertently undermine the fence's stability.

■ Ah, but there stands the shrewd **little ol' register**—a sage in the art of discernment. They recognize that precision requires alignment. Their scope narrows, focusing on the experts—the fence contractor, the landscape artist, the security strategist. They understand that mastery lies in specialization, that the symphony demands virtuosos.

And so, the fence project unfurls—a ballet of wood, earth, and wire. The fence contractor measures twice, hammers once. The landscape artist weaves blooms into lattice. The security strategist ensures every angle guards against intrusion. Despite the diverse approaches, they remain steadfast within the boundaries of their expertise.

The property owner watches, knowing that within these boundaries, magic happens. A fence emerges—not just a barrier, but a testament to purpose, skill, and vision. And in its sturdy embrace, dreams find shelter, fears retreat, and the world outside yields to sanctuary. May the fence stand tall, its story etched in every knot and grain.

In the turbulent waters of business, it's not uncommon for entrepreneurs to find themselves diluting the essence of their core competencies in pursuit of expansion or diversification. Much like "The Empty Boat" parable below, where the boat owner's initial mistake leads to an unforeseen and chaotic outcome, businesses can easily lose sight of their strengths and values amidst the frenzy of growth. The empty boat, drifting aimlessly without direction or purpose, serves as a poignant metaphor for companies that stray too far from their foundational principles.

Conversely, just as the boat owner eventually realizes his error and takes decisive action to regain control, entrepreneurs can course-correct by reassessing their strategies and realigning with their core competencies. By acknowledging that **sh*t happens** and embracing the lessons learned along the way, businesses can navigate the unpredictable currents of entrepreneurship with resilience and determination.

In the ancient Chinese philosophy of Taoism, there is a well-known parable called "The Empty Boat."[71] The story goes that there was an old farmer who lived on the banks of a river. One day, his only horse, which he used for plowing and transportation, accidentally wandered into the river and disappeared. The neighboring villagers sympathized with the farmer, lamenting the loss of his only means of livelihood. However, the old farmer remained surprisingly composed, simply stating, "We'll see."

A few days later, to everyone's astonishment, the lost horse returned, leading a group of wild horses with it. Now, the farmer had not only recovered his original horse but gained several more. The villagers were overjoyed and congratulated the farmer on his newfound wealth. Yet again, the old farmer maintained his calm demeanor, responding with a nonchalant, "We'll see."

The next day, his son attempted to ride one of the wild horses but was thrown off it, breaking his leg. Again, the villagers said, "Such bad luck" only to receive the same reply from the farmer, "We'll see." A few days later, military officials arrived at the village to draft young men into the army, to fight for their Kingdom which had just declared war on another. Seeing the farmer's son's leg was broken, they excused him from service and went on their way. The villagers, shocked, once more said, "Such good luck." to which the farmer, ever stoic and unconcerned, said, "We'll see."

This Taoist wisdom encourages a perspective that transcends immediate judgments, emphasizing the importance of embracing the flow of life without being overly attached to individual outcomes. The moral of the story lies in the farmer's ability to accept life's uncertainties with equanimity, understanding that events are neither inherently good nor bad—they simply are: **sh*t happens**.

> In the quietude of dawn, where the river meets the sky,
> There sails an empty boat—a vessel unburdened by cargo or cry.
> Its wooden hull, weathered and wise, glides upon the ripples,
> A lone figure at the helm, eyes fixed on distant constellations.
>
> Who is this boatman, this keeper of emptiness?
> He is no ordinary mariner, no seeker of fortune or fame.
> His hands, calloused by tides and tempests, steer not toward harbor,
> But into the heart of uncertainty, where waves birth both chaos and clarity.
>
> The empty boat farmer, they call him—a paradox in flesh and bone.
> His fields lie fallow, yet his spirit tills the soil of wisdom.
> He does not sow seeds of certainty; instead, he tends the soil of surrender,
> Knowing that harvests come not by force, but by grace.
>
> When storms gather, and thunder drums across the water,
> He does not curse the heavens or cling to the mast.
> He stands tall, arms outstretched, and lets the rain baptize his brow,
> For he understands that every drop carries a secret
>   —a lesson whispered by clouds.
>
> And when the sun emerges, painting the sky with hues of gold,
> He does not hoist a flag of victory or tally his gains.
> No, he simply turns his face toward the warmth, eyes half-closed,
> And breathes in the fragrance of possibility.
>
> "Stay true to the vision," he murmurs, "but befriend the unknown."
> His boat, a vessel of paradox, dances between worlds.
> It is empty, yet full of stories—the echoes of forgotten voyages,
> The laughter of dolphins, the tears of lost sailors.

And so, dear business owner, as you navigate the currents of commerce,
Remember the empty boat farmer. Embrace the unforeseen.
For in the gaps between profit margins and balance sheets,
Lies the fertile delta of innovation—the birthplace of resilience.

When shit happens (and it will), do not build higher walls,
But widen your heart's harbor. Let setbacks be stepping stones,
And losses, lanterns guiding you home.

"C'est la vie," whispers the empty boat farmer, as he sails toward the horizon. May your **little ol' register** thrive, anchored in wisdom (acceptance and adaptability) and buoyed by possibility.

FOUNDATIONAL FRAMEWORK: CREATING YOUR BUSINESS

Success is the goal and as a director, there has been a keen awareness of the level of trust that stakeholders have shown by placing faith in the role. This trust is reciprocated by paying attention to their concerns, proactively keeping them informed of any issues that might positively or adversely affect the company or project, and by a willingness to assist at every level, take on any task, and help ensure each detail is being handled. The results have been substantially worth the extra time and effort at every level, serving as a humbling reminder of the embodiment of trust.

Ah, the joys of being a director! It's like being the ringmaster of a circus, juggling the expectations of stakeholders with the grace of a ballet dancer dodging tomatoes. From proactively addressing concerns to willingly diving into the trenches to tackle any task, it's all about earning that trust like a squirrel hoarding nuts for winter. And let me tell you, seeing the fruits of that labor is like finding a pot of gold at the end of a rainbow - worth every hair-pulling moment!

GENESIS

In the discovery of your **little ol' register**, you've unearthed more than just a product; you've found the essence of an idea, the framework of a **system**, and the solution to streamlining your business operations. Now, as you stand at the threshold of formalizing your **little ol' register**, the crucial question arises: Where do you begin?

The initial step in the formalization process involves deciphering the unique needs and nuances of your business. Your **little ol' register** is not a one-size-fits-all solution; rather, it's a versatile tool waiting to be tailored to the specifics of your enterprise. Consider the nature of your transactions, the volume of sales, and the intricacies of your financial record-keeping. This preliminary assessment sets the foundation for customizing your **little ol' register** to align seamlessly with your **end in mind**.

Once you've gauged the intricacies of your business landscape, the next step is to define the parameters of your **register's** functionality. Defining the *purpose* of its birth; needs arise. Does it need to process various payment methods? Should it generate detailed sales reports? Does it play a role in inventory management? Answering the **"why"** to these questions provides the clarity needed to design a **system** that not only captures transactions but enhances your operational efficiency to match the needs of the business.

Now, envision your **register** not just as a point-of-sale device but as an integral component of your business ecosystem. It becomes a hub for financial transactions, a guardian of accurate record-keeping, and a catalyst for business growth. Formalizing your **little ol' register** is not merely a procedural task; it's a strategic move towards optimizing your business processes, fostering accountability, and setting the stage for future success.

In essence, the formalization of your **little ol' register** marks the transformation from a simple transaction recorder to a tailored solution that mirrors the heartbeat and soul of your business. It's a journey of understanding, customization, and integration, guided by the principle that every button, every function, and every entry is a deliberate step towards operational excellence in the empire of entrepreneurship.

The question of **why** you need a company arises, and it is a pivotal juncture in the entrepreneurial journey. It's like admitting that you're not lost; you simply haven't figured out your exact location. In Jack's pursuit of answers to these very questions, he found himself seeking guidance from a trusted authority on the subject—the Small Business Administration (SBA). It was during this quest that Jack encountered a seasoned SBA Agent, a sage in the domain of business wisdom.

At the tender age of 17, Jack absorbed a piece of advice that would become a cornerstone of his entrepreneurial philosophy: "Run your company as if you were public and pray you never have to." These words, uttered by the seasoned SBA Agent, resonated with profound significance. They encapsulated the essence of strategic foresight, urging entrepreneurs to adopt a mindset that transcends the immediate needs of a startup and extends into the scope of long-term *vision*.[72]

The analogy of running your company as if it were public embodies a commitment to transparency, accountability, and meticulous governance. It suggests a proactive approach to business operations, one that anticipates challenges, welcomes scrutiny, and adheres to the principles of sound management. This approach, similar to prayer, acknowledges the unpredictable nature of entrepreneurship, where external factors beyond our control may come into play.

In essence, the counsel from the SBA Agent was a call to embrace the dual nature of entrepreneurship—bold and calculated. It emphasized the importance of instilling discipline and structure in the initial stages of a venture, with an eye on scalability and resilience. By adhering to the notion of running your company as if it were public, you not only set a high standard for your own business practices but also position yourself for sustained success in the uncharted waters of entrepreneurship. So did Jack listen; NOPE and public Jack went.

Embarking on the journey to become a public company typically involves the initiation of an initial public offering (IPO), where shares of stock are offered to the public as a means to secure additional capital. While this path is not the starting point for most, with many opting for the trajectory of a traditional startup, it's essential to note that the Securities and Exchange Commission's (SEC) regulations have evolved.

The recent adjustment to the SEC rule, shifting the threshold for public reporting requirements from 500 shareholders to 2000, marks a significant evolution in financial regulations.[73] However, it's essential to note that even with this change, there are still considerations to be made, such as the inclusion of up to 35 potential non-credited individuals in a room for solicitation purposes. This adaptation underscores the fluid nature of regulatory frameworks and highlights the importance of staying informed and adaptable in the financial landscape.

For startups seeking investment, the significance of a compelling pitch deck cannot be overstated. Beyond presenting a solid business case through a traditional business plan, the pitch deck serves as a vital tool for capturing the attention and interest of potential investors. Whether delivered in a formal presentation or as a succinct elevator pitch, the goal is to evoke an emotional response that resonates with investors. Emotion, after all, is the true driving force behind trading markets, whether it be stocks, bonds, or commodities.[74] While financial decisions may be grounded in data and analysis, it is ultimately the perception of future potential gains (greed) or losses (fear) that influences investor behavior.[75]

In crafting a pitch deck, your **little ol'** startup must focus not only on presenting your business model and financial projections but also on articulating your *vision* and passion for the venture. Investors are not just looking for a sound investment opportunity; they are seeking to align themselves with entrepreneurs who demonstrate drive, conviction, and a clear understanding of your market and audience. A compelling pitch deck should therefore weave together a narrative that not only showcases the startup's value proposition but also communicates the founder's authenticity and commitment to success.

In essence, the adjustment to SEC regulations signals a broader shift in the financial landscape, one that emphasizes the need for startups to master the art of persuasion and emotional engagement in their fundraising efforts. By crafting a pitch deck that speaks to both the rational and emotional dimensions of investing, startups can enhance their chances of securing the funding needed to fuel their growth and success in the competitive marketplace.[53]

Part 2: Building the Register

Navigating the complexities of the highly regulated financial realm, companies can even engage in various legal yet baffling strategies, such as buying off market makers, to enhance the overall stock position of the company. While these maneuvers may seem like schemes, they are legitimate actions within the corporate framework, diverging from what would lead a normal individual to legal consequences.

Transport yourself in the opulent ambiance of a luxury hotel, two executives found themselves immersed in a world of possibilities, their dreams materializing with the success of their first Initial Public Offering (IPO). The day was marked by a celebration brunch, overlooking the city skyline as the market played out its last moments. With bated breath, they watched the stock ticker, their hearts echoing the rise and fall of the numbers that held the fate of their venture.[76]

As the market closed, the jubilant duo witnessed their company's stock soaring to new heights, each uptick bringing a surge of excitement. The euphoria intensified with every milestone reached, unlocking tranches of funding that had been meticulously structured based on the daily float and stock price markers. The sunlit terrace echoed with laughter, toasts, and the clinking of glasses as millions flowed into their venture, a testament to their hard work, innovation, and strategic *vision*.

In this moment of triumph, surrounded by the opulence of their surroundings, the executives reveled in the realization of their entrepreneurial journey. The brunch table, adorned with delicacies, mirrored the abundance that their company was poised to achieve. With each success, they envisioned not just financial prosperity but a legacy of innovation and impact. The luxurious setting became a backdrop to their aspirations, symbolizing the heights they had reached and the even greater summits that awaited their conquering spirit.

However, the decision to go public is a substantial leap for any company, prompting careful consideration of the reasons that drive such a choice. Post-IPO, the company becomes subject to public reporting requirements, marking a pivotal transition.

Now, following the trajectory of a typical startup, securing funding becomes a pivotal aspect as it progresses through various rounds. The initial seed round, often fueled by personal savings or contributions from friends and family, lays the foundation. As the startup gains traction and develops a more concrete business model, it may move on to a Series A funding round or traditional debt financing from a bank.

During this phase, external investors, such as venture capitalists, become key players, injecting substantial capital in exchange for equity or debt. This infusion of funds empowers the startup to scale operations, enhance product development, and reach a broader market. Each funding round represents a milestone, with subsequent rounds—Series B, C, and beyond—reflecting the company's growth, market validation, and evolving financial needs. Further insights into raising capital will be explored in Part 5: Counting the Drawer.

The likelihood of someone personally writing you a multimillion-dollar check is slim, and even if it were to happen, it might not be the wisest course of action. Hence, the necessity for your **little ol' register** is evident. In navigating the intricate landscape of business entity formations, you'll encounter a myriad of options, with over 11 different types in the United States alone. The mere mention of terms like Limited Liability Corporation, S Corporation, Partnership, and Sole Proprietorship can be daunting. Each structure comes with its own set of advantages and disadvantages, creating a complex decision-making process for entrepreneurs.

Amid this complexity, limited liability companies (LLCs) and corporations emerge as the stalwarts, chosen most frequently. The primary allure of these structures (**vehicles**) lies in their ability to shield personal assets from the inherent risks of the business world. However, it's crucial to note that this protection doesn't create an impenetrable fortress. While it won't completely absolve you from potential legal entanglements or personal accountability for your actions within the company, it does establish a critical layer of defense commonly referred to as the "Corporate Shield."

The "Corporate Shield" serves as a fundamental safeguard, setting boundaries and protecting your personal assets from the potential fallout of business-related challenges. It delineates the separation between your personal finances and those of the business entity, providing a degree of insulation against financial liabilities and legal disputes.

Understanding the nuances of these entity formations becomes paramount, as each structure offers a unique blend of flexibility and protection. As an entrepreneur, investigating the intricacies of LLCs, corporations, and other entity types is a strategic imperative, guiding you towards a choice that aligns with your business goals and provides the necessary safeguards for your entrepreneurial journey.

In the annals of corporate history, the cautionary tale of the Exxon Valdez oil spill stands as a stark reminder of the consequences of operational missteps and the importance of strategic company structuring. The colossal spill, a result of a tanker accident off Alaska's Prince William Sound, unleashed approximately 11 million gallons of oil, creating an ecological disaster that spanned 1,300 miles of coastline. The legal aftermath saw environmentalists embroiled in court battles seeking accountability. [77]

The intricacies of the corporate veil became evident as the ownership of the vessel shifted hands. Initially owned by the Exxon Shipping Company, the Exxon Valdez underwent a transformation after the spill. It resurfaced under a different name, Exxon Mediterranean, and later as SeaRiver Mediterranean in the early 1990s.[77] Exxon strategically transferred its shipping business to a new subsidiary, River Maritime Inc., safeguarding its assets while navigating the tarnished reputation left in the wake of the incident.

The question of fault pointed squarely at the ship's captain, Joseph Hazelwood, whose intoxication, and negligence were key contributors to the disaster. The revelation that an unlicensed third mate was steering the ship further underscored the lapse in oversight. Exxon, facing the repercussions, paid a hefty $507.5 million in punitive damages and lawsuit costs by December 15, 2009, a financial consequence borne by the company.[78]

Remarkably, the Exxon Valdez continued its maritime journey for over two decades, adapting to the tarnished brand by assuming different names. This strategic metamorphosis mirrored a corporate survival tactic—bankruptcy and brand replacement while the operational entity holding the assets remained unchanged. The Exxon Valdez saga serves as a poignant lesson in the intricate dance of corporate structuring, asset protection, and reputation management, demonstrating the enduring impact of a single operational misstep, a small **landmine**, on a company's trajectory.

The art of structuring and stacking companies within a hierarchical framework is a strategic endeavor aimed at enhancing asset protection, maintaining a veil of invisibility, and optimizing tax efficiency—at least for now. This multifaceted approach often involves the establishment of distinct entities, each serving a specialized purpose in the business landscape. An operating company, positioned at the forefront, engages in day-to-day operations and holds visible assets. In contrast, holding companies, strategically layered behind the scenes, act as guardians of wealth, housing assets, and intellectual property.

By segregating functions and assets across different entities, this structure shields the core business from potential risks and legal liabilities. Furthermore, incorporating entities in jurisdictions known for favorable tax conditions adds an additional layer of financial optimization. The synergy of these structures creates a robust and agile **system**, fortifying the business against various threats while maximizing its overall efficiency.

Now can this shield be pierced? Of course! One of the fundamental ways is with an "alter ego," in other words treating it as if it is you and not a separate person.[79] Especially if one is siphoning funds personal from corporate façades. [80] Remember, putting your money in the same pocket as your company's is a No-No commingling of funds. Making choices that benefit you personally rather than in the best interest of the company violates your fiduciary responsibilities, leading to malfeasance, misfeasance, or nonfeasance—-fraud. You have a moral and ethical duty to the company, as well as to the other stakeholders. If you are the only one to that duty it belongs then "more power to you," nevertheless it still is a separate **little ol' register** that has **the system** it must follow.

That being said, there are many ways to strengthen these protections. The main is to comply with basic corporate formalities, one can create a problem from a corporate separateness perspective. Form a board of directors (managing structure) for each subsidiary. Hold regular board meetings where the board considers substantive matters in depth. Document the election of officers and directors on an annual basis or, as needed, to address vacancies. No majority overlap of board members among parent and its subsidiaries.[79] Document the corporate decision-making process as necessary (e.g., keep contemporaneous minutes for meetings, or support board action with properly executed written consents and resolutions).

Certain renowned companies have, in essence, surpassed the structure in which they are contained. Some company names and product brands have become ingrained in our everyday lexicon, woven into the fabric of today's society as norms—think Kleenex versus tissue paper, Band-Aid for an adhesive bandage, or Q-tip as opposed to a cotton swab. These corporations, still flourishing today, have navigated diverse paths, and undergone a myriad of growth and adaptation. Some transitioned to being wholly owned by employees, others were bought out, and some merged with other entities creating a conglomerate.

"A word to the wise," the tenure of the Chief Executive Officer (CEO), the head figure of your **little ol' register**, is finite. Even founders can see their roles terminated within their lifetimes. We reflect on figures like Steve Jobs, the founder of Apple, and more recently, Sam Altman of OpenAI, both of whom were ousted from the companies they birthed. CEOs, while serving as figureheads, are fundamentally employees of the company, distinguished only by the public-facing role they play. This underscores the importance of cultivating a distinct identity for your **little ol' register**, recognizing that, over time, "Everyone is and will be replaced."

Summarizing our exploration, a business entity stands as a distinct legal entity, separate from its owner and founder, offering several advantages.[81] This separation encompasses business assets from personal assets, personal debt from business debt, and business liability from personal liability. In essence, you are bringing forth a distinct business entity—a unique **little ol' register**. However, with each birth and increased complexity, there comes an inherent cost. These costs may involve individual fees for each company, the necessity for separate bank accounts, distinct tax filing requirements, unique addresses, phone numbers, and dedicated sites.

Choosing the right legal structure for your business is paramount, and the decision on when and where to establish it influences the rules it operates under. Considerations include state regulations and the desired longevity of your **little ol' register**—hopefully, a perpetual existence.

VEHICLE

This lengthy discussion is about the choice of entity and primarily applies to U.S. companies, but the analogy remains consistent across different jurisdictions. Just as chicken is chicken, whether it's an IBC like a Seychelles or Belize IBC, or a Gmbh, the birthplace of your **little ol' register** can be anywhere around the globe. Despite the diverse global models available, we'll concentrate on some traditional structures commonly found in the USA to assemble the necessary components. When selecting the entity for your **little ol' register**, the end goal should steer your decision, regardless of the state or country.

You'll need to decide on various aspects when setting up your **little ol' register.** First and foremost, what type of entity do you need? This decision is just like selecting a graduation **vehicle** for your **little ol' register**, and once registered, it's likely to stick with that model and location for its entire existence. Even if its purpose is to be a holding company, related to the red-headed stepchild locked in the closet that never comes out, extracting the **register** from the **vehicle** later is possible, but it comes with associated costs. It's crucial to consider the long-term implications and the flexibility needed for your **little ol' register's** journey.

■   **THE SEDAN.** Commencing with the fundamentals, Sole Proprietorships represent the quickest and most cost-effective gateway into the sphere of business ownership, although not necessarily the most economical. This business structure operates on the premise that the owner and the business are a single legal entity, often referred to as a business entity. The key advantage of being a sole proprietor lies in the expeditious and straightforward establishment of the business. It allows for the filing of income with personal tax returns, and in some states, you can even operate a sole proprietorship without incurring fees.

Under this structure, you can easily write off home expenses, and financial matters can be co-mingled since it operates from the same pocket. However, the convenience comes with significant drawbacks, including unlimited personal liability for business decisions. This exposes the owner to the risk of personal assets being seized in the event of a business lawsuit, potentially jeopardizing personal financial stability—and the inverse is also true. Despite the initial ease of entry, the inherent risks make it imperative for entrepreneurs to carefully consider these downsides when opting for a Sole Proprietorship.

■ **THE MINIVAN.** Partnerships come in two main types: General Partnerships and Limited Partnerships. In a General Partnership, there are at least two active participants in the business, each contributing to its operations. On the other hand, a Limited Partnership involves at least one silent partner who typically invests capital but has a limited role in management. Additionally, there's the option of Limited Liability Partnerships (LLPs), which offer a layer of protection against liability for the actions of others within the partnership. While this shields partners from certain liabilities, it's important to note that both partners remain exposed to the same risks, similar to the risk-sharing athleticism found in a sole proprietorship. Understanding the nuances of each partnership structure is crucial for determining the most suitable model for your **little ol' register's** journey.

■ **THE PICKUP TRUCK.** The Limited Liability Corporation (LLC) presents itself as the quintessential choice, particularly suitable when a hands-on founder envisions a prolonged commitment to the venture or when the business aligns seamlessly with personal passions, quasi-buying your job, akin to investing in a reliable pickup truck for the long haul. However, as the business progresses and attracts additional investors from within the industry, ranging from smaller stakeholders to larger players, the LLC's structure may begin to exhibit limitations. While the LLC offers flexibility and simplicity in its initial stages, accommodating diverse investor interests and contributions can prove challenging as the company expands.

In scenarios where the LLC expands its membership to include multiple stakeholders, it undergoes a metamorphosis like upgrading to a sophisticated minivan—equipped to accommodate various needs and adapt to the demands of a growing team. The management structure transitions to involve managing members or officers overseeing the interests of stakeholders, fostering a collaborative partnership reminiscent of navigating a complex family **vehicle**. This evolution enables the LLC to embrace a more sophisticated approach to governance, with shared responsibilities and a collective focus on achieving common goals.

However, despite its adaptability and collaborative framework, the LLC model still carries certain drawbacks, reminiscent of the limitations encountered when relying on a versatile but ultimately constrained pickup truck. One notable disadvantage lies in the complexity that arises as the number of members increases. With multiple stakeholders involved, decision-making can become cumbersome, leading to potential conflicts of interest and operational bottlenecks.

Additionally, the LLC's structure may lack the hierarchical clarity found in more traditional corporate setups, potentially hindering efficiency and accountability, just like navigating rough terrain without the benefit of clear road markers. Furthermore, while the LLC offers liability protection for its members, this shield may not be as robust as that provided by a corporation, leaving personal assets vulnerable in certain legal scenarios, comparable to relying on a pickup truck's sturdy frame but lacking the full protection of a fortified **vehicle**. As such, while the LLC serves as a versatile and adaptable choice for many entrepreneurs, its limitations become increasingly apparent as the business grows and navigates more complex terrain.

■ **THE SEMI-TRUCK.** Corporation also known as the C-Corp, presents an excellent exit strategy with a beneficial tax rule that allows you to sell your stock after a five-year period. This strategic timeline is particularly advantageous, providing flexibility for future decisions, such as potentially going public or seeking substantial funding for scaling or innovative projects. By adhering to this five-year rule, you position yourself favorably for various financial opportunities, maximizing your potential gains and ensuring a smoother transition into new phases of business growth. This approach not only allows for strategic flexibility but also aligns with sound financial planning for your business journey.

The downside of a C-corporation extends beyond just the renowned issue of double taxation, although that is a significant concern. Double taxation occurs when the corporation's profits are taxed at the corporate level, and then shareholders are taxed again on any dividends or distributions they receive from those profits. This can significantly reduce the amount of income shareholders ultimately receive from their investments.

Additionally, C-corporations are subject to more extensive regulatory requirements and compliance obligations compared to other entity types. They must adhere to strict record-keeping standards, hold regular shareholder meetings, and file separate tax returns, all of which can be time-consuming and costly.

Another drawback is the lack of flexibility in allocating profits and losses among shareholders. Unlike other entity structures, such as S-corporations or partnerships, C-corporations do not allow for pass-through taxation, meaning shareholders cannot directly report the corporation's profits or losses on their individual tax returns. This can limit tax planning opportunities and make it more challenging to optimize tax efficiency for shareholders.

Furthermore, C-corporations may face challenges in attracting investors or raising capital compared to other entity types in the preliminary stages. Potential investors may be deterred by the double taxation structure and the complexities associated with C-corporation ownership. Additionally, venture capitalists and other investors may prefer to invest in pass-through entities like S-corporations or LLCs to avoid the double taxation burden.

Finally, C-corporations are subject to certain restrictions on ownership, particularly regarding foreign ownership and the types of shareholders they can have. These restrictions can limit the corporation's ability to expand internationally or secure funding from foreign investors.

In summary, while C-corporations offer limited liability protection and potential for growth, drawbacks such as double taxation, regulatory burdens, limited tax planning options, challenges in raising capital, and ownership restrictions should be carefully considered before choosing this entity structure for the inadept.

■ **THE SUV.** An ingenious hybrid of **vehicle** types, epitomizes versatility, offering the robustness of an off-road **vehicle** with the comfort and convenience of a family sedan. Similarly, in the demesne of business entities, achieving the perfect blend of characteristics is as simple as making an IRS tax election—a decision that can transform your business from a traditional LLC or C-corporation into a dynamic S-corporation. Transitioning to an S-corporation marks a strategic move, heralding a shift towards a more diverse and knowledgeable decision-making framework.

One of the primary advantages of transitioning to an S-corporation is the ability to tap into a wider pool of expertise and perspectives. By expanding the circle of shareholders, your **little ol' register** gains access to a wealth of insights and experiences, enriching the strategic planning process and enhancing the overall resilience of the business. This diversified decision-making approach empowers your company to navigate challenges with greater agility and creativity, leveraging the collective wisdom of its stakeholders.

Moreover, the strategic move to an S-corporation enables your business to enjoy the best of both worlds—the flexibility and simplicity of an LLC combined with the tax advantages associated with an S-corp. The IRS tax election serves as a bridge between these two entity types, allowing your **little ol' register** to navigate the regulatory landscape with greater ease and efficiency. This harmonious balance ensures that your business remains well-protected while maximizing its tax efficiencies, paving the way for sustainable growth and prosperity.

However, like any transformative decision, transitioning to an S-Corporation also comes with its considerations and potential drawbacks. One such concern is the added administrative burden and compliance requirements associated with S-Corp status. From maintaining accurate shareholder records to adhering to stringent IRS regulations, the transition entails a commitment to meticulous record-keeping and regulatory compliance. Additionally, S-Corporations are still subject to certain eligibility criteria and ownership restrictions, which may limit the company's ability to attract investors or expand its shareholder base. Always remember for both the Sole Proprietorship and the S Corp, all profits pass through to your personal taxes. However, they are treated differently once they get there.

Despite these challenges, the strategic benefits of transitioning to an S-Corporation often outweigh the potential drawbacks, especially for businesses seeking to optimize their tax planning strategies and streamline their operations. By embracing the versatility of the SUV model—combining the protective features of an LLC with the tax efficiencies of an S-Corp—your **little ol' register** can chart a course towards long-term success and resilience in today's competitive business landscape.

■ **THE OTHERS.** Exploring less conventional business structures that cater to unique business needs, a Co-Op emerges as a distinctive entity. Essentially, a Co-Op embodies a collective effort where individuals or businesses collaborate to achieve a common goal. Co-Ops are categorized under Subchapters C, K, S, and/or T of the U.S. tax code, depending on the legal structures they adhere to. What sets Co-Ops apart from other business models is the mechanism of distributions—rather than being based on investment, they are determined by usage.

Now, let's delve into the implications of this structure on your **little ol' register**. The Co-Op's cash flow is intricately tied to usage patterns within the collective. Instead of returns on investment, the financial dynamics revolve around the active involvement and utilization by the members. This unique approach underscores the cooperative nature of the business, reflecting a shared commitment to the common goal. As a result, the cash **register** becomes a barometer not just of financial investments but also of active participation and collaborative efforts within the Co-Op structure.

Having discussed the intricacies of choosing the right entity type for your business, it's time to delve into the sweetest part of the entrepreneurial journey—equity, often likened to the cherished dessert, pie. Just as selecting the perfect entity type lays the foundation for your business's structure and governance, determining the allocation of ownership—or slices of the pie—is essential for defining roles, responsibilities, and financial stakes within the company. As we transition from entity type to equity, we enter the land where stakeholders eagerly await their share of the pie, each slice representing a piece of the company's success and future prosperity.

■ **THE PIE:** Dividing ownership and determining the percentage of equity involves allocating shares or ownership stakes among stakeholders in a venture. This process revolves around distributing the ownership of a business or project among its participants. It's essentially a method of sharing the overall ownership or value of the enterprise, with each party receiving a specific portion or percentage based on their contribution, investment, or agreed-upon terms. This equity allocation is a crucial aspect of establishing a fair and transparent structure that aligns with the interests and contributions of all involved parties.

Regardless of the instrument, the concepts of share price, stocks, and member equity are fundamental in understanding how ownership is distributed in a business. Think of your **little ol' register** as having a pie, and the ownership shares represent slices of that pie. There are various methods to slice this metaphorical pie, and a common scenario is when two individuals decide to embark on a business venture together.

In a 50-50 partnership, each person gets an equal slice of the pie, meaning they share ownership equally. Alternatively, in a two-member limited liability company (LLC), ownership is divided between the two members, each getting a portion of the pie reflective of their agreed-upon terms.

Stocks, represented by shares, offer another way to divide ownership. For instance, if a company has 1000 shares of stock, and two individuals hold 500 shares each, they effectively have an equal share of the ownership of the business.

In essence, the "pie" represents the total ownership or value of the business, and how it's divided depends on the chosen structure—be it a partnership, LLC, or stock ownership. The worth of each slice is determined by the agreed-upon terms, whether it's an equal split, a percentage share, or a specified number of shares. So, when exploring business structures, it's crucial to consider the various ways to slice the pie and determine the worth of each slice in terms of ownership or equity. How you're going to spit it up?

Now, should someone attempt to convince you that a particular **vehicle** structure is unequivocally superior, recall the lessons of the **blind men** trying to perceive an elephant. The choice of structure is highly contextual, contingent on your **little ol' register's** specific goals and the puzzle piece you currently require. While most incline towards the standard corporation structure with an S election, particularly for those initiating their inaugural business endeavors, it's vital to acknowledge that this approach holds a more formal and structured demeanor.

However, it's equally essential to recognize that an LLC serves as a sophisticated partnership, finding its niche, especially when two corporations embark on a joint venture. Each **vehicle** choice comes with its set of advantages and drawbacks; for instance, an LLC provides flexibility but may have implications on tax payments or investments.

Not only the tax burden that may be imposed for the choice of and where to organize at, the federal or state level, but the Uniform Commercial Code (UCC) provides a standardized set of rules governing commercial transactions across the United States, encompassing various aspects of business dealings such as sales of goods, contracts, negotiable instruments, and secured transactions. However, while the UCC establishes general principles applicable nationwide, the rules and interpretations may vary among individual states, adding a layer of complexity to compliance and business operations for your **little ol' register**.

Each state, governed by its respective agency, may adopt its own variations or amendments to the UCC, leading to differences in interpretation, enforcement, and application of commercial laws. These variations can significantly impact the ability of your **little ol' register** to conduct business efficiently and effectively in different jurisdictions.

For instance, certain states may offer more favorable terms for contracts or sales transactions, providing greater flexibility and protection for businesses. Conversely, other states may impose stricter requirements or limitations, posing challenges or hindrances to the operations of your **little ol' register**.

Understanding the nuances of UCC provisions in each state is essential for your **little ol' register** to navigate the legal landscape successfully and capitalize on opportunities while mitigating risks. By conducting thorough research and analysis, your business can identify jurisdictions with regulations that align with its goals and develop strategies to optimize compliance and operations accordingly.

Furthermore, staying informed about changes or updates to UCC rules in different states enables your **little ol' register** to adapt its practices and contractual arrangements proactively. This proactive approach ensures that the business remains compliant, competitive, and well-positioned to achieve its objectives in a dynamic and evolving commercial environment.

To play in this sandbox, just as in the upkeep and maintenance required for any **vehicle** or essential equipment, a **little ol' register** has its own set of responsibilities to fulfill, especially in the regulated playground of business. In this context, most states mandate the appointment of a resident agent—the initial point of contact who bears the brunt of scrutiny if the **little ol' register** happens to step out of line. This individual serves as a crucial liaison between the business entity and the regulatory authorities, ensuring that the **register** complies with local regulations and navigates the intricate legal landscape effectively.

Taking a spread of the most common US choices we can match up the **wants-needs** and choices of **rich thinking** that would be prudent, with insight of **end in mind**—to get **water from the river—system**.

Pro / Con Matrix	Sole	LLC	S-Corp	C-Corp
Gross Sales	200	200	200	200
Cost & Expenses	60	60	65	65
Owner Salary W2 (payroll)	-	-	70	70
Profit (EBITDA)	140	140	65	65
Distributions	140	140	65	0
Self-Employment / Payroll Tax	19.8	19.8	9.8	9.8
Federal Taxes (individual)	15.8	15.8	16.2	-
Federal Taxes (company)	-	-	-	11.6
Total Tax Paid	35.5	35.5	26.0	22.4
Personal Liability	Yes	Partial	None	None
Admin. Complexity	♦	♦♦	♦♦♦	♦♦♦
Setup Complexity		♦	♦♦♦	♦♦♦
Investors	-	~	US<200	✓All
5-Year Exit	No	No	No	Yes<$50M

These calculations are for illustrative purposes only in order to show you how these general scenarios differ. For simplicity, this example does not include the 20% deduction for "Qualified Business Income" that became available to owners of pass-through businesses under the Tax Cuts and Jobs Act in 2018. Always consult a tax professional about how changes might affect your particular tax situation.

The tax implications, accounting practices, and variations in deductions will be revisited later in the chapter titled "Counting the Draw," where we will go deeper into some of these topics in greater detail.

Keeping true to our analogy, recognizing that it's not you personally securing the contract, but rather your **little ol' register**, opens up new possibilities. Perhaps your **little ol' register** ventures into the construction industry. Now, instead of being the worker, you're tasked with ensuring the contract is fulfilled, whether it's providing a framer or overseeing the entire framing and wall construction process. The responsibility extends beyond yourself; it could be Frank one week and Juan the next, as long as the work is getting done. Your **little ol' register** has made a commitment and given its word to fulfill the obligations of the contract.

Why don't scientists trust atoms? Because they make up everything! Now that we've lightened the mood, let's cruise into discussing some interior options and choices for your **vehicle**.

■ **HOME.** In the world of your **little ol' register,** the concept of residence closely aligns with the primary place of business. Just as your residence is your home base, the primary place of business serves as the hub for your **little ol' register's** activities or where the bulk of the paperwork lays. It's where decisions are made, transactions occur, and the daily operations unfold. Whether you're managing things from a cozy home office or a bustling commercial space, the primary place of business is the heartbeat of your **little ol' register**, anchoring its existence in the vast landscape of business ventures.

The physical address of your **little ol' register** carries substantial significance weight in establishing its credibility and professionalism. You have several options to consider, each with its own set of implications. One straightforward and cost-effective approach is to use your home address for both personal and business purposes. Alternatively, you may choose to enhance your company's image by acquiring or leasing a **shiny** and distinguished business address tailored to your operational needs. Additionally, renting a mailbox, securing space within an executive office suite, or employing mail forwarding services are viable alternatives that can elevate your **little ol' register's** facade without incurring excessive overhead costs. For those prioritizing anonymity, utilizing an attorney's address remains a tried-and-true method, offering an additional layer of privacy. It's essential to carefully evaluate these options to ensure that your **little ol' register's** image aligns effectively with its overarching business objectives and the rules there under.

■ **NANNY**. Resident Agent takes on the role of a diligent nanny, ever watchful and responsible. Similar to a nanny sending a note home if a child misbehaves, the Resident Agent plays a crucial role in communication between the state and your **little ol' register**. This legal caretaker ensures that important notices, legal documents, or updates from the state government are promptly delivered to your business's metaphorical doorstep. Just as a nanny keeps parents informed about a child's well-being, the Resident Agent helps your **register** stay in compliance and maintain a harmonious relationship with the state authorities, allowing your business to thrive in a structured and well-monitored environment. The attorneys for your **little ol' register** are always a good idea, we know they love to argue.

■ **ALIAS**. On occasion, you might find it desirable for your **little ol' register** to operate under a name different from its original one. In personal terms, this alternate moniker is often referred to as an Alias or Also Known As commonly known as AKA. In the business context, however, we use the term Doing Business As (DBA).

An exception for sole proprietors, incorporating a DBA is crucial for handling transactions and depositing checks in the name of the sole proprietorship. It establishes a formal link between the individual and their business identity.

Moreover, this relationship between a company and its brand is integral. The company's name can give rise to a brand, which may eventually evolve into a distinct entity. This transformation allows the brand to operate as its own company, with its unique identity and business activities while still maintaining a connection to the original company.

PRO TIP: When brainstorming names for your **little ol' register**, conduct a thorough search for domain names and website addresses. This step is particularly crucial if your **register** is destined for a public, consumer-facing role. By checking the availability of domain names within the state where you'll operate, you ensure a seamless and professional online presence. Remember, your website serves as a virtual storefront, and securing a relevant domain enhances your brand's visibility. Dive deeper into the intricacies of website color branding and create a simple yet effective logo. For an in-depth exploration of color theory, refer to Chapter 4: Working the Register - In Front of the Counter: Sales Marketing.

■ **MORALS**. The bylaws, member agreements, and partnership agreements serve as the fundamental guidelines that shape the behavior and operations of your register. Whether you're a sole proprietor or part of a larger team, these documents embody the ethical and moral compass of your business. While initially appearing as boilerplate language, they eventually evolve into the book of life for your company, determining the "how" and "when" of decision-making.

Regardless of the contract's name, it's the blueprint for when and how choices are made within the company, establishing the boundaries for you and other stakeholders.

Without clear governance, you risk undesirable outcomes, like former spouses becoming unexpected partners or a newly appointed CEO making extravagant expenditures. These rules, encapsulated in Robert's Rules of Order, are not static; they adapt over time, shaping the enduring legacy of your **little ol' register** and ensuring you remain a proud parent long into the future.

You may not always be in charge, even though you might have been that person at the start of your business. This is where structuring the pecking order and rules becomes prudent.

■ **FAMILY TREE.** For the ruling council, there are many different hierarchical structures that any business or organization may take to arrange their business unit. The type that is usually leaned towards is a C-level structure or variation thereof within scalable companies. Names and titles, themselves, are truly arbitrary. They are just **shiny stickers** with **the sweetest thing** conveying how that **hat** and **chess** piece should act and play in your **little ol' register's system**.

This setup bears a resemblance to the American government **system**: the Chief Executive Officer (CEO) acts as the company's public representative, the Chief Operations Officer (COO) handles the daily operations, and the Chief Financial Officer (CFO), affectionately known as the bean counters, manages finances. The board of directors guides decisions, to be carried out by these officers, in line with shareholders' interests, similar to the separation of powers.

The other two roles, normally seen, for your **little ol' register**, are the secretary, who handles administrative duties and documentation and welds the seal, while the treasurer manages financial affairs, and assets, as in company stock, and basically serves as a financial risk manager.

Titles, in essence, serve as ambiguous placeholders that often fail to capture the essence of an individual's role (**hat**) or responsibilities. They can be arbitrary labels assigned based on tradition, hierarchy, or organizational structure, rather than accurately reflecting the contributions or expertise of an individual. In many cases, titles are interchangeable and lack intrinsic meaning beyond their superficial designation.

Indeed, the significance of a person's role or accomplishments cannot be encapsulated by a mere title. Instead, individuals should be recognized and valued for their unique skills, expertise, and contributions to the organization, regardless of the label assigned to them. Ultimately, it is the actions and impact of individuals that truly define their worth, not the titles they hold.

This leads to fiduciary responsibilities, especially in the context of financial management, which is of paramount importance in ensuring the trust and confidence of stakeholders. The Sarbanes-Oxley Act (SOX) of 2002, enacted in response to corporate accounting scandals, imposes stringent regulations on financial reporting and accountability. Under SOX, corporate executives and board members are held accountable for the accuracy and integrity of financial statements, requiring them to act in the best interests of shareholders. This legislation aims to enhance transparency, mitigate fraud, and uphold ethical standards within organizations, thereby safeguarding investors' interests and promoting market integrity. Compliance with SOX entails rigorous internal controls, independent audits, and transparent disclosures, underscoring the critical role of fiduciary duties in maintaining the integrity and trustworthiness of financial **systems**.

Can you go at it alone? YES! Referred to colloquially as a one-man corporation, the one-man band, you have the flexibility to assume all the key roles—President, Vice President, Secretary, and Treasurer—any of the titles (**hats**). Considering this from the **little ol' register paradigm**, you wear multiple **hats**, being its father, mother, teacher, and nanny. It's crucial to remember that, per the rules, these roles can be terminated immediately after the appointment, even within the first day, or shortly after filing the necessary forms on behalf of the company. While the initial team may be a solitary individual, prudent and wise practice entails keeping the authorities updated with any personnel changes, ensuring compliance, and the smooth operation of your **little ol' register**.

■ **BIRTH CERTIFICATE.** To obtain a birth certificate for your register, you'll need to request one from the state where you plan to establish your business. This certificate of good standing means the company has been formed with all the property documents and most importantly fees paid to the state. Different states offer varying advantages, with Wyoming, Nevada, Texas, and Delaware being popular choices, particularly for those aiming to stay incognito or to go public.

Similar to the details provided to capture a newborn's vital statistics, the initial documents such as the doctor's report, articles of incorporation, or operating agreement provide the state with a comprehensive overview of your company—details resembling a newborn's weight, height, eye color and who the parents at the birth of your **little ol' register**.

Remember every state (governing authority) usually requires having one point of contact, a nanny, for your **little ol' register** to send a note home if it acts up and receives a bad report card.

■ **SOCIAL.** Just like any upstanding taxpayer in America, your **little ol' register** needs a Social Security Number. "But I already have one," you might say. That's true; you have one attached to you as an individual, but it won't do for your new young cash register. You don't want to be directly tied to and held liable for the taxes of your new company, even if it's a separate entity.

Consider the Employer Identification Number (EIN) as the business equivalent of the Social Security Number (SSN). While an individual's SSN is a unique identifier crucial for personal transactions and engagements, the EIN plays a similarly pivotal role for businesses. Whereas the SSN links to personal identity for participation in various aspects of civic life, the EIN serves as the distinctive marker for a business entity in the eyes of the government and financial institutions. Both numbers are fundamental for navigating their respective domains, ensuring smooth operations and compliance within the vast waters of personal and business affairs.

And, of course, don't forget about State and Local Taxes (SALT). These are essential considerations to ensure your **little ol' register** remains on the right side of financial regulations and responsibilities within the jurisdictions it operates. We all must pay the piper for "nothing can be said to be certain, except death and taxes" said Benjamin Franklin yet the certainty of mortality within the realm of business remains a topic of debate.

■ **PASSPORT.** In the sphere of corporate travel and expansion, the passport serves as a fitting analogy to the concept of foreign corporations for your **little ol' register**. When your company decides to venture beyond its home state borders, just as individuals require a passport to explore foreign territories, your business needs to file a foreign corporation certificate. This document acts as your corporate passport, granting the authorization and recognition needed to operate in a jurisdiction other than your company's state of origin. It allows your **little ol' register** to navigate the intricate playgrounds of various states or countries, ensuring compliance with local regulations and establishing a legal presence as it ventures into new corporate sandboxes to play in.

■ **DRIVER's LICENSE.** Just as a driver's license serves as a testament to an individual's ability to navigate and operate a **vehicle**, a business license functions similarly for your **little ol' register**. This license is the proof of your company's competence and authorization to engage in specific activities within a given industry or jurisdiction. It encapsulates the skills, qualifications, and adherence to regulations that validate your **little ol' register's** capability to drive its operations on the business highway, ensuring a smooth journey and compliance with the rules of the road in the corporate landscape.

At times, acquiring licenses is essential for various activities; for instance, driving a car necessitates a driver's license. Similarly, your **little ol' register** might need authorization from relevant authorities to engage in specific activities it desires. Analogous to a learner's permit, these licensing agencies may require a principal to oversee and guide your **little ol' register's** endeavors.

■ **INSPECTION.** Certification of occupancy for your **little ol' register** address can be likened to the inspection process for your license plates. Just as your **vehicle** undergoes scrutiny to ensure it meets safety and regulatory standards before hitting the road, the certification of occupancy ensures that your business premises comply with local building codes and regulations. This crucial step not only signifies that your **little ol' register** has a legal and safe space to operate within but also aligns with the meticulous checks and balances that a **vehicle** undergoes to ensure its roadworthiness. It's a stamp of approval that allows your business to navigate the corporate landscape smoothly and with the assurance that it meets all necessary requirements.

■ **LIBRARY CARD** In the jurisdiction of the **little ol' register**, obtaining a professional license can be likened to acquiring a library card. Just as a library card grants you access to a wealth of knowledge within the library's vast collection, a professional license provides entry to specific fields and industries. The library card allows you to borrow books, explore new subjects, and contribute to your intellectual growth, much like how a professional license empowers individuals to engage in specific professional activities, contributing to their career development. Both serve as gateways to valuable resources, whether it be information or professional opportunities, enriching the journey of your **little ol' register** or the eager reader alike. Sometimes you need to find someone who has one to put in these places.

■ **CREDIT SCORE.** Serves as the individual's financial report card, reflecting their creditworthiness. Much like this, the Dun & Bradstreet (D&B) Credit Rating acts as the report card for businesses, encapsulating their creditworthiness in the corporate landscape. Just as a good personal credit score opens doors to credit cards, lines of credit, and even mortgages for individuals, a favorable D&B Credit Rating grants businesses access to financial opportunities, such as credit lines and loans. Both scores play a crucial role in shaping financial narratives, determining the extent to which individuals and businesses can engage in financial transactions and secure resources for their respective wants-needs.

Finally, let's peek into a intriguing concept: What if the shares of the corporation were issued to "bearer"? Would it be equivalent to writing a check payable to "cash" or the iconic "bearer bonds" seen in movies, complete with attached coupons? This raises the fundamental question: Who would have the authority to cash the check? Moreover, considering that the figureheads of the company are employees who don't necessarily have ownership stakes, who would be listed on official filings and appear in a search if they were fired?

HATS

Anyone who has started a new business on their own, knows they are the head pot washer and the master floor sweeper, the first in the morning and the last to leave, only to go home worrying about everyone else's paycheck and the next marking campaign or product, all in the hope there something left to feed themselves. The mounts of blood, sweat, and tears, oh, that good ol' "sweat equity."

Your **little ol' register** is going to require assistance in its journey to maturity. Various aspects of the **system** must be nurtured for it to expand and reach its maximum potential. Staying true to the metaphor, think of your **little ol' register** as needing a caregiver, instructor, mentor, nanny, tutor, and more—sometimes simultaneously, and at other times, in a sequential manner. This diverse support network is essential for the holistic growth and development of your **little ol' register**.

Let's address the initial and straightforward question—who is willing to step into the role of president or CEO? Despite external perceptions, most onlookers often envision wealthy individuals enjoying opulent lifestyles in our expansive homes, seemingly indifferent to the struggles of the common person. This image may cast the president as the head whip-cracker, overseeing and directing the entire operation.

However, it is crucial to dispel misconceptions and recognize that each member of the leadership, even those in the upper echelons, has made unique sacrifices and navigated different challenges to achieve our collective goals. The burden of responsibility is substantial, particularly for the head of the table, as they bear the weight of decision-making and strategic direction for the entire enterprise where lies the feet of responsibility and accountability. Understanding and appreciating these sacrifices and responsibilities is essential in shaping a cohesive and effective leadership structure within your **little ol' register**.

It's crucial to recognize that, left to its own devices, your **little ol' register** cannot initiate action. As we delve into the assignment of various roles (**hats**) and the individuals suited for them, it becomes apparent that many employees tend to disengage their cognitive faculties upon entering the workplace. This shift is driven by the desire for a predictable, steady income—a fair choice within their rights. Their **wants-needs** are met, and they may not be inclined to shoulder the true weight of responsibility required to operate the company.

For some, the pursuit of excellence in a specific skill is satisfying, and the professional quest is fulfilling, becoming **kings of their own domains**. Others, however, may not be willing to jeopardize their livelihoods for an uncertain venture. The idea of sacrificing the present for future gains doesn't resonate with everyone. Then there are those who find fulfillment in roles that can only be found by government employment, aspiring to such as a congressperson or president. The variety of employee motivations and aspirations underscores the need for thoughtful **hat** assignments in your **little ol' register** to ensure that each **hat** is filled by someone aligned with the responsibilities and goals it entails.

Continuing on the path of transformation from "I" to the regal "We," the focus shifts to viewing each **hat** (role, duty, and title) within the organization as a mini-**system**. This approach recognizes that every business unit, role, and job has a unique set of functions, responsibilities, and workflows, undifferentiated to its own **little ol' system** within the broader framework.

Within these mini-**systems**, the concept of "**pushing paper**" comes to life. The salesperson, for instance, only sees the documents directly related to their sales activities, while the individual responsible for packing boxes is immersed in information exclusively concerning the contents of those boxes. Each role operates within its silo, unaware of the intricate details of other roles—such as the janitorial staff's compensation for sweeping up after them. These distinct **systems** have their specialized tools, processes, and specifications tailored to achieve specific goals, resembling gears in the overall machinery of your **register**.

As the collective heartbeat of your **little ol' register** reverberates through the organization, distinct characteristics begin to surface. Amid the diverse **hats** and mini-**systems**, one central persona emerges—the embodiment of your **little ol' register**. This persona is like a cybernetic neuro-net, a manifestation of collective thinking enveloped in a concrete exoskeleton. It is the unifying force that gives coherence to the myriad functions, ensuring that each mini-**system** works harmoniously towards the common goal and success of your business.

Layering paper pushing over the same desk is a necessity in the preliminary stages, especially when your **little ol' register** is a one-person show. Files neatly categorized by job initially share a common desk, creating a semblance of order amid the solo hustle. However, as your business gains momentum and complexity, this unified workspace will inevitably evolve to accommodate the growing demands of various functions.

Walks in the bookkeeper or secretary to help, the initial two layers—job and accounting—mark the first separation, acknowledging the distinctive requirements of each domain. As the enterprise expands, a three-tiered structure emerges, allocating dedicated desks to sales, operations, and accounting within the same file ecosystem. This partitioning is a crucial step in streamlining workflows and ensuring that each department has its designated space and process to thrive.

Much like the drafting table for a spunky drafter in an architectural firm or the stove for a chef in a restaurant, each desk represents a specialized station tailored to the unique needs of the respective department. This granular approach acknowledges the importance of individual workflows, and the different steps, within the larger **system**. As your **little ol' register** matures, these separate workflows become even more pronounced yet replicable, fostering efficiency and scalability. Each desk is a vital cog in the machine, ensuring that the entire operation runs smoothly, and each department has the tools it needs to contribute effectively to the overall success of your business—developing the "cookie cutter" approach to your **system**.

The **system** still stays the same even in an inverted scenario, where the dynamic often shifts, making the user of a platform like Google Search more of a provider of information to advertisers, contributing to the platform's overall revenue through targeted ads and big data. Similarly, in the land of temporary employment agencies, individuals seeking job opportunities may find themselves inadvertently becoming the resource, as these agencies may prioritize upselling their services to companies listed on platforms like "Indeed." Yet **chicken is chicken** and, in these situations, the job seeker or user becomes a valuable commodity in the business transaction between the agency and the companies seeking the service or information. Regardless the need for replicability during growth is paramount, you do not want to engineer the **system** each step of the way.

In the congested jurisdiction of union philosophy, particularly within the esteemed Teamsters, the concept of wearing multiple **hats** takes on a unique significance. Consider this scenario: if you find yourself needing to reach a destination but lacking the necessary driver, you can't simply hop into your personal car and take care of it yourself. This perspective highlights a fundamental belief: there's a finite number of **hats** available, and if there aren't enough to go around, the solution isn't to stretch yourself thin but rather to bring more people on board.

In practical terms, this means recognizing the limitations of individual capacity and skill sets. Instead of expecting one person to juggle an excessive number of responsibilities, the emphasis is on expanding the team to ensure that each task is adequately covered. This approach aligns with the ethos of collective effort and mutual support, where success is viewed as a collaborative endeavor rather than a solitary pursuit.

By embracing the philosophy of not wearing multiple **hats**, your **little ol' register** can cultivate a culture of teamwork and specialization. Each member of the team contributes their unique expertise, allowing the group to function more effectively as a whole. This not only maximizes efficiency but also fosters a sense of camaraderie and shared purpose among team members.

Moreover, it underscores the importance of strategic delegation and resource allocation. By assigning tasks based on individual strengths and capabilities, organizations can optimize their operations, achieve better outcomes, and by value increase revenue. This proactive approach to task management ensures that no one person is overburdened, and that the workload is distributed equitably among team members—producing a superior product or service.

In essence, the concept of not wearing multiple **hats** serves as a reminder that success is not solely dependent on individual effort but rather on the collective contributions of the entire team. By recognizing the value of each person's unique skills and talents, organizations can harness the power of collaboration to overcome challenges, **solve the solutions**, and achieve the **end goal in mind**.

Suddenly, the focus shifts from the mechanics of task management to the intricacies of human dynamics. As the CEO, you're not just overseeing a team; you're stewarding an entire family, and perhaps even more than one. In this role, you become the heartbeat of the company, the vital force that keeps everything pulsating and alive.

As a CEO, you stand at the crossroads of duty, burden, and privilege:

> In the hallowed halls of corporate might,
> Where decisions echo through day and night,
> The CEO stands, a sentinel of fate,
> Balancing burdens heavy and dreams innate.

Part 2: Building the Register

> The realization dawns, stark and clear,
> Not mere cogs, but souls inhabit here.
> Each heartbeat, each whisper, a universe unfurls,
> Aspirations, fears, and dreams—their precious pearls.
>
> The weight upon your shoulders, oh CEO,
> Is Atlas' burden, a cosmic ebb and flow.
> Their well-being entrusted, livelihoods in your care,
> A symphony of lives, a tapestry rare.
>
> Yet, woven within this weighty mantle,
> Lies a privilege profound, a sacred candle.
> For in your hands, the power to ignite,
> To shape destinies, to steer toward light.
>
> Impact and transformation, your canvas vast,
> Brush strokes of vision, resilience steadfast.
> The privilege to uplift, to forge a legacy,
> In this delicate dance of responsibility.
>
> So, carry the burden, but wear it as a crown,
> For leadership's path is both thorny and renowned.
> And remember, amidst the weight and strife,
> You hold the keys to a metamorphic life.

May your journey as a leader be filled with purpose, empathy, and transformative grace. Assuming the mantle of leadership, you become the central figure around which the entire organization revolves. Your decisions ripple outwards, shaping the culture, direction, and destiny of your **little ol' register**. Every choice you make, every word you speak, reverberates throughout the organization, influencing the lives of those under its care.

This realization underscores the profound importance of leadership in fostering a positive and nurturing work environment. As the heart of the company, you have the power to inspire, empower, and uplift those around you. Your leadership sets the tone for the organization, shaping its culture and guiding its collective journey towards success.

But with this power comes great responsibility. As the CEO, you must lead with integrity, empathy, and *vision*. You must champion the values of transparency, fairness, and respect, creating an environment where every individual feels valued, heard, and supported. In doing so, you not only strengthen the bonds within your organizational family but also lay the foundation for sustainable growth and prosperity.

Ultimately, the role of CEO is more than just a title; it's a sacred trust—a commitment to serving the greater good and advancing the collective welfare of all those who depend on you. It's a journey of self-discovery, growth, and transformation—one that requires courage, compassion, and unwavering dedication. As the heartbeat of the company, your leadership has the power to shape destinies and change lives. Embrace this responsibility with humility and grace and let your leadership shine as a beacon of hope and inspiration.

A tale of caution, in the high-stakes world of corporate finance, a nefarious stock manipulation scheme unfolded, drawing the attention of the FBI, DOJ, and SEC[82]. The masterminds behind the fraudulent activities were top executives at a prominent corporation. As the regulatory net tightened around them, the corporate officers found themselves caught in the web of the classic Prisoner's Dilemma.

The day of reckoning arrived with a dramatic raid orchestrated by federal agents. The offices echoed with chaos as files were seized, computers confiscated, and the once-confident executives realized the harsh reality of their actions. Faced with the impending consequences, the authorities presented the executives with a choice—cooperate and reveal the full extent of their wrongdoing or face severe legal repercussions.

The crooked executives found themselves at a critical crossroads, where each had to carefully consider their options: confess to the crimes, accept responsibility, and possibly secure a more lenient sentence, or maintain their silence in the hope of salvaging whatever shreds of dignity remained.

However, for some executives, the dilemma was even more challenging, as they were innocent of any crime. They found themselves confronted with a harsh choice: either embrace victimhood and risk losing every hard-earned dollar they had built, or become unwitting accomplices, facing the prospect of three-square meals, a place to stay, and the glint of **shiny** new handcuffs. The weight of this decision bore heavily on each executive, unveiling the intricate interplay of morality, self-preservation, and the unforgiving realities of the legal crossroad.

In a room filled with tension, some chose to cooperate, providing the authorities with valuable information to dismantle the intricate web of deception. Others, motivated by fear, loyalty, or desperation, chose to remain silent, hoping to protect themselves and their ill-gotten gains. When **s*t happens**, hitting the proverbial fan, their true nature played out in real-time as each executive grappled with the decision that could alter their lives forever.

The fallout of the investigation would lay bare the interplay of choices, consequences, and the enduring allure of the Prisoner's Dilemma in the stockades of white-collar crime. It underscored the glaring reality that individuals, regardless of their relationships or professed loyalties, will often act in their own self-interest. Despite pledges of loyalty or friendship, when faced with the stark choices presented by the dilemma, each person's instinct for self-preservation ultimately takes precedence. It's like that age-old saying: "In business, it's every man for himself—especially when there's a **shiny** pair of handcuffs involved!"

In the elaborate yarn ball of organizational dynamics, each **hat** worn by the roles of the company, including the CEO **hat**, represents the unique facets of leadership, responsibility, and *vision*. As you navigate the multifaceted landscape of executive leadership, remember that each **hat** carries its own weight and significance. Whether you're donning the strategist's cap, the diplomat's **hat**, or the mentor's crown, approach each role with diligence, wisdom, and compassion.

In the end, the true measure of leadership lies not in the number of **hats** you wear, but in the impact, you have on those around you. By embracing the diverse roles and responsibilities that come with the title, you have the opportunity to shape the destiny of your **little ol' register** and inspire greatness in others. Wear your **hats** with pride, lead with purpose, and let your *vision* guide the way to a brighter future for all.

Part 3: Programming the Register

"A man must be big enough to admit his mistakes, smart enough to profit from them and strong enough to correct them."

– John C. Maxwell,
Founder of The John Maxwell Company

LEARNING OBJECTIVES, THE EXECUTIVE PERSPECTIVE

From the Executive Perspective, as the earth rapidly approaches, prepare to don the CEO crown and wield the scepter of strategic vision! Here, we'll full-fight into the exhilarating grounds of top-level decision-making, where every choice echoes through the corridors of power. From honing negotiation skills and balancing the truth of advertising to nurturing a culture of innovation and mastering the art of delegation, each learning objective is a golden star on your shoulders, unlocking the secrets of executive excellence. So, summon your inner tycoon and get ready to lead your company to the zenith of success—because in the realm of CEOs, the sky's not the limit; it's just the beginning of your cosmic conquest!

■ **Strategic Leadership and Decision-Making:** Develop the skills necessary to provide strategic leadership and make informed decisions that drive the long-term success and growth of your organization.

■ **Effective Communication and Stakeholder Management:** Learn how to communicate effectively with internal and external stakeholders, including employees, investors, customers, and regulatory bodies, to build trust and foster positive relationships.

■ **Change Management and Adaptability:** Acquire skills in change management and adaptability to navigate through periods of transition and uncertainty, and lead your organization through successful change initiatives.

■ **Innovation and Entrepreneurial Thinking:** Foster a culture of innovation and entrepreneurial thinking within your organization, encouraging creativity, risk-taking, and continuous improvement.

■ **Ethical Leadership and Corporate Social Responsibility:** Explore the principles of ethical leadership and corporate social responsibility, and learn how to integrate these values into your business strategy and operations.

■ **Strategic Partnerships and Alliances:** Identify opportunities for strategic partnerships and alliances that can enhance your organization's capabilities, expand its market reach, and drive innovation and growth.

■ **Performance Metrics and Key Performance Indicators (KPIs):** Understand the importance of defining and tracking key performance metrics and KPIs to measure progress towards organizational goals and drive performance improvement initiatives.

Notes:

MANAGING THE STORE: LEADERSHIP AND GOVERNANCE

Every perspective presented, if an executive believes their job is to manage, then they are only partially correct. Indeed, the ability to "get the job done" and make sound financial decisions based on foresight and analysis is how one grows into the role in the first place. Nevertheless, until one masters the art and science of managing the relationships they maintain in that role, they aren't going to provide maximum value.

The role of leadership in business is analogous to the captain navigating a ship through uncharted waters. A skilled leader provides direction, instills a sense of purpose, and charts a course toward shared objectives. Beyond merely steering the ship, true leadership involves inspiring the crew to weather storms, fostering a resilient spirit, and ensuring that every member contributes their unique strengths to the collective journey. A successful leader doesn't command from a pedestal but stands shoulder to shoulder with their team, cultivating an environment of trust, collaboration, and continuous growth. In essence, leadership is the compass that not only guides the company through challenges but also empowers individuals to discover their own potential amid the vast sea of opportunities.

Welcome to the kingdom of Managing the Store: Leadership and Governance, where we delve into the intricate **paradigms** of how we perceive ourselves and others, and how to inspire these perceptions within our teams, customers, and stakeholders. Through sections like "**Blink**," "**Take My Job**," and "**Chess**," we'll unravel the complexities of decision-making, empathy, and strategic planning that underpin effective leadership and governance in the retail landscape. Join us on this journey as we navigate the subtle nuances of human behavior and organizational strategy to unlock success in the retail department.

BLINK

In Malcolm Gladwell's book "**Blink**," the notion of the adaptive unconscious and its impact on our decision-making process takes center stage. Here, Gladwell delves into the power of thinking without thinking, emphasizing the significance of split-second judgments and snap decisions. Within the fabric of our unconscious lies a reservoir of insights and instincts, capable of swiftly assessing situations, people, and circumstances with remarkable accuracy. [83]

Malcolm challenges the conventional wisdom that suggests careful deliberation leads to better decisions. Instead, he posits that our intuitive responses, made in the **blink** of an eye, often yield outcomes that rival or surpass those achieved through prolonged analysis. Through compelling anecdotes and scientific research, Malcolm demonstrates how our minds possess an innate ability to distill complex information into rapid-fire assessments, shaping our perceptions and influencing our actions. [83]

The book illuminates the nuances of first impressions, shedding light on the subtle cues and signals that inform our unconscious judgments. Whether navigating social interactions, evaluating products, or making critical business decisions, the adaptive unconscious plays a pivotal role in guiding our responses. By exploring the interplay between intuition and analysis, Malcolm invites readers to reconsider the value of rapid cognition and embrace the power of instinctive thinking.[83]

Nevertheless, the principles explored in "**Blink**" extend beyond split-second decisions and apply to various facets of information processing, including reading and comprehension. Take speed reading, a technique that trains individuals to absorb text at an accelerated pace, harnesses the power of rapid cognition aligned with viewing a picture worth a thousand words.

By honing the skill of speed reading, individuals can enhance their cognitive abilities and optimize their capacity to extract meaning from written content with efficiency and precision. Much like the swift assessments made in the **blink** of an eye, speed reading allows readers to quickly assimilate information, discern key insights, and grasp the essence of complex ideas without getting bogged down in minutiae.

Just as our adaptive unconscious sifts through sensory inputs to form instantaneous judgments, speed reading enables readers to navigate through texts with agility, extracting pertinent details and synthesizing overarching themes in a fraction of the time it would take through conventional reading methods. [84] This accelerated mode of information processing not only fosters greater comprehension but also cultivates a deeper appreciation for the art of reading as a powerful and transformative intellectual endeavor.

Yet can the word choice lead to incorrect thoughts or actions? Indeed, the distinction between using "I" versus "We" can significantly impact the message conveyed, even in solitary endeavors. While one may currently operate solo, opting for the inclusive "We" instead of the singular "I" fosters a sense of collaboration, unity, and shared responsibility. This subtle shift in language sets the tone for collective engagement and implies an openness to collaboration and teamwork, laying the groundwork for future partnerships and alliances.

However, the influence of communication extends beyond mere word choice. Our senses play a crucial role in interpreting messages, with body language often overshadowing verbal cues. According to the 7-38-55 Rule, only 7% of communication is conveyed through words, while tone of voice accounts for 38%, and body language constitutes a whopping 55%.[85] This underscores the significance of nonverbal cues in conveying intention, emotion, and meaning, highlighting the importance of aligning verbal and nonverbal communication to ensure clarity and coherence in our interactions.

The significance of language choice lies in its ability to strike a delicate balance between conveying truth and inspiring action. We possess the innate capacity to swiftly assess messages and situations, drawing upon our intuitive instincts and cognitive biases. Yet, this process is not solely influenced by what we hear or see; our presumptions and maladaptive thoughts also shape our perceptions, alike the parable of the **blind men** and the elephant. In essence, it's the accumulation of these predispositions, seemingly insignificant details—the nuances in language, the subtleties of body language, and the underlying assumptions—that collectively shape our understanding and interpretation of the world around us, all in the **blink** of an eye.

Definitely, to trust our gut instincts and make swift decisions, we must train our minds accordingly. The philosophy of "slow is smooth and smooth is fast" underscores the importance of taking deliberate actions to prevent errors and promote efficiency, especially in high-pressure situations.[86] This principle can be extrapolated to our perceptions and business strategies, enabling us to align our thoughts, direction, and strategies effectively. By adopting this approach, we can clarify our thinking, articulate our *vision* to others, and gain a deeper understanding of the realities of the world around us all in a **blink**.

By cultivating this mindset, we develop the ability to navigate the complexities of our environment with clarity and purpose. Just as a skilled craftsman hones their technique to achieve mastery, we sharpen our mental faculties to enhance our decision-making process. This entails not only refining our cognitive skills but also cultivating emotional intelligence and intuition.

In the mind of business, where rapid decisions can often determine success or failure, the ability to trust our instincts and make quick yet informed judgments is invaluable. By embracing the concept of "slow is smooth and smooth is fast," we can streamline our thought processes, minimize hesitations, and seize opportunities with confidence.

Moreover, this approach fosters a deeper connection with our intuition, allowing us to tap into our subconscious knowledge and insights. Rather than succumbing to analysis paralysis or overthinking, we learn to trust our instincts and act decisively in a **blink**.

In essence, training our minds to embrace this philosophy empowers us to navigate uncertainty with grace and agility. It enables us to remain calm under pressure, make sound judgments, and adapt to changing circumstances with ease. As we refine our ability to think swiftly and purposefully, we unlock new levels of effectiveness and resilience in both our personal and professional lives.

Indeed, in the rough and tumble playground of business, where decisions must often be made swiftly and with precision, the importance of implementing guiding principles cannot be overstated. By establishing governing rails that align with the core values and objectives of your **little ol' register,** you create a framework for navigating the inherent complexities of the market with poise and effectiveness.

Much like the concept of "slow is fast" emphasizes the value of deliberate action over haste, these governing rails serve as a blueprint for promoting thoughtful decision-making and strategic planning within your organization. They provide a set of guidelines and standards that help mitigate the risks associated with impulsive reactions or uninformed choices.

Moreover, just as speed reading trains the brain to process information rapidly and efficiently, these governing rails equip your team with the tools and techniques needed to interpret market signals, assess opportunities, and respond decisively to emerging trends. By instilling a culture of agility and adaptability, you empower your **little ol' register** to stay ahead of the curve and capitalize on new opportunities for growth and innovation.

In essence, by embracing the principles of deliberation and foresight, you create a foundation for sustainable success and resilience in the face of uncertainty. By incorporating these governing rails into your business strategy, you establish a framework that not only promotes efficiency and effectiveness but also fosters a culture of continuous learning and improvement.

Effective governance serves as the nerve **system** of a well-functioning organization, acting as the flashlight that guides decision-making and ensures the smooth operation of your **little ol' register**. Governance encompasses the set of policies, processes, and structures through which an organization is directed, controlled, and held accountable. It provides the framework for decision-making at all levels, from strategic choices to day-to-day operations.

In the context of your **little ol' register**—the executive prefrontal cortex of the company—governance plays a crucial role in safeguarding assets, maintaining financial integrity, and mitigating risks. A robust governance structure includes mechanisms for financial oversight, internal controls, and transparency. Board members, executives, and financial professionals must collaborate to make informed decisions that align with the organization's mission and strategic objectives.

The governance framework also extends to compliance with legal and regulatory requirements, ensuring that the cash **register** operates within ethical and legal boundaries. By adhering to governance principles, companies build trust with stakeholders, including investors, employees, and customers, contributing to the overall health and sustainability of the business.

In essence, effective governance is the guardian of the cash **register's** accuracy, reliability, and integrity. It ensures that financial decisions are aligned with the company's purpose, safeguarding the interests of all stakeholders, and fostering a resilient and prosperous financial foundation. Alleviating any snap judgment in the light of an emotional decision.

It was just another day shooting on location of one of America's most infamies crime shows, the crew meticulously orchestrating the dramatic reenactment of a notorious criminal's elude from all.[87] Little did they know that irony was about to take center stage in a twist that no scriptwriter could have concocted. As the cameras rolled and actors passionately brought to life the story of a notorious criminal's escape, fate had a different script in mind.

As the actor ranted describing the gripping scene, the real criminal, unbeknownst to the crew, fate had orchestrated a twist no one could have predicted. In a stroke of surreal happenstance, the very criminal they were portraying emerged from the shadows and unwittingly stepped onto the set. Oblivious to the cameras and lights, he became an unwitting participant in his own narrative. The crew, believing it to be just another extra, a breathing prop, continued with the shoot.

However, in a **blink**, keen-eyed of set law enforcement officers, trained in the mindset of criminality, watching at video village recognized the fugitive instantly. What began as a scripted reenactment swiftly transformed into a real-life arrest, with the cameras capturing every moment in vivid detail.

In a surreal turn of events, the arrest unfolded right there on the set, with the cameras rolling and the actors seamlessly transitioning from their scripted lines to stunned silence. The criminal, thinking he had found a haven among the cast and crew, found himself in the unexpected spotlight of justice. It was a moment of ironic poetic justice, where reality seamlessly blended with the staged portrayal of crime, leaving everyone on set in disbelief at the serendipity of capturing on television's very own stage of life.

In the journey of business leadership, it's essential to strike a delicate balance between trusting your instincts and tempering emotional responses with logical deduction. While intuition can often provide valuable insights and guide decision-making in the **blink** of an eye, it's equally important to cultivate the executive governance of the prefrontal cortex within your **little ol' register**.

By honing the cognitive processes that govern rational thought and strategic planning, you empower your team to navigate complex challenges with clarity and precision. Through disciplined training and continuous learning, you can enhance the speed and efficiency of decision-making across every facet of your business, from operational workflows to strategic initiatives.

Ultimately, by integrating instinctual wisdom with cognitive discipline, you create a harmonious synergy that propels your **little ol' register** towards sustainable growth and success. So, trust your gut, but also invest in the cognitive infrastructure and guidelines that enable your **little ol' register** to thrive in the ever-evolving landscape of business.

CHESS

In the intricate game of business, attire serves as the strategic **chess** piece, a crucial element in dressing your **little ol' register** for success. Embrace the reality that judgments are often made based on appearances, and recognize that your presentation carries significant weight, sometimes even surpassing the importance of your product and brand. The key lies in projecting an image that mirrors a national brand supported by a multitude of investors. "Walk the walk—talk the talk," exuding the confidence and stature of a substantial company, even if your **little ol' register** is just starting its journey.

With wide-eyed wonder and a heart pounding with anticipation, Jimmy embarked on his very first bus ride ever to the famous Miami Beach, accompanied by his spirited aunt. The rhythmic hum of the bus engine marked the beginning of an adventure that would etch memories into the canvas of his childhood.

As they neared their destination, the air grew thick with the scent of salt and excitement. Miami Beach unfolded before his eyes like a vibrant collage. A symphony of colors and sounds danced along the bustling streets. His aunt, a seasoned traveler, guided him through the lively scenes, from the pristine beaches to the eclectic boardwalk.

Amidst the lively atmosphere, Jimmy encountered the hustle and bustle of street performers engaging in card games and lightning-fast speed **chess**. Mesmerized, he observed the nimble fingers of the three-card Monte dealers, their sleight of hand captivating the attention of onlookers. The **chess** experts, on the other hand, orchestrated moves with a precision that left him in awe.

What struck Jimmy most was the vast diversity among the people. Faces from all walks of life mingled on the vibrant streets—a true kaleidoscope of humanity. The contrasts were striking, from the sun-kissed beachgoers to the strategic **chess** players absorbed in their mental battles.

With each step, Miami Beach revealed itself as a melting pot of cultures, where the rhythm of life pulsed through the streets. Jimmy and his aunt savored every moment, immersing themselves in the vibrant energy that permeated the air. The bus ride, far more than a simple journey, became a voyage into a world where diversity thrived, and the richness of experience unfolded at every turn.

What seemed to be a magical world and each person cast into their roles the sun dipped below the horizon, casting hues of orange and pink across the Miami skyline, Jimmy and his aunt made their way back to the bus stop. Eager to carry the day's vibrant experiences with him, Jimmy couldn't help but notice the stark contrast between a few individuals awaiting the same bus. On one side stood an elderly street artist, his weathered hands still clutching the remnants of a well-loved paintbrush. On the other, a young tech enthusiast was engrossed in the glow of his tablet. Intrigued by the diversity encapsulated within those waiting for the bus, Jimmy struck up a conversation with both and inquired about the next stop. The artist shared tales of his colorful journey, while the tech-savvy young man unfolded a digital narrative of innovation and progress. In that brief exchange, the bus stop became a microcosm of life's varied chapters, each person carrying a unique story and perspective on the ride back home.

As they walked back towards the bus area, Jimmy realized in an instant **why** he listened to one guy and not the other. The young tech in the aisle was dressed sharply. The young man looked like he was on his way home from work in a fancy office downtown. The other was wearing sweatpants, had a dark stain on his t-shirt, and looked like he might have skipped showering that day.

At this moment, Jimmy realized just how many preconceived notions and stereotypes were built into his own assumptions of other people. **Why** was he judging based on clothes—can Jimmy trust the instructions of someone who can't be trusted to even keep food off themselves? Jimmy didn't mean to make this **blink** judgment, was it simply the years of parochial schooling conditioning taking over? His decision process went into autopilot. If you want people to listen to you, there's an important lesson here: Dress the message.

The clothes you wear and the way you groom yourself will change the way other people hear what you say. It will subconsciously tell them if you're like them or if you're different. It will determine whether they listen or ignore. Trust or distrust. As memoirist and writing coach Adair Lara says, "Tone is what the dog hears." Consider the audience and the message. Think carefully about who it is you're trying to influence and **why**. What do they care about and **why** is it important?

In the art of effective communication, the mantra "listen first, speak second" encapsulates a fundamental principle that underpins meaningful dialogue and connection.[88] By prioritizing attentive listening over immediate response, individuals cultivate empathy, understanding, and respect in their interactions. This approach allows one to grasp the nuances of another's perspective, concerns, and emotions before formulating a thoughtful and considerate response. In both personal and professional settings, embracing this practice fosters constructive communication, facilitates conflict resolution, and strengthens relationships. Moreover, it demonstrates humility and openness to learning from others, enriching one's own perspectives and broadening horizons. In essence, by heeding this timeless advice, individuals lay the foundation for authentic and impactful communication that transcends barriers and fosters genuine connections.

When you know this, you can present yourself and communicate in a way that focuses on those ideals. The way you'd dress at a business conference full of middle-aged folks is different from how you would dress at a high school sports game. Think about who you're talking to and what would make them trust you. The most expensive route is not always the most effective one. Take the case for a standard business suit, a cheaper suit smartly trailered to your form is better than an ill-fitting expensive mop. A clean scrubbed pair of tennis shoes is better than un-shined scuffed dress shoes. A well-fit tucked-in polo is better than an overblown button-up untucked and untidy appearance. When you make it, you can wear whatever you want, until then play the game.

You may not like this reality but remember those who succeed are not those who complain about "the way it is" or "the way it should be." You find a way to play the game. You can "Hem" and "Haw" all you want or do you want that grass-fed cheddar?[45] Winners are the ones who accept reality for what it is and use that reality to their advantage—seize the day! They also don't fool themselves into thinking that things today will be the same as tomorrow.

With the **End in Mind**, don't dress where you're at; dress where you want to be. Here's **why**: "Self-Perception." Primarily, dressing well changes how you see yourself. The clothes we wear not only reflect our personality and values but also shape the perception in our minds. This phenomenon, known as "self-verification theory," suggests that we tend to seek clothing that aligns with our self-concept, reinforcing our desired identity.[89]

Moreover, research shows that clothing significantly influences first impressions and social perception, affecting how others perceive our personality traits, credibility, and even competence; irrespective of the surrounding bus windows. When we dress well, we experience a psychological phenomenon known as "enclothed cognition."[90] This theory suggests that our clothing choices directly impact our mood, self-esteem, and overall cognitive processes.[91]

Wearing outfits that make us feel attractive and put-together can enhance our posture, body language, and non-verbal communication, signaling confidence to ourselves and others. You appear more put-together, sophisticated, and in control. This altered self-perception can give you a psychological boost, leading to increased confidence. Even when a woman dyes her hair, a release of dopamine showers her for days, no matter the color.[92] Even though the color does have some impact on our perceptions and the perceptions of others, the **blink** of radiation from oneself will shine brighter.[93]

Ever noticed how someone wielding a clipboard seems to exude authority effortlessly? It's almost as if they could stroll into any establishment, clipboard in hand, and not be questioned about their access or purpose. But let's not veer off into discussions about physical penetration testing and stealing trade secrets just yet; we'll save those for later sections.

The clipboard changes the **paradigm** because it symbolizes organization, authority, and purpose. People tend to associate clipboards with official tasks, whether it's conducting surveys, performing inspections, or overseeing operations. When someone holds a clipboard, others instinctively assume they have a legitimate reason for being there and are authorized to carry out their activities. It's a psychological phenomenon where the mere presence of a clipboard can alter people's perceptions and behavior, granting the holder an unspoken level of authority and credibility.[94]

Every role is cast through those vibrant streets of humanity. In turn, every **hat** has a uniform. Uniforms influence customer perception and play a vital role in shaping brand image and customer experience. When customers encounter employees in well-designed, cohesive uniforms, it creates a positive first impression and reinforces brand values. Uniforms communicate authority and professionalism, instilling a sense of trust in individuals who interact with uniformed personnel. The presence of a uniform creates an immediate perception of competence, expertise, and credibility. Whether it's a doctor in a lab coat or a police officer in their distinctive attire, uniforms evoke the same sense of authority and expertise, establishing trust between the wearer and those they serve.[95]

They also have the power to enhance performance by creating that same psychological shift in the individual who wears them. When people put on the uniform associated with their roles or professions, they experience this cognitive **paradigm** shift subconsciously all in a **blink**. This phenomenon triggers behavioral patterns linked to the uniform's symbolism, enabling individuals to embody the qualities and expectations associated with their roles, and specific psychological associations.[95] By creating effective uniforms, employees can feel a sense of purpose, professionalism, and accountability, which can improve their performance and productivity. This can be simply a uniform-colored t-shirt and matching jeans, as the collective conformity needed to inspire the troops and the masses.

A vital role that plays in fostering unity and team cohesion within organizations are uniforms. When employees wear uniforms that represent a collective identity, it fosters a sense of belonging and promotes a team-oriented mindset. Uniforms eliminate visual barriers and create a level playing field, emphasizing that everyone is part of a unified team working towards a shared goal. The psychology of uniforms goes beyond mere attire it produces into the most mundane and innocuous aspects that **blinks** in our subconscious. It encompasses the power of symbolism, perception, and behavioral influences.

Many may resonate with the experience of navigating the remote work landscape during the Covid years, parallel to the 2022 version of the 1980 garage startup. It offers a glimpse into the world of launching a business from the comfort of home. In this setting, certain phrases can either bolster or impede the progress of your **little ol' register**. Consider phrases like "Allow me to reach my office," even if that office is currently nestled amidst the confines of your trousers and dress shirts in the shared section of your wife's closet that she graciously lends you. These days, many have set up "sets" and applied filters for their in-home offices for those Team-Zoom meetings, blurring the lines between professional and personal spaces.

When you answer, respond with a touch of professionalism: "Hello, this is Robert. How may I assist you on this wonderful day?" Ensure you have a concise and professional voicemail on that shared line, temporarily concealing your **little ol' register's** brand within your personal line. This approach extends to even those mysterious calls from unknown numbers—never let unfounded fear (**mind-killer**) dictate your responses and never miss an opportunity due to hesitation.

This extends beyond you and to everyone helping your **little ol' register**. When training staff, emphasizing phrases like "yes sir," "no sir," and "thank you, ma'am," along with promoting proper respect and etiquette, becomes a priority. Onboarding into this philosophy may be smoother for some, especially those naturally accustomed to it, as seen in the cultural norms of the South.

Statements like "Only big companies have to do that" or "We don't have to do that around here" often stem from a contrast between the perceived norms of corporate entities (B-type) and the reality of being a sole practitioner or small business (J.O.B) owners. This contrast highlights the different **paradigms** at play in the business world. While larger corporations may have dedicated departments and resources to handle certain tasks or comply with specific regulations, smaller businesses often operate with limited personnel and resources, leading to a different approach to addressing challenges.

Additionally, the mindset of "we don't have to do that around here" may reflect a reluctance to adapt to new practices or processes due to ingrained habits or a resistance to change. However, it's essential to recognize that embracing best practices and compliance measures, regardless of business size, can contribute to long-term success and sustainability.

As we speak, verbal pauses filled with "Um," "Ah," and "You Know," breaks the valuable golden silence, and the rippling resonance of words like "Yo," "Yeah," and "Dude" extends beyond mere language; it becomes a component of both attire (image) and perception.[96] The way we express ourselves, from the refined eloquence of a snobbish Englishman to the warm drawl of a good ol' Southern speaker, profoundly influences how others perceive us.

Consider the dichotomy between these linguistic styles. Picture a scenario where you require brain surgery, and the doctor, in a heavy Southern drawl, casually remarks, "Well butter my butt and call me a biscuit, we're fixin' to cut that little noggin open." It's hard not to entertain the thought of seeking a second opinion. While this is a jest about the Southern upbringing, it's crucial to recognize that certain words in different regions can wield significant impact. This isn't a commentary on the doctor's qualifications or their surgical prowess, but rather an exploration of the nuances carried by regional expressions and the manner in which one speaks.

Another linguistic subtlety that resonates with many is the distinction between "Ya'll" and "You Guys." For those who have navigated between the Texan and Californian territories, these linguistic preferences can be perplexing.

While one might expect "y'all" to be favored in California for its gender-neutral quality, the complexities of regional language endure. As the saying goes, "When in Rome."

Now, what if one were to consider that every industry possesses its own specialized language? Undoubtedly, this observation hits the mark. Within each sector, a distinct jargon, a coded language, exists, familiar only to those fully clothed and immersed in that specific line of business. It constitutes a clandestine lexicon that transcends verbal expression, encompassing both language and appearance. For example, a request for a pair of half-apple boxes, a joker, a c-stand with a gobo head, and some B52's for Video Village might confound those outside the showbiz. This underscores the notion that effective communication in a professional context not only hinges on the words employed but also demands a profound comprehension of the specialized language and visual cues inherent to each industry.

An apron for a waiter, a hard **hat** for a construction worker, and a clipboard for an inspector—these distinct attires are the embodiment of the **chess** pieces on the grand board of professions. Each outfit conveys a specific role, much like the moves of **chess** pieces in a strategic game. The waiter's apron symbolizes service and attentiveness, the construction worker's hard hat signifies diligence and safety, and the inspector's clipboard represents meticulous examination and assessment. Just as **chess** pieces have unique functions and contribute to the overall strategy of the game, these work attire contribute to the professional landscape, signaling the wearer's role and responsibilities in the intricate game of industry and service.

Just as each **chess** piece has its unique moves and significance on the board, the way we dress our **little ol' register** becomes a crucial move in the business arena. The attire becomes a visual representation, communicating the essence and professionalism of our venture. It sets the tone for how the world perceives and interacts with our business, influencing the moves we make on the grand chessboard of commerce. So, let's choose our attire wisely and make a powerful opening move in the intricate game of business.

TAKE MY JOB

In the intricate dance of business, from the initial hire to the ongoing training, and the aspirations to climb the corporate ladder, the responsibility ultimately falls on your shoulders. Whether you're a solo entrepreneur or the captain of a larger enterprise, the success or failure of your **little ol' register** hinges on the decisions and actions you make. In this domain, the adage "it's always your fault" serves as a powerful reminder of the accountability that comes with the entrepreneurial territory.

Knowing that your **little ol' register**'s performance relies on a well-informed leader, the quest for knowledge becomes paramount. If you lack information, it's your duty to seek it out—whether that means personally acquiring the knowledge or surrounding yourself with the people who do. Blindly, delegating the task to someone within your organization is a valid option, yet don't become ignorant or complacent with this option alone. The flow of wisdom must not be obstructed, and the learning curve must be continually traversed for the betterment of your business and yourself.

Aiming for just a 1% improvement in a specific goal might not sound like much, but believe it, it's like compound interest for your achievements! You start with that tiny 1%, and before you know it, you're skyrocketing toward success faster than a cat chasing a laser pointer! It's like trying to teach a monkey a new trick—seems small at first, but give it time, and you'll have a primate that will be slicing bananas over calculus! So, remember, even if you're making progress at a snail's pace, at least you're not standing still. After all, slow and steady wins the race... unless you're racing against a hare on roller skates!

Nevertheless, understanding what needs to be done and actually executing those tasks are two distinct realms.[97] The gap between intention and action often separates those who merely aspire to success from those who tangibly achieve it.[98] The ability to bridge this gap becomes a defining factor in the journey of your **little ol' register**. So, let's dive into the intricate details of navigating this space and ensuring that your aspirations materialize into concrete results.

The chasm between intention and action is where many dreams go to take a long nap. It's like wanting to climb Mount Everest but only making it as far as the local hill—there's a big difference between dreaming about success and actually putting on those climbing boots! That's why it's crucial to bridge that gap with concrete, actionable goals. It's like having a treasure map but actually digging for the gold instead of just staring at the X and daydreaming about riches. So, let's stop admiring the view from the edge of the cliff and start taking steps to soar among the stars!

To achieve these results, we must first design these crucial components by creating the definitions and expectations of each job and role (**hats**), analogous to gears in a machine. Each job is a resource necessary for the smooth functioning of the entire **system**.

Part 3: Programming the Register

In this process, it's essential to teach the nuances of the job to the designated individuals, transforming them into subject matter experts who understand the intricacies of the domain within your **system**. Building the **system** involves creating a comprehensive structure with all the necessary roles, each functioning like a specific **hat**. The organization operates as a unified entity, breaking down into miniaturized subunits, with each station having specific tasks and requirements. The overarching management objective is to craft a box from the outside, concealing the internal workings while ensuring that every input results in two valuable outputs, promoting efficiency and cohesion.

The notion of "that's not my job" is counterproductive; instead, it's about embracing the union mindset where each member works collaboratively for the greater good.[99] The goal is to identify individuals who not only fit the role but also resonate with it on a personal level—those who wear the **hat** willingly and passionately, answering the age-old question of what they aspire to be when they grow up.

In evaluating the viability of various roles and responsibilities, it's crucial to take into account the overall costs associated with each **hat** worn within your team. While initially, performing a specific role might appear to be a cost-saving measure for the company, it's imperative to closely examine whether these apparent savings inadvertently result in personal gains for the individual donning that particular **hat**. However, strategically performing the more costly job at certain times and facilitating training for potential replacements ensures a sustainable and efficient progression up the hierarchical ladder. For instance, if one **hat** incurs a cost of $10 per hour and another $50, it makes more financial sense to allocate the $10 task to someone else, saving the company $50, rather than the inverse scenario.

Don't worry, according to the IRS, as a working founder, you too are considered an employee of the company.[100] When you perform a task on one hand and then withdraw money from the **register** for personal use, it's like taking a draw or borrowing against future distribution payments. In the beginning, especially with no partners, the money involved is "essentially" your own, or representing your portion thereof. However, the manner in which this is done, both presently and in the future, is regulated by your **little ol' register's genesis** doctrine–the company's bylaws. It's crucial to remember the concept of commingling funds—mixing personal and company finances, symbolized by placing coins of different ownership in the same pocket.

As the gears of your system evolve and responsibilities are delegated to the other employees, such as ensuring nightly deposits or managing payroll, complications may arise.[101] Granting someone the authority to write checks may pose a risk, especially if that individual has the potential to deplete the company's bank accounts. This becomes particularly problematic itself or if, for instance, you decide to terminate their employment. Releasing internal controls can be a challenging and exceedingly risky situation. To protect your **little ol' register's** financial integrity, having a well-defined check and balance **system** in place is mandatory, particularly if your goal is to step away from day-to-day operations.

Every decision is a step forward on your journey, and the culmination of these choices propels you toward your **little ol' register's** *vision*, your ultimate goal. Reflect on the past, learn from it, and let each moment guide you as you forge ahead. Remember daily, the first good decision is the one you've just made today, embracing the daily opportunity to shape your future. Keep your eyes on the **end goal**, let it fuel your determination, and know that every decision inches you closer to the realization of your dreams, for today's decisions are tomorrow's successes.

As we have dipped our toe the Madhatter's world of **hats**, the adage "do it first" stands as a guiding principle for effective leadership. Leading by example means embodying the work ethic, dedication, and standards you expect from your team. It's about diving headfirst into the challenges, tasks, and responsibilities, setting a precedent for others to follow. When you demonstrate a willingness to get your hands dirty and tackle the nitty-gritty aspects of the job, it not only earns the respect of your team but also fosters a culture of shared commitment and mutual effort. By immersing yourself in the work, you eliminate any room for ambiguity or misinformation about the job requirements, allowing you to lead and govern with authenticity and credibility.

This principle of leading by example is intrinsically tied to the idea that you should never ask anyone to do something you wouldn't do yourself. This principle establishes a foundation of trust and transparency within the team. If you've walked the same path, faced the same challenges, and overcome similar hurdles, there's a mutual understanding that transcends mere instruction. Your guidance carries the weight of firsthand experience, and your team can trust that your directives are grounded in practical wisdom. This approach not only strengthens the leader-follower relationship but also ensures that expectations are realistic and rooted in a genuine understanding of the work at hand, not to mention the fact you become quite aware of what that role takes.

Don't be a know-it-all. The delicate balance between being a subject matter expert and understanding what a founder needs to build a **system** is a crucial dynamic in the entrepreneurial landscape. While being a subject matter expert

provides invaluable insights and a deep understanding of the industry, it's equally essential for a founder to grasp the broader aspects of business operations. Founders often wear multiple **hats**, and their role extends beyond specialized knowledge. They need to navigate various facets of the business, from strategic planning to team leadership and financial management. Recognizing the need for a well-rounded skill set, founders must decide whether to find or train new experts who complement their expertise. Building a successful venture requires not only depth in a specific **domain** but also the ability to orchestrate a harmonious ensemble of skills and perspectives to drive the business forward.

Building a robust business **system** involves meticulously crafting a structure that accommodates all the necessary roles and responsibilities, analogous to wearing different **hats**. Each **hat** symbolizes a unique skill set or function crucial for the smooth operation of the venture. From the visionary **hat** of the founder to the financial strategist's cap, and the operational manager's headgear, each plays a pivotal role in creating a comprehensive and well-functioning **system**. The process involves identifying key functions, allocating responsibilities, and ensuring that every aspect of the business is covered. Whether it's developing products, managing finances, or fostering a positive workplace culture, the art lies in designing a **system** where each **hat** fits seamlessly into the overall structure, contributing to the success and sustainability of your **little ol' register**.

Is your business starting to resemble an adult day care center, where you find yourself stuck in a loop of repeating instructions, fixing mistakes, and constantly firefighting to keep things together? The frustration of an owner-dependent, chaotic scenario can be overwhelming. But fear not, as there's a transformative process that can turn your business into a well-organized machine that operates smoothly.

Drawing inspiration from the Marine Corps, which has been refining leadership since 1775, remember that leaders are made, not born. It's a journey that requires time and commitment. Take a bold step: consider handing over your role. Identify the tasks that cost the most in terms of your time and energy, wear the "Today's **Hat**," and focus on building a **system** that someone else can seamlessly take over. The ultimate goal is to create a business that runs efficiently even when you're not at the helm. Believe in yourself and the potential for change.

Managing the Store: Leadership and Governance

Within your team, you'll find a diverse spectrum of motivation and ambition. Some members are hungry for growth and eager to climb the corporate ladder, while others may exhibit complacency. The key lies in identifying and nurturing the hunger for advancement. Channel your efforts into inspiring those individuals with a fervent drive, propelling them toward loftier goals within the company.

As Covey astutely observes, many individuals exert tremendous effort in their work but lack the clarity and *vision* needed to make substantial progress. In homage to Sisyphus the myth, it's similar to pushing a rope with all one's might—an arduous task with minimal results. To foster a culture of support, envision the workplace as a staircase of life where each person occupies a different step. Encourage a collective effort to reach down and assist those on lower steps, injecting a dose of camaraderie, vast amounts of **Kool-Aid**, and mutual upliftment.

Moreover, as the visionary, implore the profound role of leadership throughout your **little ol' register**, emphasizing interdependence in every role to eliminate co-dependence and discourage lone-wolf mentalities. The ultimate goal is to create a cohesive team that collaborates seamlessly, understanding that success is a collective solo endeavor—true interdependence.

One of the great leaders known for his exceptional military and strategic skills was Attila the Hun, often known as the "Scourge of God." Attila rose to power as the leader of the Huns, a nomadic **warrior** people, in the 5th century. His prowess in military leadership was unparalleled during his time. He demonstrated an extraordinary ability to unite diverse and often fractious tribal factions under his rule, by speaking directly to their souls, creating a formidable and disciplined force.

One of Attila's key leadership skills was his strategic *vision*. He exhibited a profound understanding of geopolitical dynamics, allowing him to capitalize on the weaknesses of the Roman Empire and other adversaries. He knew his enemy as he knew himself.[102] This strategic brilliance was evident in his ability to plan and execute military campaigns that struck fear into the hearts of even the most powerful civilizations of his era. His leadership was marked by decisiveness, adaptability on the battlefield, and an uncanny ability to motivate his troops.[103]

Attila's charisma and communication skills were also noteworthy. He could inspire loyalty and obedience among his followers, fostering a sense of unity and purpose within the Hunnic horde.[103] While his leadership may be controversial due to the devastation wrought by his military campaigns, there is no denying that Attila's strategic acumen, tactical brilliance, and ability to lead a diverse coalition of **warriors** contributed to his historical legacy as a great leader in the annals of military history.

Leadership in any institution, much like in the military, is only as effective as the principles that underpin it. The bedrock of successful leadership lies in a commitment to integrity, accountability, and a clear sense of purpose. Military history teaches us that great leaders are those who lead by example, earning the respect and trust of their subordinates. They instill a shared set of values that guide decision-making and actions, creating a cohesive and disciplined unit. In business or any other organization, the same principles apply. A leader's ability to inspire, communicate effectively, and uphold a strong moral compass becomes the linchpin for success. When leaders embody these principles, they cultivate a culture of excellence, loyalty, and resilience, echoing the time-tested foundations found in the military.

A well-crafted *mission* statement serves as a compass guiding the organization through its journey. Beyond a mere declaration of *purpose*, it encapsulates the essence of the organization's reason for existence, communicating its intentions, *values*, and overarching goals. This concise yet impactful statement becomes the touchstone for decision-making, aligning the collective efforts of employees, customers, vendors, and other stakeholders with a shared sense of *purpose*. It serves as a unifying force, fostering a sense of identity and direction within the organization. A *mission* statement, when effectively formulated and embraced, becomes a source of inspiration, driving individuals at every level to contribute to the fulfillment of the organization's larger objectives. It not only clarifies the organization's role in the broader landscape but also shapes its identity in the eyes of those it serves and engages.

Values are the foundational pillars that provide steadfast guidance, whether navigating the complexities of the business battlefield or steering the course of your **little ol' register** through the varied landscapes of its communities. In the intricate dance of business, which mirrors the strategic maneuvers of warfare, the significance of well-defined values cannot be overstated. Drawing wisdom from Sun Tzu's timeless treatise, "The Art of War," unveils a treasure trove of strategies and rules of engagement that resonate with the challenges faced by businesses. The ancient proverb, "The enemy of my enemy is my friend," echoes through the corridors of time, serving as a testament to the enduring relevance of strategic alliances and collaborative approaches.[102] These age-old principles offer valuable insights into the dynamics of both external and internal conflicts, shaping a framework that not only guides decision-making but also fortifies the ethical core of your business endeavors.

Purpose goes beyond mere existence; it encapsulates the soul and essence of your **little ol' register**. Just as a military unit rallies around a shared mission, your business must have a clear and compelling *purpose*. This overarching goal serves as a north star, guiding decision-making and actions. A well-crafted *purpose* statement not only articulates the "**why**" behind your business but also resonates with stakeholders, instilling a sense of belonging and motivation. It becomes the heartbeat of your organizational culture, influencing how teams collaborate and customers perceive your brand. In essence, purpose transcends the mundane transactional aspects of business, infusing it with meaning and creating a narrative that extends far beyond the balance sheet. It's a beacon that unites the collective efforts of your team, forging a path toward shared aspirations and a lasting legacy for your **little ol' register**.

Throughout history, individuals have demonstrated a profound willingness to sacrifice for causes they deem worthy of such sacrifice. Death, in these contexts, is not the most fearsome prospect—living in perpetual humiliation, stripped of one's humanity, is far more daunting. However, when people are presented with the chance to lay down their lives for the sake of their children, grandchildren, neighbors, or the nation to which they hold a legitimate connection, they often embrace this sacrifice willingly. This sentiment has been evident since the dawn of history. Those defending fundamental principles are not driven by a desire for death, but rather by a commitment to noble ends—protecting their nation or family and preserving the lives of others.

In summary, the essence of leadership lies in the ability to forge *purpose*, articulate a compelling *mission*, and envision a future that aligns with the collective aspirations of a business. Leaders serve as the architects of a company's destiny, shaping its purpose to transcend mere existence. Through a well-defined *mission*, they communicate the organization's reason for being, fostering clarity and direction. A visionary leader, armed with a clear *purpose* and *mission*, charts a course for the future—giving life to the business's overarching *vision*. In the grand tapestry of leadership, *purpose, mission,* and *vision* are interwoven threads that, when artfully crafted, propel your **little ol' register** forward with resilience, purposefulness, and a collective commitment to a higher cause. As the baton of leadership is passed, the mantle of responsibility becomes a beacon illuminating the path toward shared goals, ensuring that the journey is not just profitable but also purposeful.

Part 3: Programming the Register

AT THE WATER COOLER: CONVEYING THE FEELING

Challenge; the heart of the workplace, where the hum of productivity harmonizes with the cadence of camaraderie—at the water cooler. In this section, we probe into the nuanced art of conveying feelings, exploring how businesses can tap into the emotional reservoirs that shape perceptions, foster inspiration, and create a sense of belonging.

In the business empire, inspiration is the currency that fuels innovation and propels ventures toward greatness. Here, we unravel the power of selling the dream—painting a compelling *vision* that transcends products and services. Whether you're a startup founder, a seasoned entrepreneur, or a visionary leader, the ability to inspire is the cornerstone of transformative leadership. We explore the techniques and narratives that breathe life into dreams, galvanizing teams, and stakeholders to rally behind the shared *vision*—the **End in Mind**.

The workplace is more than a collection of desks and chairs; it's a community—a family. We unravel the profound impact of fostering a sense of inclusion, where every member feels valued, heard, and integral to the collective journey. From team dynamics to corporate culture, we navigate the strategies that transform a group of individuals into a cohesive and supportive family. Inclusion is not just a buzzword; it's a powerful catalyst for productivity, creativity, and the overall well-being of an organization.

The water cooler conversations are not mere interludes between tasks; they are the threads that weave the fabric of workplace culture. Here, we underscore the importance of encouraging individuals to observe their surroundings. From the layout of the office space to the subtle cues in communication, fostering observational skills cultivates a deeper understanding of the workplace ecosystem. It's a journey into the nuances that often go unnoticed but profoundly shape the collective experience.

Join us as we navigate the waters of workplace dynamics, exploring the art of inspiration, the essence of inclusion, and the transformative impact of keen observation. At the water cooler, where ideas flow freely, and relationships are nurtured, we uncover the intangible elements that define the soul of a thriving workplace.

PYRAMID

The memory escapes me regarding who shared this epic tale with me or where it initially imprinted itself in my mind. Regardless, it stands as one of the most impactful experiences that contributed to my comprehension of the fundamental motivation of the common worker.

Amidst the monumental endeavor of constructing the Great **Pyramid** of Giza in Egypt, a diligent human resource manager approached three different workers to inquire about their perspective on their laborious tasks. The first worker, beads of sweat glistening on his furrowed brow, responded with frustration, "Look! I'm breaking these stupid rocks in horrendous working conditions and barely get paid for my time and effort."

In contrast, the second worker, while acknowledging the challenges, expressed a more balanced view. "It's hard work, no doubt, but it allows me to make enough to pay my bills and provide for my family. It's a means to an end."

However, it was the response of the third worker that resonated with a profound sense of purpose. Standing tall, he proudly proclaimed, "Can't you see? We are building a **pyramid**!"

His words echoed not just the physical act of laying stones, but a *vision* of contributing to something far greater—the creation of an enduring symbol that would stand the test of time. This powerful expression highlighted the transformative impact of having a *vision*, infusing even the most challenging tasks with a sense of *purpose* and significance.

Look closely, and you'll see it: **pyramids**, not the ancient stone structures but a metaphorical one representing three different types of people. Now, let's engage those cognitive muscles! This one's also known as the "The Bystander Effect": one person obliviously walks by a piece of trash lying in their pathway, completely unaware. Another notices it and loudly proclaims the need for it to be picked up, drawing attention to the issue. Then there's the third type—the one who carelessly walks by but takes the initiative to pick up the trash and throw it away without a fuss.

Now, let's apply this analogy to the field of work. We have the same three types of workers: the one who sees a task that needs to be done and vocalizes it, the one who doesn't even notice the task, and the one who quietly takes action to resolve it. Regardless of how others may perceive them, the true measure of humility lies not in grand gestures but in the willingness to roll up one's sleeves and get the job done.

So, who's building the **pyramid**? It's not just about individual contributions; it's about a collective effort that transcends personal ego and ambition. It's about working towards something bigger than oneself, driven by a shared *mission*, *vision*, and *purpose* for your **little ol' register**.

At the foundation of this **pyramid** lies the essence of your **little ol' register**—the mission *statement*, *vision*, and *purpose*. Again, we see these elements serve as the foundational blocks upon which your business stands, guiding every decision and action, and giving way to your *motto*. Let's delve into each one:

- **Mission Statement:** This succinctly articulates the core purpose of your **little ol' register**. It answers the question: **Why** does your business exist? Your *mission* statement should capture the essence of what you aim to achieve and who you aim to serve. It's the North Star that guides your company's direction and aligns everyone's efforts toward a common goal.

- **Vision:** While the mission statement defines your present purpose, the *vision* paints a picture of your desired future. It outlines what success looks like for your business in the long term. Your *vision* statement should be aspirational, inspiring, and ambitious, providing a clear direction for where you want to take your **little ol' register**—the **End in Mind**.

- **Purpose:** Beyond the mission and *vision*, the purpose delves into the "**why**" behind your business. It's the deeper meaning that drives you and your team forward. Your purpose statement reflects your *values*, passions, and the positive impact you aspire to make in the world. It's about connecting with something greater than just turning a profit—it's about making a difference.

- **Motto:** Lastly, the motto encapsulates the spirit and ethos of your **little ol' register** in a concise phrase or slogan. It's the rallying cry that encapsulates your values and motivates your team. Your *motto* should be memorable, resonant, and reflective of your company culture.

Defining these elements requires introspection, collaboration, and a deep understanding of your business and its place in the world. It's about distilling your essence into words that resonate with both your team and your customers. By articulating your *mission*, *vision*, *purpose*, and *motto* clearly and authentically, you provide a guiding framework that shapes every aspect of your business journey, from strategic planning to daily operations.

Indeed, keeping the **end goal in mind** and staying true to the foundational *mission* of your **pyramid** is crucial in all facets of your **little ol' register's** endeavors. Whether it's developing new products, engaging with customers, or making strategic business decisions, aligning every action with your *mission*, *vision*, and *purpose* ensures coherence and consistency.

For instance, when crafting marketing campaigns or designing products, ask yourself: Does this initiative resonate with our *mission* statement? Does it reflect our *vision* for the future? Does it serve our *purpose* and embody our values? By constantly referring back to these guiding principles, you ensure that your actions are purpose-driven and contribute meaningfully to your overarching goals.

Moreover, integrating your *mission* and values into your company culture fosters a sense of alignment and shared purpose among your team members. When employees understand and believe in the *mission*, *vision*, and *purpose* they are more motivated, engaged, and empowered to contribute to the success of your **little ol' register**.

Additionally, communicating your *mission* and *values* effectively to your customers can differentiate your brand in a crowded marketplace. Consumers are increasingly drawn to businesses that stand for something beyond just making a profit.[104] By authentically embodying your *mission* and *values* in your interactions with customers, you build trust, loyalty, and goodwill.

In essence, the *mission*, *vision*, *purpose*, and *motto* serve as guiding lights that illuminate the path forward for your **little ol' register**. By anchoring every decision and action in these foundational principles, you create a roadmap for success that leads not only to financial prosperity but also to fulfillment, purpose, and positive impact.

In essence, what are we? We're a team with a unified purpose, keeping the **end goal in mind** with every action we take. "Can't you see? We are building a **pyramid**!" As Robert Bolton Ransford, the inventor, aptly put it, "A belief is not merely an idea the mind possesses; it is an idea that possesses the mind." The power of your *vision* can be harnessed and weaponized as a mind virus for growth and exaltation. It's about everyone seeing and feeling the company's *mission* and *values*, fully embracing what it stands for—a collective sipping of the company **Kool-Aid**—if you will.

KOOL-AID

As previously explored, the power of inspiration and *vision* cannot be understated in shaping one's perspective. On set, a recurring joke emerged when common folks would quip, "You're living the dream," met with a knowing corner smile and a wink from the eye, responding, <u>"No, we are making the dream."</u> Even from a bungalow nestled miles away along a stretch of all-white sandy beach, the amusement of overhearing people discussing the latest celebrity gossip magazine, only to realize it happened six months ago on the last set, unfolded while sipping a beverage adorned with an umbrella.

Making the Dream requires a lot of **Kool-Aid**. The phrase "drinking the **Kool-Aid**" has evolved into a colloquial expression, often used metaphorically to describe unquestioning acceptance or allegiance to a particular belief, ideology, or group, even in the face of potential risks or negative consequences. The origin of the term dates back to the tragic Jonestown Massacre in 1978, where members of the People's Temple cult, led by Jim Jones, died by mass murder-suicide in Guyana after consuming a poisoned drink.[105] Although the actual beverage involved was a cyanide-laced fruit punch, the phrase "drinking the **Kool-Aid**" has become symbolic of blind loyalty and conformity within various contexts, cautioning against unquestioning adherence to a particular doctrine or leadership.

Yet can we wield this power for good? The image of the **Kool-Aid** man, frantically delivering sugary beverages to children, might seem comical at first, but it draws a parallel to historical practices that aimed to boost productivity. During the Industrial Revolution, the introduction of coffee breaks emerged as a strategy to enhance worker efficiency.[106] Employers realized that providing employees with short breaks for caffeine consumption not only improved their mood and alertness but also contributed to increased focus and output. Much like the **Kool-Aid** man delivering sugar-infused drinks, the caffeine from coffee served as a stimulant to keep workers energized and engaged.

Caffeine, a natural stimulant found in coffee and many energy drinks, has been known to enhance cognitive functions, such as alertness and concentration.[107] This heightened mental state translates into improved productivity and output in a work setting. The **Kool-Aid** man's sugary offerings, while whimsical, symbolize the broader trend of recognizing the impact of consumables on human performance. Just as coffee breaks became institutionalized to support productivity during the Industrial Revolution, the provision of energy-boosting substances like sugar and caffeine remains a prevalent strategy in various contexts today.

These substances act as agonists, triggering the release of dopamine, and various actions can elicit the same response. Whether it's pursuing personal goals, being part of a collective endeavor, or even seemingly benign and illicit substances, the common thread is the surge in dopamine release.[108] Understanding this shared neurochemical pathway allows us to explore ways to optimize both personal and collective efficiency within the workforce.

When we pursue goals, engage in collaborative efforts, or even partake in certain substances, the brain's reward **system** responds by releasing dopamine. [109] This neurotransmitter, often referred to as the "feel-good" chemical, plays a central role in motivation and pleasure. By recognizing the similarities in how the brain responds to these different stimuli, we can strategically leverage these mechanisms to enhance not only individual performance but also the overall efficiency of a team or workforce.

In essence, the section emphasizes the potential alignment of personal and collective motivations, exploring how understanding the underlying neurobiology can inform strategies for fostering productivity, motivation, and a sense of accomplishment within both individual and team contexts.

Stimulating employees, cultivating inspiration, and instilling a shared corporate *vision* are essential elements that collectively shape and influence individuals' perceptions and actions within an organization. The process of Stimulating employees involves creating an environment that mirrors real-world scenarios, allowing individuals to navigate challenges and develop problem-solving skills. Inspiration serves as a driving force, sparking creativity and motivation among employees, and leading to a positive impact on their perceptions of their roles and contributions. A cohesive corporate *vision* acts as a guiding light, aligning individual efforts with organizational goals and fostering a sense of *purpose*. Analogous to drinking the corporate **Kool-Aid**, employees immersed in a shared *vision*, a shared **end in mind**, become part of a collective mindset, fostering unity and commitment toward achieving common objectives. These elements, when seamlessly integrated, contribute to a dynamic and harmonious corporate culture that shapes how individuals perceive their roles and the overall *mission* of the organization.

In the aspect of catalyzing motivation, the essence lies in the profound sense of inclusion, fostering a feeling of being part of something—a part of a family. **Kool-Aid**, in its symbolic representation, transcends individual desires, emphasizing fulfilling collective **wants-needs**, aligning with a shared identity, all for the common **end in mind**.

As Winston Churchill aptly noted, "The price of greatness is responsibility." This principle underscores the understanding that true leadership goes beyond personal aspirations; it entails a commitment to the well-being and objectives of the collective. Whether the drive comes from financial goals, a sense of purpose, or the pursuit of recognition and vanity, individuals possess unique motivational buttons—be they honor, guilt, or fear.

At the Water Cooler: Conveying the Feeling

Motivation, a multifaceted force, propels individuals into action. Recognizing the diverse sources of motivation, a leader can navigate the complex landscape of human drive. People fight for various reasons, and as a leader, tapping into and leveraging these motivations becomes a potent tool in building cohesive and effective teams. The **Kool-Aid** forces us to dive into the endless power of motivation, urging leaders to decode the individual narratives that propel their teams forward.

Throughout history, individuals have shown a willingness to sacrifice their lives for causes they deem worthy. The fear of death pales in comparison to the horrors of living in perpetual humiliation or slavery. The key lies in offering people the opportunity to fight for something larger than themselves—whether it be their children, grandchildren, neighbors, or the nation to which they feel a legitimate connection. Defending principles and noble causes instills a courage that transcends the fear of death.

Irrespective of the specific **register** or business **system** being developed, fostering a pack mentality within the team is a strategic imperative. While individual team members will be considered replaceable, the collective strength and resilience of the pack contribute significantly to overall success. The true strength of a wolf isn't fangs, speed, and skill. It's the pack. This analogy to a wolf pack underscores the idea that the true strength lies not just in individual attributes like fangs, speed, or skill, but in the cohesive unity of the pack. This principle remains true in business—the strength of your **little ol' register** is not solely in its individual components but in the synergy of a unified and loyal team. Find ways to inspire loyalty and ambition in a few capable individuals—**warriors**.

Your **little ol' register's** requirement for leadership and building a strong foundation, the analogy of a wolf's strength being in its pack holds true. The true power doesn't solely reside in individual capabilities but in the cohesion and loyalty of a well-knit team. "Build a pack" has the importance of cultivating loyalty and ambition among a select group of capable individuals. Identifying and nurturing these key contributors can create a core team that becomes the backbone of the business, enhancing its stability and adaptability. With plenty of **Kool-Aid**, this will help maintain workforce loyalty and engagement. It goes beyond providing just a paycheck, offering intangible qualities that keep employees invested in the company's *mission* and values.

Mitigate the "brain drain," a common challenge of employers, turnover. While it may be impossible to completely eliminate turnover, using strategies inspired by the **Pyramid** and **Kool-Aid** philosophies can significantly contribute to retaining valuable team members. By keeping the workforce engaged and motivated, your **little ol' register** stands a better chance of sustaining its momentum and achieving long-term success.

Sip under those cheerful umbrellas as you embrace and encourage your team to joyfully "drink the company **Kool-Aid**." Remember, it's not about conformity; it's about nurturing and fostering a shared sense of *purpose* and commitment. Cultivate a community within your **little ol' register** where each member isn't merely an employee but a vital part of a collective journey. Align individual motivations with the broader goals of the business, crafting a workplace culture that transcends mere tasks and transactions, evolving into a shared experience of growth and success. So, go ahead, whip up a metaphorical batch of that special **Kool-Aid**, share it with your team, and witness the bonds of loyalty and dedication fortify, turning your **little ol' register** into an unstoppable force in the business landscape. Here's to raising a glass to drinking the company **Kool-Aid**—making the dream! Cheers!

LOOK UP

The dapper man descends the steps of the Gulfstream, catching sight of his dedicated staff member waiting at the bottom. A wave of joy washes over the employee as his boss approaches, throwing an arm around his neck with a genuine smile. "What's on the agenda today?" the eager young man inquires. In a moment of camaraderie, the well-dressed man's arm rises, making circular motions in the air as the plane's stairs retract, and the aircraft begins its descent down the runway, gathering speed. With a whisper "**Look up**," and a camera handed to the enthusiastic young blood and instructions to capture the plane's chase, the unpredictable nature of filmmaking unfolds. In making the dream filming an American talent show, an impromptu decision on landing led to the realization that an introductory shot was needed to captivate the home audience. [110] What captivates your attention?

If you haven't gathered from the subtle hints scattered throughout, the author of this book grapples with dyslexia and ADHD.[111] This unique combination of cognitive characteristics provides a distinctive lens through which the author navigates the intricacies of daily life, business, and the pursuit of success.[112-114] Despite the challenges posed by these conditions, the author embraces them as part of his identity, recognizing that these unique perspectives offer valuable insights and unconventional approaches to problem-solving. It serves as a testament to the resilience, adaptability, and creativity that can emerge from navigating a world that may not always align with traditional expectations.[113]

Encouraging positive reinforcement, particularly from an early age, is crucial in reshaping the perception of learning and ability. Instead of labeling it as a disorder or disability, framing it as a learning difference (which we all do) can be transformative.[115, 116] This mindset shift underscores the diversity in how individuals learn, emphasizing that everyone has their unique strengths and weaknesses. Drawing inspiration from the culinary world, the concept of "Mise en place," borrowed from our junior Olympic-winning chefs, teaches the importance of putting everything in its place. On the buffet table of people and skills, this philosophy encourages recognition and appreciation for the varied ways individuals approach tasks and challenges, fostering a more inclusive and understanding environment.

Once upon a time, in a whimsical dimension where the laws of logic took a backseat, there existed a legendary short bus, in which Jack rode—safety helmet in hand, that traversed the corridors of history. This wasn't just any ordinary short bus; it was the chariot of the most renowned individuals who had a unique relationship with learning disabilities.

Picture this: Albert Einstein, with his unruly hair and mischievous grin, sat at the front, his mathematical equations scribbled on the window in marker. Despite his inability to compute basic arithmetic, he dazzled his fellow passengers with his groundbreaking theories on relativity, all while struggling to remember which stop was his.

Nikola Tesla, the eccentric inventor, could often be found tinkering with gadgets in the back, oblivious to the chaos around him. While his mind buzzed with ideas for revolutionary inventions, he frequently missed his stop due to the birds, lost in the labyrinth of his own mind.

And who could forget Pythagoras of Samos, the comedic bean-loving genius whose quick wit and boundless energy filled the bus with laughter. With his trademark humor and penchant for spontaneous improv, he turned every ride into a rollicking adventure, much to the delight of his fellow passengers.

Together, this unlikely ensemble embarked on a series of misadventures, from accidentally launching a rocket powered by rubber bands to staging impromptu science experiments that left the bus teetering on the edge of disaster. But through it all, they embraced their quirks and celebrated their unique perspectives, proving that genius comes in many forms, even if it arrives on a short bus.

Now we ask, can lacking skill be offset by other strengths? Indeed, the beauty of collaboration lies in the complementary nature of diverse skills. Each individual brings a unique set of strengths to the table, and by harnessing these collective abilities, a team can compensate for the skills that may be lacking in one member. It's like assembling a puzzle where each piece contributes to the overall picture, some may focus on the piece and others the entire picture.[112]

A person may excel in visionary thinking, innovation, and conceptualization, while another may possess the meticulous skills required for detailed tasks, such as writing or arithmetic unlike our friend Albert. Recognizing and embracing these differences allows for a well-rounded team where each member's strengths offset the weaknesses of others.

In the context of a business, a poor writer can collaborate with a skilled secretary for polished press releases, and someone less adept at drawing can enlist the help of an illustrator to visually convey ideas. This collaborative approach not only enhances the quality of output but also fosters a culture of mutual support and shared success within the team.

Developing tools and methods that align with one's preferred learning style is imperative, regardless of an auditory, visual, or tactile learner. Often, Jack has thoughts that race ahead of his ability to articulate them coherently, resulting in blended and truncated sentences. Jack's mouth is too slow for his brain. Despite this, Jack holds a conviction that traditional language use is markedly inefficient in the context of today's communication landscape, which is often characterized by evaporating attention spans.

Verbal communication, with its inherent verbosity, tends to lose the listener's focus quickly. Consider a detailed sentence like "Thelma, her hair dancing in the wind, takes control of the wheel, steering the pink convertible with the top down across the dirt road. The car accelerates, soaring over the high cliff, leading them to their ultimate demise." Now, let's contrast that with a more concise version and hopefully in the correct order: "Car, Cliff, Dead!" This reduction captures the essence of the message without the verbosity, highlighting the potential for a more streamlined and impactful form of communication tailored to the demands of our attention-deficient world.

One of the techniques employed by Jack in enhancing daily functioning and preventing a drift into a state of distraction, a method he affectionately terms "Feeding the Beast," involves proactive engagement with his surroundings. In situations where anxiety might be looming, like standing in line, he finds it helpful to deliberately scan the environment. Whether it's observing the room, looking at photographs on someone's desk, examining the shine on their shoes, or even gazing at the pathways tracing throughout the ceiling, this intentional act serves as a form of stimulation for managing any deficit in attention.

However, the significance of this seemingly simple technique extends beyond managing attention. It also enables keen observations of different **systems** in the living environment, fostering a deeper understanding of their workings. By employing this approach, Jack not only copes with attention challenges but also gains valuable insights into the intricacies of various **systems** that surround us.

This also includes acknowledging others as unique individuals, Jack connects with them on a personal level, asking about their day, empathizing with their challenges, and acknowledging shared human experiences. This usually leads to a vast outpouring of thoughts, swimming through the nonsensical, emotion-saturated venting session. Yet sometimes, Jack finds hidden nuggets of knowledge that aid his next move.

By integrating these elements into his interactions, Jack not only fosters a more positive and nuanced understanding of the observed environment but also alleviates struggles with attention and focus. An additional perk is that sometimes, the actions of an engaged conversationalist may result in receiving free items, extra assistance, and the coveted ingredients of the secret sauce—numerous future possibilities.

Keep in mind, strive for authenticity in your character, and don't be duplicitous in your nature, but also acknowledge that everyone and everything in our surroundings has the potential to evolve into a valuable resource, an information treasure, and an opportunity that favors the prepared mind.

Additionally, as our esteemed acquaintance Steve Jobs pointed out, Microsoft may have bit off Apple, as he reminds everyone with his words, likely inspired by the (mis)quoted words of Pablo Picasso, who suggested, "Lesser artists borrow; great artists steal." The essence lies in recognizing the transformative power of inspiration and how innovation often involves drawing from diverse sources to create something uniquely valuable.

In essence, the **Look Up** technique encourages one to observe their surroundings, absorb relevant information, and uncover details that others might have overlooked. This approach helps one stay grounded, engaged, and attuned to the nuances of one's environment, ultimately enhancing the ability to navigate the complexities of daily life. Observe, Absorb, and Find: what others have missed. **Look up!**

Part 3: Programming the Register

IN FRONT OF THE COUNTER: SALES & MARKETING

Unveils the journey of entrepreneurship, instructing your **little ol' register** to spread its wings, forge new alliances, and foster collaborative efforts to enhance prosperity. In more colloquial terms, it's the same as your **little ol' register** pulling out a couple of dollars, instructing them to go out, make more friends, and inviting them all home to stay and join in on the fun.

Beginning with a core principle that guides one approach: Equal opportunity exploitation. This means regardless of sex, gender, creed, or personal preferences. Whether it's a female or a male, tailor your storefront window or the warm smile of your server to meet the **wants-needs** of your potential customer, ensuring a successful sale and a satisfied customer.

In the bustling world of business, the knife's edge between success and failure often balances on a fundamental truth: the lifeline of any enterprise is its customers. The most common pitfall that leads to business failure is a dearth of patrons. While many entrepreneurs successfully bring their products or services to market, the mere existence of offerings does not guarantee triumph. Thus, well before the birth of a new business, it is paramount to meticulously deliberate on the strategies employed to attract customers in a manner that is both predictable and reliable.

Enter the scope of Sales & Marketing—the dynamic duo charged with the formidable task of transforming potential into reality. Sales serve as the heartbeat, the direct interface between the product or service and the eager consumer. Here, the art of persuasion and the science of understanding human behavior converge, creating a synergy that propels transactions forward. However, the front line alone cannot stand resilient without the strategic artillery provided by Marketing.

Marketing is the primary architect, crafting the narrative, constructing the brand, and strategically positioning the business in the marketplace. It is the silent conductor of a symphony of messages, orchestrating a harmonious blend that resonates with the target audience. Effective marketing not only attracts attention but also builds relationships, fostering a sense of trust and loyalty among consumers. A well-designed marketing strategy aligns the business with the aspirations and **wants-needs** of its audience, creating a symbiotic relationship that transcends transactional exchanges.

In essence, the Sales & Marketing section of this **little ol'** playbook is the compass that guides entrepreneurs through the uncharted waters of customer acquisition. Understanding the intricacies of this dynamic duo is not just a prerogative; it is the very heartbeat that sustains a thriving business. Continuing our journey through the Everet cliffs of business success, our focus shifts to the realm of cultivating exceptional user experiences and fostering enduring customer relationships. It's not just about attracting customers—it's about retaining them and ensuring their ongoing satisfaction with your **little ol' register's** brand.

Creating a seamless and enjoyable user experience is analogous to crafting a masterpiece—a delicate blend of functionality, aesthetics, and intuitive design. Whether it's your website, mobile app, or brick-and-mortar space, each touchpoint with your brand should evoke a positive response. By prioritizing user-centric design, frictionless interactions, and all the company **Kool-Aid** they can drink, your **little ol' register** can transcend mere transactions, offering customers an immersive journey that resonates with their **wants-needs** and preferences.

Reinforcing these relations, the journey doesn't end with a one-time transaction. Customer retention is the linchpin that transforms sporadic engagements into lasting relationships. The secret lies in understanding the pulse of your customer base, staying attuned to their evolving **wants-needs**, and proactively addressing concerns. Personalization becomes a powerful tool, tailoring interactions to individual preferences and demonstrating that your brand is more than just a product—it's a thoughtful companion on their journey.

Hitting the point home, ensuring the sustained happiness of your customers is a multifaceted endeavor. Beyond the product or service, itself, it extends to the overall brand experience. Clear communication, timely support, and a genuine commitment to customer satisfaction become the pillars that fortify your brand's reputation. Satisfied customers are not just repeat customers; they evolve into brand advocates, amplifying your business through positive word-of-mouth and organic growth—spreading the company propaganda exponentially.

In the pages that follow, we will delve deeper into strategies, tactics, and best practices that empower businesses to not only attract but retain a loyal customer base. The journey to business success is paved not only with transactions but also with the enduring connections forged through exceptional user experiences and unwavering customer satisfaction.

MILKING

Every day, we believe we're making informed choices, especially when it comes to our purchases. However, the reality may not be as straightforward as we think. Let's simplify this concept. What is the color of a doctor's lab coat?

What is the color of the moon? The primary color of a swan? Copy paper? Tissue paper? On a sunny day, what color are clouds? Now, ask yourself, what do cows drink? If you said **milk**, you were primed! In reality...cows drink water.

Priming is when a stimulus is presented, and it influences a person's later response. Priming words or images is the psychological phenomenon where exposure to a stimulus influences a person's response to subsequent stimuli. This involves presenting information or cues that can shape a person's thoughts, attitudes, or behaviors in a specific direction as you just witnessed.

As an additional illustration, if you give someone the list of the words wolf, cat, and pet, and then ask them to think of a word that rhymes with "log," they're likely to answer "dog." A wolf might remind someone of a dog, the word cat is often paired with the word dog and a dog is a common pet. In other words, that list of words gets the mind ready to choose "dog."

These Neurolinguistic programming techniques (NPL), including priming, can influence a customer's decision-making process by framing their mindset in a certain way. This can be for any of our senses. In turn using specific language, images, or themes, you can create positive associations with your **little ol' register's** product and brand. These positive associations can influence how customers perceive and evaluate the product when making purchasing decisions. For example, presenting positive and success-oriented messages can prime customers to view a product or service more favorably.

Milking can be used to establish trust and credibility. Providing customers with information about the quality, reliability, or positive experiences of others with the product can prime them to trust the brand and be more receptive to the sales message. Regardless in the middle of the sales process, walking in the store, or cold calling, "priming," also called predisposing, your market can be powerful.

One of the common NLP techniques, Priming, is more manipulative. Priming is a technique to adjust your thoughts. In psychology, priming is a technique in which the introduction of one stimulus influences how people respond to a subsequent stimulus. An example of priming is when you are in a wine shop, and they play Italian music to subtly influence you to purchase Italian wine.

Even affirmations are priming and can be used in the enrichment of one's life or pocketbook. Take a look at the great burger joint McDonald's. They have implemented this tool at the heart of the company for decades, inundating their customers from the age of adolescents with one simple phrase, "I'm loving it." The more times you hear, say, or sing this affirmation, the more you have solidified this in the minds from the youngest age, indoctrination.

We all know what the "Most important meal of the day!" is, but the fact it was coined by Dr. John Harvey Kellogg to sell his new Seventh-day Adventist breakfast cereal for the masses of the newly industrialized factory worker has continued influence till this day.

The man known as the "father of propaganda" in the 1900s is often attributed to Edward Bernays. Bernays, an Austrian-American pioneer in the field of public relations and propaganda, was a nephew of Sigmund Freud. He is recognized for his influential work in shaping public opinion and behavior through strategic communication and manipulation of information.[117] One notable campaign orchestrated by Bernays involved associating cigarette smoking with women's liberation and empowerment.

In the 1920s, he worked on behalf of the American Tobacco Company to break the social taboo against women smoking in public. Bernays linked smoking to notions of equality and freedom, coining the phrase "torches of freedom" to promote cigarettes as a symbol of women's rights. His efforts significantly contributed to the cultural shift in which smoking became more socially acceptable for women.

By setting expectations, priming plays a crucial role in shaping the value regarding a product or service. Sales professionals utilize this technique by highlighting specific features, benefits, or unique selling points to steer customers towards a favorable perception of the offering that cannot be compared to any other available.[53] This process is closely linked to the anchoring and adjustment heuristic, where initial information acts as an anchor that influences subsequent judgments and decisions.

Consider a scenario where a customer walks into a car dealership and sees a luxury sedan priced at $80,000. This initial price acts as an anchor, shaping the customer's perception of the car's value. Subsequently, when shown a slightly less expensive model priced at $70,000, the customer may perceive it as a great deal compared to the $80,000 option, despite still being a significant investment. In this example, the initial anchor of $80,000 influences the customer's judgment, leading them to adjust their expectations and perceive the $70,000 model as more affordable and desirable. This demonstrates how anchoring and adjustment heuristics can impact decision-making processes, even in contexts beyond pricing.

In front of the Counter: Sales & Marketing

By strategically highlighting the benefits and unique aspects of a product or service, sales professionals can effectively prime customers to perceive the offering as more valuable than they initially might have. This priming process influences the perceived value of the product or service in the customer's mind, potentially justifying a higher price point. Despite these subjective value additions, customers may be inclined to adjust their perception of the offering's worth based on the primed information provided by the sales professionals. This demonstrates the significant impact that framing and priming techniques can have on profound influence on the consumer and the perceived value of products or services.

Priming makes certain concepts, **milk** in this case, or information more accessible or not in a person's mind making the desired answer more cognitively accessible. We already know how lazy brains are and like to take shortcuts. Sales messages that prime customers with positive and relevant information make it more likely that those thoughts will be activated and influence the decision-making process. Predisposing questions that are yes, prime the individual for the final sales question to purchase.

Consider the scenario reminiscent of the classic impulse buy at the cashier's checkout counter. Whether it's strategically placed right in front of you or prompted by the cashier's inquiry—like asking if you'd like to add a candy bar to your purchase—it's similar to a subtle nudge towards making an unplanned purchase. Since they prayed on priming, did they fraudulently induce you to buy that candy bar or were you just **milked** throughout the store?

Priming is effective in leveraging emotional responses. Emotional cues in sales presentations can prime customers to connect emotionally with the product and brand, influencing their decision-making based on emotional factors and its appeal which we all do with **shiny** things. As we will see in the Peanut butter section, **milking** can tap into social norms and the principle of reciprocity. For instance, mentioning social norms related to responsible buying behavior or emphasizing reciprocity in terms of added value can prime customers to feel obligated to reciprocate with a positive response.

In essence, priming leverages the psychological tendency of individuals to be influenced by their subconscious exposure to certain cues or information, messing with one's **blink** directly. Your sales team can strategically use priming (**milking**), to create a positive and receptive mindset in your customers, increasing the likelihood of successful sales outcomes.

In the realm of presentation, perception can often be just as important as reality. It's not always about the size of your company, but rather the image you

Part 3: Programming the Register

project to the world. This is where the power of looking bigger than you are comes into play.

Consider the scenario of a small startup with just a handful of employees. They find themselves in need of more trained staff at a moment's notice, a challenge that seems daunting given their limited resources. However, they recognize an opportunity to tap into the pool of union workers, known for their specialized skills and reliability.

Despite the hesitations and complexities associated with dealing with unions, the startup decided to take a bold step. They approach the largest union controlling 80% of the Las Vegas strip, with over 60,000 members. What unfolds next is a testament to the art of perception and persuasion.

Through a chance encounter with the union president, who happens to be a wonderful well-seasoned lady, the startup is able to make a lasting impression. With charm, sincerity, and a genuine willingness to collaborate, they win over the hearts and minds of the union leadership.

Weeks later, the startup receives an unexpected opportunity that catapults them into the big leagues. They are offered the chance to take over and manage services for one of the 18 major hotels on the Las Vegas Strip, a move that requires them to become a unionized company.[118] Despite their humble beginnings, they are now welcomed into the echelons of industry giants, all because they dared to look bigger than they were and seized the opportunity to make a lasting impression.

In the business world, the adage "look bigger than you are" underscores the importance of projecting a professional and established image, even if your company is relatively small or in its early stages. This strategy is rooted in this **milking paradigm** and has several strategic advantages. A company that appears larger can instill confidence and trust among potential clients, partners, and investors. A polished and professional image primes competence and reliability, influencing stakeholders to view your **little ol' register** as more credible and capable. In today's competitive business world, there's nothing more important than standing out from the crowd.

Additionally, looking larger can enhance a company's competitive position, showing the strength in numbers. A **little ol' register's** larger-looking image may attract a broader customer base, more significant relationships, and better talent, all of which contribute to growth and success. Perceived size can be a powerful tool in negotiating strategic alliances or securing deals, as larger entities are often perceived to have greater resources and stability. It's a **chess** piece for your **system**. By showcasing your strength in numbers, you can gain a significant advantage over your rivals. Don't let your size hold you back - take advantage of this powerful strategy to enhance your competitive position and achieve greater success.

While staying true to your authentic self is paramount, leveraging strategic branding, marketing, and communication tactics is akin to adorning your **little ol' register** with **shiny stickers** that project an image of grandeur and scale, perfectly aligned with your ambitious aspirations. These tactics not only create favorable impressions but also open doors for growth and triumph in the fiercely competitive business arena. After all, in the battle for attention and market share, a **little ol'** sparkle can go a long way.

SHINY

Advertising, marketing, and sales are an ever-ongoing endeavor. Much like moths drawn irresistibly to a flame, our species exhibits an undeniable fascination for all things **shiny** and appealing.

In the glamorous world of fashion shoots, where celebrities are often the selling point for the same pair of jeans, an amusing scenario unfolded during the filming at the Liberace Museum. Picture this: a stunning blonde, the kind that could make heads turn on any street, was the desired face to flaunt those denim wonders. The crew orchestrated the perfect shots amid the dazzling backdrop of Liberace's extravagance. The jeans, of course, took center stage, but the celebrity's allure was the secret ingredient.

Fast forward two years later, and it was déjà vu on set. The same jeans, the same client, and the same crew found themselves in another whirlwind of fashion frenzy. However, this time, a new celebrity stepped into the limelight, ready to don those coveted denims. It was almost comical how the jeans seemed to have their own celebrity rotation, with each star bringing their unique charm to the timeless denim allure. The crew couldn't help but chuckle at the cyclical nature of the fashion world, where even jeans had their moment in the celebrity spotlight, twirling in the glitzy aura of Liberace's legacy.

People are more likely to choose products that are endorsed by a celebrity rather than a non-celebrity, and they spend less time deliberating their choices and are more confident about their decisions. A study on marketing psychology yielded this significant finding and one more tantalizing tale.

Gaze-cueing is stronger in non-celebrities. When non-celebrities look at a product, viewers more often follow their gaze toward that product and linger on the item. When a celebrity is featured in an ad, viewers tend to linger on the face of the famous person regardless of whether the star is gazing at the product or back at the viewer. "It turns out that even though viewers aren't looking at the product as much, the celebrity is still building consumer confidence. These are where preferences are more swayable on purpose, in fact, eye-tracking alone just proves that viewers look longer at the celebrity than the product.[119] That's known in marketing as "The Vampire Effect," which posits that celebrities can overshadow and steal consumer attention away from the brand.

Most believe the ability of celebrities to persuade is rooted in evolution and biology. Both humans and primates will follow the lead of high-status, high-prestige individuals in their group by aligning their gaze or copying their decisions.[120] This behavior is seen in the wild, when monkeys turn to look at whatever a higher-status monkey is looking at in the trees, or in the office, when employees model their work after the top-rated employee. When the leader is successful, others require less evidence to make the same choice. But **why** do we put so much weight into these?

We have already established that our minds are inherently lazy, and heuristics are mental shortcuts (**milking**), that can facilitate problem-solving, simplify decision-making, and probability judgments. These strategies are generalizations, or rules-of-thumb, that reduce cognitive load.[60] They can be effective based on a more limited subset of the available information and making immediate judgments; however, they often result in irrational or inaccurate conclusions and they can also lead to cognitive biases.

The cognitive bias known as the "Goldilocks Principle" or the "Center-Stage Effect" often influences decision-making when faced with three options, such as Small, Medium, and Large. This heuristic suggests that individuals are inclined to choose the middle option, viewing it as a balanced compromise between the extremes. Psychologically, the medium option seems to offer a sense of safety, avoiding the potential regret of making an extreme choice. This bias is frequently observed in consumer behavior, impacting choices ranging from meal sizes to clothing. Companies leverage this cognitive tendency when presenting options, strategically placing the medium choice as the most appealing and commonly chosen selection. Understanding and applying such cognitive biases can be a powerful tool in marketing and sales to guide consumer choices.

This cognitive bias is also evident in social dynamics when requesting assistance as in the "Big little, little Big" principle. When someone is initially approached with a large daunting ask, then a seemingly small favor, they are more likely to agree.[60] However, if additional requests are added incrementally, the initial small request is followed by a larger one, the person is more likely to comply with those asks as well. This phenomenon can be explained by the principle of "Commitment and Consistency." Once an individual has committed to helping in a small way, they feel psychological pressure to maintain consistency by agreeing to subsequent requests. This tactic is often used in persuasion and negotiation, demonstrating the significance of understanding cognitive biases not only in consumer behavior but also in interpersonal interactions and influence strategies.

Shiny objects attract inquisitive minds. Okay! Most minds. It's a trait we acquire very young browsing the multi-colored sweets in the corner store. In the world of business and marketing, understanding heuristics can be invaluable. Your **little ol' register** can do more than just hope; it can tailor its strategies and strategically employ these heuristics to appeal to the cognitive biases of your customers, leading to more effective marketing campaigns and product designs—effectively guiding emotionally-based decisions.

Consider the scenario of standing in line, an activity that, ironically, many, including some who are known herein, might not find appealing. Picture a line extending beyond the building, visible to every passing car. What might the onlookers be pondering? What's the allure that warrants such a lengthy wait? Now, transpose this to a restaurant setting. An extensive line implies exceptional food, doesn't it? Conversely, a bar with an empty parking lot might be assumed to offer subpar experiences. This heuristic, rooted in perception, can manifest in various interpretations depending on individual perspectives and messages we choose to highlight. Now you're ready to apply this strategy to your first home Tupperware Party.

Tupperware Parties was the Suburban Women's Plastic Path to Empowerment. The parties swept the nation during the 1950s and 1960s—and were more than they seemed. "Tupperware was a disruptor in the market and in households nationwide when its plastic storage containers launched in 1946," said Venkatesh Shankar, professor of marketing and e-commerce at Texas A&M University's Mays Business School.[121] "The famous neighborhood house parties where Tupperware products were sold by the host to her family and friends was a new way of marketing, combining socializing with direct sales."

In a cozy living room filled with anticipation, Sarah prepared for her home sales meeting, ready to showcase the features of the charming Tupperware she grew to love. As she meticulously arranged the chairs, she hesitated for a moment, contemplating whether to set out the extra folding chairs stored in the corner. Remembering a piece of sales wisdom, she decided to only leave a few chairs out, creating an atmosphere of exclusivity and scarcity. The prospective buyers arrived, and as they settled into the available seats, only to pull out more chairs as people arrived, the room subtly conveyed a message of desirability. A sense of limited availability stirred a heightened interest, and soon enough, inquiries about the product and business opportunity poured in.

The strategy proved to be a subtle yet effective sales tactic. By strategically limiting the seating, Sarah had sparked a perception of high demand, subtly implying that this product was in great demand, leading to potential buyers recognizing its value and acting swiftly to secure their spot in the competitive Tupperware market. The "Scarcity" principle had worked its magic, turning a simple living room meeting into a demonstration of market demand and the allure of exclusivity.[53]

In navigating the intricate terrain of decision-making, our emotions often wield a remarkable influence, sometimes surpassing the sway of logic or reason. This phenomenon, as we've observed, is inherently subjective, raising the question of its objectivity. Consider the sway of pathos in written expression—the deliberate use of language, examples, diction, or images to evoke emotional responses in the reader. Pathos encompasses a spectrum of emotions, from anger at societal injustices to sympathy for misfortune and laughter in the face of humor or illogical situations.[54] Intriguingly, fear emerges as a prevailing emotion strategically harnessed by many advertisements.

Dipping our toe into the psychology of fear-based decision-making, loss aversion stands out as a powerful force. It illuminates our inherent tendency to fear the prospect of loss more intensely than we cherish the acquisition of something of equivalent value. For instance, the frustration stemming from losing $10 surpasses the joy we experience when unexpectedly finding $10 in the back pocket of our jeans.

This powerful psychological dynamic, however, must be approached with caution, as unwavering belief can sometimes border on fanaticism—a phenomenon alike to our metaphorical drinking of the **Kool-Aid**. This mindset, akin to sunk cost bias, compels individuals to persist in their investments of time or effort, reluctant to see their initial commitment go to waste. It's the impulse that whispers, "I chose this jean brand, so they must be the best."

When your **little ol' register** uses this or other ploys, realize emotions can have a powerful impact on our actions, sometimes leading us to act against our best interests. Great marketing campaigns don't convert people by accident;

they guide users through an effortless decision-making process with decisive messaging. It's not about deceiving people or tricking them into buying something. It's about understanding how people's minds work and presenting your brands in the most effective way—something that's increasingly difficult in a competitive and always inundating market.

As the curtains draw close, the allure of **shiny** things extends beyond mere aesthetics; it penetrates the core of human psychology, influencing our preferences, choices, and ultimately, our purchasing decisions. Marketers and **little ol'** businesses, armed with this understanding, can craft strategies that resonate with the innate biases and preferences of consumers. Embracing the power of **shiny** marketing goes beyond surface-level appeal; it's about tapping into the deep-seated tendencies that drive human behavior. By consistently innovating and presenting products and services in a way that captivates the human desire for novelty and attractiveness, businesses can not only attract attention but also create a lasting imprint in the minds of their audience. In the red-blooded view of consumerism, the pursuit of the **shiny** is not just a fleeting trend but a perpetual force that your **little ol' register** can harness to shine brighter in the competitive market.

SOUNDS GOOD

In everyday language, **sounds good** serves as an informal means of expressing positivity or agreement in reply to a suggestion, idea, or proposal. It suggests that the speaker finds the proposal agreeable, acceptable, or appealing. However, what unfolds when something "**sounds** too **good**" introduces a layer of skepticism or consideration about the proposal's authenticity or feasibility. This shift in the phrase implies a cautious reflection on whether the presented idea or offer may be overly optimistic or might involve unforeseen challenges.

In the heart of the bustling Las Vegas Strip, amidst the glittering lights and cacophony of a thousand dreams, stood a man in a perfectly tailored blue suit. His chiseled face, a mask of exhaustion and weariness, betrayed a desire for escape from the relentless demands of his **little ol' register**. Determined to find a brevity of solace, he checked into the renowned hotel-casino that was notorious for its lively bachelorette parties and dazzling shows.

As he navigated the lively casino floor, the frenetic energy of the crowd seemed to part around him. In the midst of the chaos, he was the embodiment of a moment of tranquility—a fleeting oasis within the wild seas of the casino.

There, a most beautiful woman locked eyes with him, and to her, he seemed to emerge from the mist, a beacon of calm in the swirling storm.

Her gaze met his, and in that instant, her world hushed. His bespoke attire radiated self-confidence and charisma, a silent assurance that spoke volumes. With just one look, he granted her peace amid the bustling spectacle. As if drawn by an unseen force, she approached, and their worlds collided.

What began as a chance encounter on the casino floor unfolded into an unexpected adventure. In the **blink** of an eye, they found themselves in a penthouse suite overlooking the vast expanse of the Las Vegas Strip. From their lofty perch, they observed the miniature world below—a sea of lights and bustling activity, a city that never slept.

As they stood together, hand in hand, the man and the woman marveled at the intricate dance of glistening life below. The tiny ant-like figures scurrying around were chasing dreams, desires, and elusive fortunes. In that moment, high above the glittering spectacle of the **shiny** lures, the man in the blue suit and the woman found a shared respite, a sanctuary far removed from the chaos of their respective worlds and an epiphany of the driving nature of the figures below—**shiny**.

Turning to our big beautiful round marble of a world is saturated in blue, and the color blue is renowned for its calming effects on the mind.[122] It is frequently linked to feelings of serenity and tranquility, creating a positive first impression when worn. In broader terms, all shades of blue are associated with calmness, stability, and trust. This psychological impact can make individuals feel more at ease when interacting with someone dressed in blue. Interestingly, women tend to gravitate towards royal blue, while men often prefer red.[123] Take, for instance, the traditional blue suit in a business setting or the little Red Lake dress at dinner.

Even hotels strategically paint the walls of service hallways in soothing tapioca hues, aiming to create a calming atmosphere for their hardworking employees. When you take a stroll through a Las Vegas casino, you'll notice a peculiar tradition—those vibrant, mind-bending carpets. The loud patterns serve a purpose: they make patrons look up, drawing their attention to the **shiny** allure of slot machines and table games, enhancing the odds that the next hopeful player will become entranced by these one-armed bandits. This intentionally disorienting design is crafted to keep tourists wide awake amid the chaos. To further disconnect visitors from the concept of time, casinos refrain from displaying clocks or windows, and staff are trained never to wish a guest "good morning." This insight sheds light on **why** savvy individuals always wear

In front of the Counter: Sales & Marketing

sunglasses, even indoors or in the club. Stepping out into the blinding desert sun after a stint in the casino is an unforgettable lesson in the power of these carefully crafted illusions.

Even though colors have a genuine effect on our emotions they can also attach us to a memory[124]. Heinz launched in 2000 a limited run of green ketchup to cross-promote the release of the movie Shrek (a green ogre). Kids went crazy for the stuff. Heinz, realizing they were on to something good, quickly ramped up production of the popular green sauce.[125] Kids wanted to be like Shrek, the big, strong, lovable green ogre they saw in the movie. Parents enjoyed the movie just as much as the kids, and they were more than willing to buy a novelty-colored ketchup (versus a sugary promotional candy) to keep the movie memory alive. Novelty items typically have limited shelf life while product extensions are hopefully built for staying power in the brand portfolio.

It's important to note that individual reactions to colors and images can and do vary, and cultural associations may differ across different regions and communities in turn, knowing your market demographics becomes very important—**Think Customer**. Take an international entertainment company's premier Resort & Casino. They had to replace the entire front facade entrance because it was in homage to their trademark logo–a lion. But why you may ask so inquisitively? Because of its design itself, Asian gamblers reportedly perceived the facade as if they were entering through the lion's mouth, which is considered bad luck in Chinese culture. As a result, they remove the lion entrance. Yet to another mouth, one may have vastly different tastes.

Speaking about tastes, the philosophy behind placing the food court or high-end restaurants within the labyrinthine expanse of a casino floor is a strategic move deeply rooted in the psychology of consumer behavior. As patrons navigate through the maze of slot machines and gaming tables, their senses are heightened, and hunger pangs are inevitably subdued by the **shiny** and the sounds of luck. In the same seminal manner, ask yourself **why** every tour or **little ol'** ride always exits through the gift shop?

At some point in time, the scent of delicious cuisine wafting through the air becomes an irresistible beacon, leading them towards the promise of culinary satisfaction. However, the reality is that these eateries are often not profit centers in themselves. Instead, they serve as "loss leaders," a term used in the business world to describe products or services sold at a loss to attract customers. Casinos recognize that offering a

Part 3: Programming the Register

variety of dining options enhances the overall experience, encouraging patrons to stay longer, indulge in more entertainment, and, most importantly, continue spending time on the casino floor. So, while the food court or upscale restaurants may not directly contribute substantial profits, they play a pivotal role in the larger strategy of keeping guests engaged and invested in the addictive casino environment.

Frequently the allure of the casino floor may lead you to momentarily appease your hunger at the nearby vending machine. You might believe you have the willpower to resist such temptations. However, studies suggest that addiction encompasses more than just substances; it extends to various activities, emotions, and sensory encounters that trigger pleasure neurotransmitters like dopamine. [126] Surprisingly, even seemingly innocent **shiny** vending snacks like Flamin' Hot Cheetos possess addictive qualities. Their irresistible allure lies in the meticulous balance of high salt, fat, and carbohydrate content, known as the "bliss point."[127] With ingredients that tantalize four out of five possible tastes detected by the human tongue, these snacks offer an unmatched flavor experience.

Let us start with the color, Red Lake #40, used in various food products, including these very same Flamin' Hot Cheetos, which has been proven to stimulate and command attention.[128] This neon pop of color makes Hot Cheetos visually one of the brightest salty snack foods available. Perceiving color intensity as flavor intensity, scientists find that the more food dye added, the more likely consumers rate the flavor as much more intense.[129]

Rockford, Illinois Public Schools, where about 150,000 bags of Flamin' Hots were sold annually, may be attributed to the crunch, a flair of multisensory marketing. Products like Flamin' Hots are designed to create a memorable and addictive sensory experience, combining taste, texture, and visual appeal to attract consumers, especially younger ones. This multisensory approach can be very effective in driving sales, as evidenced by the high volume of Flamin' Hots sold in the district.

Investigating the sonic appeal of chips, research indicates that as crispiness and crunchiness increase, so does the liking score. Soundproof studies demonstrate that the louder the chip, the fresher, crispier, and more enjoyable it's perceived, enhancing the overall sensory experience.[130]

Flamin' Hot Cheetos masterfully engage auditory aspects of sensory experience, followed by a rush of endorphins and dopamine, inducing a high or euphoria. Although anecdotal, individuals in spicy food contests report euphoria, comparable to hallucination. Despite lacking actual spiciness in the ingredients, Flamin' Hots creates a sensation through capsaicin, tricking the tongue into perceiving a literal burn. The pain of the spicy requires relief intern releasing endorphins and the production of even more dopamine.[131]

Wait there's more, Frito-Lay discovered that people love that gross orange and red dust. The dust on fingers contributes to the overall sensory experience, evoking a feeling of deviousness and a craving for more. Frito-Lay's neuroscience tests, including fMRI scans, confirm that messy Cheetle dust promotes a sense of fun and mischief, aligning with the same emotion they market through Chester and their advertisements featuring pranks and troublemaking.[132]

Yes, many **little ol'** businesses, have now jumped into the science of brain scanning to craft snacks that irresistibly tantalize the senses, capitalizing and exploiting the complexities of sensory stimulation and the allure of anticipated rewards to fuel addictive tendencies. In a world where boredom looms large, individuals seek out experiences that evoke sensation and fulfillment. Thus, they often resort to indulging in habits reminiscent of Fight Club, reaching for Flamin' Hot Cheetos, scrolling through TikTok, or lighting up cigarettes to satisfy their cravings for self-stimulation.

Interestingly, recent research delves into the intriguing sphere of human psychology, uncovering the idea that the anticipation of a reward might hold a more profound sense of pleasure than the reward itself.[133] It suggests that the pursuit, the journey towards a goal, carries an intrinsic reward that continues to fuel the human desire for the pursuit of pleasure. This phenomenon, rooted in the interplay of anticipation and the release of dopamine, forms a potent force that propels addictive behavior.

In our contemporary society, marked by instant gratification, the art of delaying gratification is at risk of fading into obscurity. However, this skill once considered a virtue, possesses a power that rivals any cherished achievement. The ability to postpone immediate rewards in favor of more substantial, delayed gains is a lost art that could wield as much influence as any ancient wisdom or spiritual practice.

Consider a simple yet insightful thought experiment often used to illustrate the concept of time preference or time discounting in economics and decision theory: imagine children are presented with a choice between receiving a small reward immediately (like one marshmallow) or a larger reward (say, two marshmallows) if they wait for a brief period, typically around 15 minutes.

This experiment vividly demonstrates the trade-off between instant gratification and delayed gratification. Some children opt to enjoy the immediate pleasure of the one marshmallow, while others exercise patience in anticipation of the greater reward. The ability to delay gratification has been linked to greater long-term success and self-discipline, and possibly a more profound sense of pleasure in the anticipation itself.

Now, let's transpose this scenario into the space of financial decision-making: would you rather have $10 today or $100 in a week? Okay, now consider this twist: would your decision remain consistent if the choice was between $10 today versus $100 in a year? These alternate setups highlight different facets of decision-making and time preference. Despite the promise of a larger reward in the future, individuals may still exhibit inconsistent behavior in their decision-making process.

This inconsistency can stem from several factors, such as the perceived value of time, uncertainty about future circumstances, and individual preferences and priorities. People may weigh immediate gratification differently against future rewards based on their unique situations and mental outlooks at the time of decision-making.

Overall, these thought experiments and real-life scenarios help to illustrate the complexities of human decision-making and the interplay between immediate and delayed gratification in shaping our choices and behaviors.

In a society increasingly focused on instant gratification and rapid outcomes, the concept of patience and delayed gratification may seem outdated. However, embracing these values could lead to a deeper and more lasting sense of fulfillment. Despite the potential for greater rewards in the future, many individuals prioritize immediate gains, reflecting the prevalent preference for instant pleasure over long-term benefits, grabbing that bag of chips.

We can see, in the intense potpourri of marketing and branding within perceived gratification, the use of **shiny** tactics, sales ploys that **sounds good**, and strategic color choices within a logo or packaging plays a pivotal role in shaping consumer perceptions and fostering brand recognition. The concept of shininess goes beyond mere aesthetics; it symbolizes novelty, sophistication, and a modern appeal that captures the attention of the audience. **Shiny** elements, whether in the form of metallic finishes or glossy textures, evoke a sense of premium quality and exclusivity.

Color, paired on the other hand, is another potent tool for conveying emotions, establishing brand identity, and triggering psychological responses. Each color carries unique connotations and can influence how consumers perceive your **little ol' register's** brands. For example, the use of red can evoke passion and energy, while blue, as we have noted, may symbolize trust and reliability. When strategically combined with **shiny** elements, colors enhance the overall visual impact, creating a cohesive and memorable brand image.

A well-designed logo, incorporating **shiny** elements and thoughtfully chosen colors, becomes a visual ambassador for the brand. It communicates your **little ol' register** brand's personality, values, and promises, making it instantly recognizable in a crowded market. By leveraging the psychology of color and the allure of **shininess**, brands can establish a strong and positive connection with their target audience, fostering loyalty and leaving a lasting impression in the competitive landscape.

Regardless of the mesmerizing allure of the Flamin' Hot Cheetos, one-armed bandits, green ogres, or the illusory man in the blue suit, the experience is like moths drawn irresistibly to a scorching flame. As we peer down, much like the curious observer observing a colony of ants, we witness a multitude of individuals scurrying around, captivated by the tantalizing symphony of flavors and sensations that these fiery snacks of endorphins offer. The **shiny** allure of the sounds that beckon, coupled with the vivid sensory experience, creates a collective fascination.

In the sphere of persuasion, where taste and texture intertwine, the soundscape of crunchiness becomes a siren song luring endorphin enthusiasts into a world of multisensory delight. The vibrant colors, the enticing crunch, and the subtle euphoria induced by the combination of flavors all harmonize to form a melody that resonates deeply within the target's senses.

Thus, as we navigate the giggles of marketing, the symphony of sounds generated by a bag of Flamin' Hot Cheetos or the exclamations of turned fortunes becomes a cultural phenomenon, drawing people into its vortex of sensory stimulation. It's a captivating journey where the **sounds good**, the tastes taste even better, and the collective experience becomes a shared indulgence in the irresistible world of instant perceived pleasure.

Part 4: Working the Register

"It takes 20 years to build a reputation and 5 minutes to ruin it. If you think about that, you'll do things differently."

– Warren Buffett, CEO of Berkshire Hathaway

LEARNING OBJECTIVES, AN OPERATIONAL OUTLOOK

From the Chief Operating Officer's Perspective, boots are on the ground! So, get ready to roll up your sleeves and crawl through the nitty-gritty of operational wizardry! Here, we'll explore the art of being squared away, from optimizing workflows to smoothing out the wrinkles in day-to-day operations. In this operational theater, each learning objective serves as your gut intuition, leading the charge through the complex terrain of efficiency, much like a seasoned commander navigating through the fog of war, where every tweak and adjustment brings you one step closer to operational nirvana. So, load your pencils, tighten your bootstraps, and get ready to orchestrate the conquest of success—because in the COO's realm, every detail counts, and every victory is sweeter than the last!

■ **Efficient Process Management:** Explore strategies for optimizing operational processes to improve efficiency, reduce costs, and enhance productivity within your organization.

■ **Supply Chain Optimization:** Understand the fundamentals of supply chain management and learn how to optimize your supply chain to minimize disruptions, improve inventory management, and meet customer demand effectively.

■ **Quality Control and Continuous Improvement**: Gain insights into quality control principles and continuous improvement methodologies such as Lean and Six Sigma, and learn how to implement them to drive quality excellence and operational efficiency.

- **Inventory Management and Demand Forecasting:** Develop skills in inventory management and demand forecasting to ensure optimal inventory levels, minimize stockouts, and maximize inventory turnover while meeting customer demand.
- **Technology Integration and Automation:** Explore the role of technology in streamlining operations and improving business processes, and learn how to leverage automation tools and systems to enhance efficiency and accuracy.
- **Workforce Training and Development:** Understand the importance of workforce training and development in building a skilled and motivated team, and learn how to design and implement effective training programs to enhance employee capabilities.
- **Team Building and Talent Development:** Understand the importance of building and nurturing high-performing teams, and develop strategies for recruiting, retaining, and developing top talent within your organization.
- **Health and Safety Compliance:** Learn about health and safety regulations and compliance requirements relevant to your industry, and develop strategies for ensuring a safe and healthy work environment for your employees.
- **Customer Experience Optimization:** Explore techniques for optimizing the customer experience, from order fulfillment and delivery to after-sales support, to drive customer satisfaction and loyalty.
- **Crisis Management and Business Continuity Planning:** Develop strategies for crisis management and business continuity planning to ensure resilience in the face of unexpected disruptions or emergencies, and minimize the impact on business operations.

Notes:

BEHIND THE COUNTER: DAILY BUSINESS OPERATIONS

Opportunities in the bustling world of business operations, where every day brings a new set of challenges and triumphs. Behind the counter lies an area of ceaseless activity, where the wheels of commerce never stop turning. From managing inventory and serving customers to balancing budgets and fostering employee morale, the daily grind of business ownership demands unwavering dedication and strategic foresight.

Specifically, I believe an executive has three important sets of relationships that must be managed just as assiduously as the operation under his or her stewardship. These three relationships represent the other employees of the company, the other professionals that he or she interacts with, and most importantly of all, the customer. Inspiring ambition, conveying feeling, and igniting passion in every member and customer are vital parts of "Making the Dream."

As we continue on this journey passing through the heart of daily business operations, it's essential to keep a keen eye on the path ahead. Like a seasoned **warrior counting each step** before battle, we must navigate through the intricacies of decision-making and resource allocation. Every move we make, every decision we take, shapes the destiny of your **little ol' register** and determines its place in the competitive terrain.

But beware, fellow **warriors**, for in this world, the line between buyer and seller can blur in the **blink** of an eye. As we tread the treacherous terrain of commerce, let us remain vigilant against the siren call of instant gratification and the pitfalls of overconfidence. Remember, it's not just about making the sale or securing the deal; it's about protecting the future sanctity of your **little ol' register**, your business, from the allure of fleeting pleasures and the threats of external forces. So, gear up, **warriors**, and let us march forward with purpose and wit, for on the battlefield of business, only the savvy and resilient emerge victorious.

NEVER SAY NO

From the earliest moments of our cognitive development, the word "no" holds a prominent place in our linguistic repertoire. [134] It stands as a sentinel at the gateway of our understanding, guarding against danger and guiding our interactions with the world. The concept that "no" is among the initial words grasped by children is a well-trodden path in the field of child psychology and linguistics.

Part 4: Working the Register

As infants begin to navigate the complex landscape of human communication, they instinctively grasp the significance of this simple yet powerful word. "No" becomes their first line of defense, a shield against harm, and a means of asserting their autonomy in an unfamiliar environment. Whether uttered by caregivers as a precautionary measure or spontaneously voiced by the child themselves, the word "no" serves as a foundational building block in the construction of language and social interaction.

Moreover, the early acquisition of "no" reflects the innate human tendency to establish boundaries and assert personal agency. It signifies a crucial milestone in the developmental journey, marking the transition from passive recipient to active participant in the exchange of ideas and desires. Through the repeated utterance of "no," children assert their preferences, assert their boundaries, and begin to carve out their identity in the world of human experience.

In essence, "no" embodies the core of human resilience and self-preservation, serving as a testament to our innate capacity to navigate the complexities of the world around us. As we delve deeper into the intricacies of your **little ol' register's** development, the significance of this seemingly simple word becomes ever more profound, offering insight into the fundamental mechanisms that shape our understanding of language, cognition, and social interaction.

In the vivacious arena of business management, the ability to combat challenges with finesse and adaptability is paramount. While the instinctive response of "no" may serve as a reflexive shield against uncertainty, it can also inadvertently close doors and stifle innovation. In contrast, adopting a solution-oriented approach fosters a culture of problem-solving and resilience, laying the groundwork for sustained success and growth.

When confronted with obstacles or requests that may initially seem daunting or impractical, reframing the conversation with a constructive "how much" opens up avenues for exploration and collaboration. Rather than succumbing to defeatism or rigidity, this mindset encourages creative thinking and resourcefulness, empowering stakeholders to explore alternatives and devise innovative solutions.

Moreover, embracing the ethos of "how much" embodies a commitment to proactive engagement and continuous improvement. By actively seeking solutions and quantifying potential outcomes, businesses can mitigate risks, seize opportunities, and optimize their operational efficiency. This proactive stance not only enhances the agility and responsiveness of the organization but also cultivates a culture of empowerment and accountability among team members.

The transformative power of "how much" lies in its ability to transcend barriers and catalyze progress. By reframing challenges as opportunities and approaching them with a solution-oriented mindset (**solving the solutions**), businesses can unlock their full potential and chart a course toward sustained success. So, the next time you encounter a roadblock or mammoth ask, remember to hold the reflexive "no" and the mantra of disclosing "how much" and watch as possibilities unfold before your very eyes.

At the same time, a fundamental tenet that emerges in this philosophy is the understanding that your word is your bond, not only to others but, most importantly, to yourself.[135] The commitment to delivering on promises and agreements is integral to building trust and maintaining integrity in business dealings. Upholding this principle creates a reputation for reliability and dependability, key elements in the success and sustainability of your **little ol' register**. Stick to your word, even if it means sacrificing today, for tomorrow's gains will blossom abundantly.

In the pursuit of effective problem-solving and constructive collaboration, it's crucial to halt the assignment of blame and channel efforts toward **solving the solutions**. The mindset that prioritizes resolving challenges over assigning fault is key to fostering a positive and productive working environment. This approach encourages open communication and teamwork, enabling your **little ol' register** to navigate obstacles with resilience and efficiency.

As Eleanor Roosevelt wisely noted, "Great minds discuss ideas; average minds discuss events; small minds discuss people." Embracing this philosophy elevates the focus of discussions within your **little ol' register**, emphasizing the importance of engaging in conversations that contribute to innovation, progress, and shared goals. By fostering a culture that values idea-driven discussions, you cultivate an environment that thrives on creativity and collective problem-solving, leaving the "neigh" sayers behind.

Dale's insight further reinforces the notion that criticism, when aimed at individuals, is counterproductive.[65] Instead of fostering growth and improvement, it tends to put people on the defensive. Recognizing the futility of criticism, your **little ol' register** can shift its focus toward constructive feedback and collaborative solutions. This approach not only preserves positive working relationships but also encourages a mindset of continuous improvement, without the **mind-killing** fear of repercussions looming, within the team.

Back in the bustling and combative world of business, where every company strives for a moment in the spotlight, the tale of your **little ol' register** unfolds with a unique approach to competition. Imagine a vibrant marketplace where businesses are like gladiators in a grand narrative, each playing a distinct role.

Part 4: Working the Register

Your **little ol' register**, guided by a strategic philosophy, refrains from casting shadows on its fellow characters.

In this narrative, the wisdom of the **little ol' register** is illuminated through the lens of both business strategy and psychological insight. Picture a boardroom where decisions shape the destiny of the company. Instead of disparaging competitors, the focus is on exuding professionalism, an unspoken acknowledgment that every player in the industry contributes to its dynamism.

As the plot thickens, the narrative weaves through the psychology behind this approach. It's not merely a business tactic; it's a psychological dance. Positivity becomes the protagonist, propagating a culture of innovation and collaboration within your **little ol' register**. The characters, representing the team, thrive in an environment where their strengths are celebrated, fostering a collective belief in the company's journey.

Enter the concept of "Attribution Theory," where the characters—be they customers, employees, or industry peers—associate positive traits with a business that exhibits positivity. Your **little ol' register**, steering clear of the negativity trap, gains favor in the hearts and minds of its audience. The narrative takes a turn towards collaboration over confrontation, understanding the other's intrinsic motivation, as the protagonist explores opportunities for partnerships, alliances that promise mutual growth. [136]

In this story, your **little ol' register** is not just a business entity; it's the protagonist with a unique narrative arc. Its journey is not marred by the pitfalls of criticizing others but is defined by a commitment to showcasing its own brilliance. As the plot unfolds, the **little ol' register** emerges as a beacon of positivity, not just surviving but thriving in the unwritten pages of the business world. And so, the tale continues, where the chapters of history are written with words of collaboration, innovation, and the unwavering belief that in the narrative of business, every character has a role to play.

Speaking positively about your competition reflects professionalism and respect within the industry. It demonstrates that your **little ol' register** is secure enough in its capabilities to recognize the strengths of others. This in turn leads to customers and their likelihood to trust and engage with businesses that maintain a positive and respectful tone. Criticizing competitors can create an atmosphere of negativity that may turn potential customers away. Rather than dwelling on weaknesses in competitors, emphasize the unique strengths and advantages of your **little ol' register**. Highlighting and focusing on your "Unique Selling Points" (USPs), something that **sounds good**, allows you to differentiate your business without engaging in a negative discourse.

"Positivity breeds positivity. Surround yourself with those who lift you higher." - KJ Dell'Antonia. When your **little ol' register** focuses on its own strengths, it cultivates a positive mindset within the team. This, in turn, contributes to a more constructive and innovative work environment. As we look at this from a psychological standpoint, individuals tend to attribute positive characteristics to entities that exhibit positive behavior; "Attribution Theory." By avoiding negativity towards competitors, your **little ol' register** is likely to be perceived more favorably by customers, employees, and industry peers.

In summary, refraining from disparaging competitors aligns with principles of professionalism, fosters a positive psychological environment, and strategically positions your **little ol' register** as a business that focuses on its unique strengths. This approach contributes to a more harmonious industry landscape and enhances the overall reputation and success of your business.

Socrates' wisdom encapsulates the essence of this ethos: "The greatest way to live with honor in this world is to be what we pretend to be." It underscores the importance of authenticity and consistency in one's actions, aligning behavior with the principles and values that define your **little ol' register**. By embodying the ideals, you aspire to, you not only foster a culture of integrity but also contribute to the long-term success and positive reputation of your business.

As we conclude the chapter on "**Never Say No**," the resounding message is clear: wisdom lies in embracing clever ideas, regardless of their origin. In the intricate dance of business, where innovation and efficiency are the choreographers, the **little ol' register** knows that negativity should never overshadow positivity. Therefore, **never say no**, just ask how much.

The narrative unfolds with the recognition that good ideas are currency in the marketplace of innovation. Whether from a seasoned executive, a fresh-faced intern, or a competitor down the street, the **little ol' register** understands the value of shedding the armor of pride and opening its gates to the influx of valuable insights.

In the grand symphony of ideas, your **little ol' register** is attuned to the melody of collaboration, the choir of "Yes." Every note, every suggestion is considered, not through the lens of hierarchy, but through the pursuit of excellence. The narrative arc of this section encourages a shift in perspective—a reputation for reliability and dependability are the key ideas, not egos, that take center stage.

As the curtain falls on this chapter, your **little ol' register** stands not as a solitary figure on a pedestal but as a collective force fueled by the synergy of diverse thoughts. It understands that the journey to success is paved with the cobblestones of collaboration, where innovative ideas, irrespective of their origins, are the currency that propels the narrative forward.

So, dear reader, as you embark on your own business odyssey, remember the echo of this chapter: **never say no**, let good ideas flow freely, and watch as your **little ol' register** becomes a beacon of innovation and efficiency in the vast landscape of commerce. Onward to the next chapter, where the saga of business wisdom continues to unfold.

WARRIORS

Embedded in the roots of Japanese morality and culture is one of the most misconstrued codes of conduct: bushido, commonly known as the 'Way of the **Warrior**.' The Samurai, integral to a **warrior** class that thrived in Japan from the 10th century C.E. until the 19th century, adhered to this ethos.[137] Their principles were deeply influenced by Confucianism, a conservative philosophy emphasizing values such as loyalty and duty. Today, the enduring impact of bushido and its connection to Japanese culture continues to shape perspectives on honor, discipline, and commitment. This historical backdrop not only reflects the Samurai's dedication to a moral code but also draws intriguing parallels to contemporary business management and operations.

In the heart of medieval Japan, the legendary warlord Oda Nobunaga stood as a beacon of leadership, his unorthodox management style leaving an indelible mark on history. Nobunaga, known for his strategic brilliance and ambitious *vision*, cultivated an environment that fostered creativity and risk-taking among his **warriors**.[137, 138]

In the hallowed halls of his castle, Nobunaga assembled a council of diverse and talented samurai, each possessing unique skills and perspectives. Unlike many feudal lords of his time, Nobunaga welcomed innovative ideas and encouraged his followers to challenge conventional thinking. He understood that true strength lay not only in the might of a sword but in the power of imaginative minds.

One fateful day, faced with a formidable adversary, Nobunaga's council proposed a daring plan that defied traditional battlefield tactics. The warlord, recognizing the potential brilliance in their unconventional strategy, not only approved it but entrusted the execution to the very samurai who conceived it.

The battle unfolded, and to the surprise of many, the audacious plan succeeded, securing a decisive victory for Nobunaga's forces. This triumph solidified the warlord's reputation as a leader who valued innovation and rewarded daring initiatives.

Oda Nobunaga's legacy extends beyond the conquests of feudal Japan; it resonates in the annals of leadership philosophy. His approach, emphasizing creativity and risk-taking, serves as a timeless lesson for leaders navigating the complexities of their own battlefields.

In the honorable words of Lao Tzu knowing others is intelligence; knowing yourself is true wisdom. Mastering others is strength; mastering yourself is true power.[137] The concept of "kaizen" the philosophy of continuous improvement centers around turning a pursuit into a way of life and understanding that when we become competent in one discipline, the skill carries over into all others. "By acquiring a broad understanding, one can perceive the essence in everything." [138] Embrace mastery within your domain while cultivating versatility across various skills. Become an expert in understanding yourself.

The Bushido code encompasses eight fundamental principles or virtues that **warriors** were held to uphold. These include values such as loyalty, modesty, proficiency in martial skills, and a commitment to honor.[139] Merged with the given insight from Nobunaga's strength, if the objective is victory, it would be foolish not to heed ideas, regardless of their origin.

Embracing the essence of the Bushido code in a contemporary business setting involves delving deeper into its core principles.[140] Loyalty, a commitment to one's principles and *values*, extends beyond personal allegiances to encompass a steadfast dedication to the company's *mission* and goals. Modesty becomes a reminder to approach success with humility, acknowledging achievements while remaining open to continuous growth and improvement, not mounted on a **high horse**.

The **warrior** spirit, as emphasized in the original code, translates into a modern context as the cultivation of skills and expertise. A commitment to continuous learning and honing one's craft is essential for both personal and professional development. Whether it's mastering new technologies, staying abreast of industry trends, or enhancing leadership abilities, the **warrior** mindset encourages a relentless pursuit of excellence.

Moreover, the virtue of honor extends beyond personal integrity to the reputation and integrity of your **little ol' register**. Upholding ethical standards and conducting business with transparency contribute to building a trustworthy and honorable brand.

In the context of the workplace, holding one's head high is a symbolic expression of confidence and self-assurance. It reflects a positive self-image, radiating a can-do attitude that inspires confidence in others. Being a go-getter aligns with the proactive spirit of a **warrior**, encouraging a mindset that actively seeks opportunities, overcomes challenges, and contributes to the overall success of the organization.

Maintaining composure and projecting a stress-free demeanor in front of your team, regardless of **hat**, conveys a sense of calmness and unruffled confidence. Adopting a playful and light-hearted approach can be remarkably effective. The significance of this quality should not be underestimated, especially in times of heightened tension and uncertainty when individuals may be on edge and conflicts may arise. Ease is an inherently attractive quality, serving to alleviate tension and create a more relaxed environment. It allows for humor without intensity, employing charm as a disarming tool to foster a positive atmosphere.[57]

Have you ever caught yourself unconsciously mirroring or mimicking someone else's behavior? This fascinating phenomenon is known as echophenomenon, derived from the Ancient Greek word ἠχώ (ēkhṓ), meaning "echo" or "reflected sound." Another term for this is echopraxia, which refers to the automatic replication of bodily movements without explicit intent. Essentially, echophenomenon involves imitating another person's actions without conscious awareness, highlighting the inherent mimetic nature of humans. It's similar to how a smiling baby can effortlessly make you break into a grin. This subconscious imitation can almost be seen as a form of flattery, underscoring the importance of holding oneself to high standards of behavior and appearance, especially for those **warriors** in leadership roles.

In recent years, the study of mirror neurons has shed new light on our understanding of imitation. Mirror neurons are specialized neurons in the brain that fire both when we act and when we observe someone else performing the same action.[98] This suggests that our brains are wired for imitation and that it plays an important role in our social interactions. Interactions between individuals involve the use of the body to communicate information and feelings.[57] Through gestures, facial expressions, and body language, we send social signals to convey messages all in a **blink**.

In the corporate empire, **warriors** stand as exemplary figures to be emulated by their peers. Their embodiment of dedication, resilience, and a relentless pursuit of excellence serves as a source of inspiration for others within the organization. Much like a ripple effect, the positive traits and work ethic displayed by **warriors** create a resonating impact, encouraging their colleagues to strive for similar levels of commitment and achievement.

The concept of echophenomenon, or the tendency of individuals to mimic observed behaviors, becomes a powerful tool in the hands of **warriors**. Through their actions and demeanor, **warriors** can effectively teach and influence those around them. By consistently exhibiting traits such as determination, teamwork, and a **solving the solution**-oriented mindset, they set a precedent that encourages others to follow suit. This creates a positive and resilient organizational culture where each member is motivated to contribute their best.

In essence, **warriors** not only lead by example but also actively contribute to the development of a collaborative and high-performing work environment. Through the echo of their actions, they become instrumental in shaping the collective mindset of your **little ol' register**, fostering a culture of excellence and continuous improvement.

Recognizing the diversity in learning styles is crucial in any organization. **Warriors** tactfully set up onboarding processes with a variety of tools to ensure that everyone has the opportunity to comprehend and master the intricacies of the **system**. Whether it's visual aids, hands-on training, or comprehensive documentation, a well-rounded approach caters to the different preferences and learning strengths of team members.[19]

In the relentless pursuit of perfection, practice becomes a cornerstone. Continuous practice hones skills, refines processes, and contributes to a culture of ongoing improvement. **Warriors**, as the driving force behind the company's success, understand the value of consistent practice, embracing the never-ending quest for excellence, regardless of being **kings of their domains**, as a collective endeavor.

Nevertheless, there is a phenomenon called "Brain Drain," where individuals are lost, wounded, or move on, and the knowledge or skill is diluted from the company. This underscores the importance of a robust **system**. The gears of the organizational machine must be well-greased to mitigate dependency on any single part or employee. Investing in comprehensive training programs becomes a strategic move to prevent the loss of critical skills. By ensuring that multiple team members are proficient in key areas, your **little ol' register** becomes more resilient and less vulnerable to the potential disruptions caused by the departure of any single contributor.

Identifying the **warriors** within your company involves going beyond the formal structure outlined in operating agreements or bylaws. While these documents provide a foundation, the essence of **warriors** lies in the individuals who excel and drive the gears of the organization forward. **Warriors** can be found at every level and in every department, transcending titles and positions.

In sales, a **warrior** might be the charismatic individual who consistently exceeds targets, demonstrating not only a mastery of selling techniques but also a passion for the products or services offered. In operations, a **warrior** could be the meticulous individual who ensures seamless processes, preventing bottlenecks and optimizing efficiency.

These **warriors** embody the company's values and principles. They exhibit qualities of dedication, resilience, and a relentless pursuit of excellence. Their influence extends beyond their immediate responsibilities, as they inspire and uplift those around them. Recognizing these unsung heroes is crucial for fostering a culture of appreciation and acknowledging the diverse talents that contribute to the overall success of your **little ol' register**.

Your **little ol' register warriors** within a business plan, the "Management Profile" is a crucial component that provides a comprehensive overview of the key individuals responsible for steering the company toward its objectives. This section typically includes detailed information about the executive team, their professional backgrounds, expertise, and roles within the organization. It serves as a snapshot of the leadership's collective experience and skills, showcasing their capacity to navigate challenges and drive the company's success.

Investors and stakeholders often scrutinize the Management Profile (**Warriors**) to assess the team's qualifications, industry knowledge, and ability to execute the business plan. Additionally, the profile instills confidence in potential partners and employees, fostering trust in the leadership's capability to guide the company effectively. Ultimately, a well-crafted "Management Profile" is instrumental in establishing credibility, instigating investor confidence, and aligning the team's strengths with the strategic goals of the business.

Understanding in the invigorated kingdom of business, resembling the constant turnover of cells within a living organism, new elements, personnel, and even leadership continuously enter and exit the scene. In the intricate dance of corporate life, the hope is that these individuals are not alike to cancerous cells, which could pose a threat to the overall health and vitality of your **little ol' register**. It becomes imperative to scrutinize these components, discerning their potential impact and swiftly addressing any anomalies that might hinder the harmonious functioning of the business.

Much like a vigilant caretaker or a **warrior** willing to fall on their sword, businesses must employ proactive strategies—whether through targeted treatment, rehabilitative efforts, or, in extreme cases, amputation—to ensure the sustained well-being and resilience of the organizational health of the whole. This constant cycle of assessment and intervention becomes a hallmark of effective business management, safeguarding against potential disruptions and promoting the overall health and longevity of your **little ol' register**.

In the empire of **warriors**, those driven by passion, loyalty, and an unwavering sense of duty are the ones who stand out. They are the individuals gazing upward, envisioning the grand **pyramid** bathed in the hues of **Kool-Aid**, adorned with gleaming **hats** symbolizing their roles in this intricate **chess** game. Together, they forge a brotherhood of **warriors**, fully aware that they are the architects of the **system**, destined to step into the shoes of those who say, **"Take my job."**

GAMES

As the sun dipped low on the horizon, casting long shadows across the suburban streets, young Sarah clutched her box of Girl Scout cookies tightly to her chest. With a nervous flutter in her stomach, she approached the first house on her list, her small hand trembling slightly as she raised it to knock on the door.

For Sarah, this was more than just a simple sales pitch; it was a rite of passage, a test of her courage and determination. She had spent weeks preparing for this moment, practicing her sales pitch in front of the mirror and memorizing every detail about the cookies she was selling.

As she waited for someone to answer the door, Sarah's mind raced with doubts and fears. What if they slammed the door in her face? What if they said no? But she pushed aside her worries and focused on the task at hand, remembering the words of her troop leader: "It's all about the law of numbers, Sarah. The more doors you knock on, the more sales you'll make."

Finally, the door creaked open, revealing a kind-faced woman standing on the other side. With a nervous smile, Sarah launched into her well-rehearsed sales pitch, extolling the virtues of Thin Mints and Tagalongs with all the enthusiasm she could muster.

To her surprise, the woman's eyes lit up with recognition as she listened to Sarah's pitch. "I used to be a Girl Scout myself," she said, her voice tinged with nostalgia. I remember selling cookies door-to-door just like you're doing now."

Encouraged by the woman's response, Sarah found her confidence growing with each passing moment. She moved on to the next house, then the next, knocking on doors and making her pitch with renewed determination.

Part 4: Working the Register

As the evening wore on and the stars began to twinkle in the sky, Sarah realized something important: it wasn't just about making sales or earning badges. It was about connecting with people, sharing a moment of joy and nostalgia, and making a difference in her community.

And as she returned home, her box of cookies significantly lighter but her heart immeasurably fuller, Sarah knew that she had taken a major step on her journey of growth and self-discovery. Knocking on doors may have been intimidating at first, but with each door she knocked on, she was not only selling cookies but also building confidence, resilience, and character. Sometimes you just have to get through your ninety-nine "Nos" to get that one "Yes."

Now, as the sun sets on another day in the bustling city, a group of eager Boy Scouts gather around their troop leader, excitement bubbling in their veins. Each one wears their uniform proudly, adorned with badges representing their achievements in camping, survival skills, and community service. The air is electric with anticipation as they prepare for their next challenge.

But this isn't just any challenge—it's a game, a chance to put their skills to the test and earn even more badges to add to their collection. Inspired by the concept of gamification, their troop leader has devised a series of tasks and missions designed to engage and motivate them like never before.

The boys eagerly set off into the city, armed with maps and instructions, their eyes alight with determination. Their first task? To navigate their way through the maze of streets to reach a designated checkpoint before time runs out. Along the way, they encounter obstacles and challenges that test their teamwork, problem-solving skills, and resilience.

With each checkpoint they reach, the boys earn points and badges, fueling their competitive spirit and driving them to push harder and go further. They tackle scavenger hunts, solve puzzles, and complete physical challenges with gusto, fueled by the thrill of the game and the promise of rewards.

But it's not just about the badges or the points—it's about the camaraderie and sense of accomplishment that comes from working together toward a common goal. As they race against the clock, the boys learn valuable lessons about leadership, perseverance, and the power of teamwork.

As the sun dips below the horizon and the city lights begin to twinkle, the boys return to their meeting place, their chests swollen with pride and their minds buzzing with excitement. They may have started as just a group of Boy Scouts, but through the magic of gamification, they've become a team, united by a shared sense of purpose and a hunger for adventure.

In these tales of youthful adventure and strategic engagement, we witness the power of the "Law of Numbers" and "Gamification" to inspire and motivate individuals towards achieving their goals. From the Boy Scouts navigating the urban jungle to the Girl Scouts collecting brownie points, both narratives illustrate the effectiveness of incorporating game mechanics into real-world scenarios. The lessons learned are clear: by breaking tasks into smaller, achievable goals and providing incentives for progress, individuals are more likely to stay engaged, focused, and motivated. Whether it's earning badges or accumulating loyalty points, the journey becomes as rewarding as the destination, fostering a sense of camaraderie, accomplishment, and personal growth along the way.

The gamification field has experienced exponential growth and improved organizational recognition, particularly in talent acquisition and retention strategy. **Games** have the power to affect, boost, and encourage specific behaviors in people. They strive to assist and inspire consumers to do tasks prompted by services offered by the company. It allows us to make even the most tedious tasks and routine activities enjoyable for consumers.

One of the best strategies of competition is incentivization of people's engagement. Restaurants have used this with wait staff for years. Offering gift cards, free meals, and even tickets to a show to the individual at the end of the shift that has the highest alcohol sales. This causes drive and competition—**game** on!

To get the most out of your sales process gamification, reward habits rather than results. The goal of the points **system** is to reward positive conduct rather than to achieve the highest score possible. Only allocate value to the tasks you believe will improve the performance of your salespeople. The use of the **stickers** on these **hats** can also motivate the individual as well as the team.

Team building activities can make all the difference when it comes to job satisfaction, employee engagement, and organizational success. But even with the best intentions, it's not sufficient to simply bring a group of people together. Effective team-building activities can help your group feel more connected and able to collaborate more effectively. By engaging in such exercises, team members learn to communicate effectively, rely on each other's strengths, and navigate challenges together.

Trust is a foundational element in any successful team. Trust-building **games** create a shared experience that transcends the workplace, allowing team members to understand each other's capabilities, communication styles, and reliability. As individuals participate in activities that require vulnerability, such as blindfolded trust walks or problem-solving challenges, they begin to break down barriers and build a sense of camaraderie. Trust **games** also instill a deeper understanding of individual strengths and weaknesses, promoting a culture of mutual support and collaboration within the team. Your **little ol' register** strength is only as strong as the weakest link in its chain.[141] Ultimately, these shared experiences create a more cohesive and resilient team, better equipped to tackle complex tasks, and navigate the ever-changing demands of the workplace.

Games are much more than merely a technique to engage your employees, users, or customers. It is a mindset that ensures even the most routine-based task becomes challenging and rewarding through a healthy sense of competition and urgency, a healthy dose of a neurochemical stimulant. Enterprise teams can imbibe gamification principles into nearly every facet of their work, from team collaboration to product design and software delivery. It can accelerate outcomes and ensure more significant satisfaction levels for every stakeholder involved.

Incorporating badges, ranks, and levels into a company's structure fosters a profound sense of achievement and loyalty among employees. These symbols of recognition not only acknowledge individual accomplishments but also promote a feeling of inclusion and belonging within your **little ol' register**. Much like a family, teams within the company strive together, celebrating victories and facing challenges as a united front.

By gamifying the workplace, **warriors** view their tasks not as mundane chores but as engaging challenges to conquer. As they advance through levels and earn badges, the sense of camaraderie and shared purpose strengthens, driving collective efforts towards common goals. Indeed, the workplace becomes a playground where teams collaborate, compete, and grow together, fueled by the spirit of friendly competition and the thrill of the journey—the game's afoot.

> In the realm of sales, where numbers dance,
> And gamification's chance to enhance,
> Reward not just results, but habits true,
> For therein lies the secret to breakthrough.

The points system, a currency of praise,
Not merely for the highest score's blaze,
But to honor conduct, positive and bright,
That fuels the sales team's relentless fight.

Stickers adorn hats, a badge of pride,
Motivating both individual stride,
And the collective force that binds them tight,
As they chase success from morning to night.

Yet beyond sales metrics and profit's gleam,
Lies a deeper truth, a team-building theme,
For job satisfaction and engagement's grace,
Require more than mere office space.

Team-building activities, purposeful and wise,
Forge connections that no spreadsheet can disguise,
In exercises shared, they learn to trust,
To communicate, rely, and adjust.

Blindfolded trust walks, problem-solving quests,
Break down barriers, put camaraderie to the test,
Strengths and weaknesses revealed in the fray,
A culture of mutual support takes sway.

And remember, dear register, humble and small,
Your strength is woven into the team's grand hall,
For the chain is only as strong as its weakest link,
In this ever-changing dance, we rise and sync.

CUSTOMER SERVICE: SATISFYING YOUR "CUSTOMERS"

To the jokester: Why did the customer bring a ladder to the store? Because they heard the prices were through the roof! Collectively smiling and shaking our heads.

Now, let's dive into the world of customer service with a grin on our faces and a determination to satisfy even the quirkiest of customers. In this upcoming chapter, we'll explore the **true power** of positive thinking, where every challenge becomes an opportunity for a win-win situation. We'll also delve into **the sweetest thing**: your own name—branding—because let's be honest, who doesn't love hearing their own name? And last but not least, we'll spread some **peanut butter** of reciprocity, reminding us all to give a little and watch the magic happen.

Customer service isn't just a department; it's a cornerstone of your **little ol' register's** success. It's the secret sauce that keeps customers coming back, spreading positive word-of-mouth, and ultimately fueling your business growth. Picture this: your **little ol' register** is like a ship sailing through the tumultuous seas of commerce. Without exceptional customer service as its compass, it risks getting lost in the waves of competition or worse, sinking altogether.

Think of every customer interaction as a chance to showcase what makes your **little ol' register** stand out from the crowd. Whether it's a friendly greeting, prompt assistance, or going the extra mile to solve a problem, each interaction leaves a lasting impression on your customers. It's about building trust, loyalty, and a reputation for excellence in the minds of your clientele.

In today's hyperconnected world, where a single tweet or online review can make or break a business, the importance of customer service cannot be overstated. Your **little ol' register** may be small in size, but its impact on customer satisfaction and retention is mighty. By prioritizing exceptional customer service, you're not just winning over individual customers; you're laying the foundation for long-term success and sustainability in the competitive marketplace.

So, strap on those boxing gloves and paint that target of a nose red, folks, because, in the world of customer service, laughter is often the best policy!

TRUE POWER

Most individuals have been conditioned to opt for the easier option and avoid making difficult choices in their everyday lives. Right now, what you need to do is make bold decisions. Right now, you need to train yourself to act, take chances, and put yourself at risk—leading to greater rewards. In those moments we discover our true self. Dig deep for the life you really want, and choose not because of the **shiny why** nor the **mind-killer** but only for the fact it is a choice and it was made by you.[25]

Nobody's interested in your fears; it's time to push past them. If your **little ol' register** aligns with your expertise, then you're already equipped to tackle it—if you can do it for them, you can do it for yourself—and if not, remember, there's truly **nothing new**; it's all been tackled before. So, tighten those bootstraps, and let's get going!

Herein lies the truth about the" Power of Negativity." The notion that one negative experience or comment can be more powerful than several positive ones in business is often related to the concept of negativity bias. Negativity bias refers to the psychological phenomenon where negative events, information, or experiences have a greater impact on one's mental state and behavior than positive ones. **Why** is this so?

Negative experiences often trigger more intense emotional responses compared to positive ones.[142] This phenomenon may be believed to offer an evolutionary advantage. In terms of survival, it's more crucial to recognize and avoid potential threats than to pursue potential benefits. Consequently, our brains are wired to react more strongly to negative stimuli, such as danger or harm, than to positive ones.

When individuals encounter negative experiences or feedback, their brains may release stress hormones like cortisol. Interestingly, despite the negative emotional state, these stress-inducing events can also lead to an increase in dopamine levels in specific brain regions. Dopamine, typically associated with pleasure and reward, plays a complex role in response to stress.[60] This intricate interplay between stress and dopamine contributes to the heightened emotional impact of negative events.

Moreover, negative experiences tend to be more deeply ingrained in our memories, particularly within the hippocampus, a brain region crucial for memory formation. This means that negative events are often stored more prominently and persistently in our minds compared to positive ones. Consequently, even minor negative experiences can leave a lasting mark on our overall perception and emotional well-being.

Neurotransmitters wield remarkable power over our daily lives, influencing not just our thoughts and actions but also our deepest desires. From the motivating surge of dopamine that propels us toward our goals to the calming embrace of serotonin that soothes our anxieties, these chemical messengers orchestrate the symphony of our emotions and behaviors. They shape our perceptions of pleasure, drive our pursuit of rewards, and even dictate our responses to stress. With such profound influence, understanding the intricate dance of neurotransmitters within our brains offers a key to unlocking the mysteries of human behavior and harnessing the **true power** of our minds.

The chemical pattern that dictates our ability to change is intricately linked to four key neurotransmitters:[143]

- **Acetylcholine** acts as the spotlight of attention, enhancing focus and concentration. When you're fully engaged in a task, acetylcholine is at work, keeping your mind sharp and alert. When you're engrossed in a book, solving a puzzle, or nailing a presentation, it's acetylcholine that takes center stage.

- **Adrenaline** (Epinephrine): This one's all about energy and alertness. When you need that extra boost—whether it's during a high-pressure situation or a thrilling adventure—adrenaline kicks in. It's like your body's turbocharger, ready to activate the fight-or-flight response.

- **Dopamine**. Ah, the life force itself. Imagine dopamine as your personal cheerleader. It fuels your motivation, stokes ambition, influences time perception, and whispers, "You've got this!" Whether you're chasing dreams, celebrating victories, or simply savoring a delicious meal, dopamine is there, clapping in the front row. When you achieve a goal, experience pleasure, or anticipate something exciting, dopamine is cheering you on.

- **Serotonin**, conversely, promotes calmness and relaxation, helping to reset and destress the mind and body. It's like a gentle hug for your nervous system, allowing you to destress and find balance. When you unwind after a long day, meditate, or bask in the sun, serotonin whispers, "Rest, my friend. You've earned it."

Together, these neurotransmitters play a crucial role in shaping our behavior, emotions, and ability to adapt to new situations. So next time you feel focused, energized, motivated, or serene, give a nod to these invisible maestros—they're the puppeteers pulling the strings of your life's grand show!

These molecules also serve as the gatekeepers of neural plasticity, determining whether your brain can adapt and change its thoughts, behaviors, skills, and even responses to anxiety and trauma. This process becomes particularly crucial after the age of 25 when the brain undergoes significant stiffening. Surprisingly, a large majority of therapists, athletic coaches, self-help gurus, and educators remain unaware of this fundamental aspect of neuroscience. Bridging the gap between neuroscience and psychology, especially in the realm of business, is

Part 4: Working the Register

essential to maximize our potential. Using cutting-edge information from Andrew we can be much more effective at reaching our full potential.

Every Navy SEAL shares one common trait, and it's not raw talent. Contrary to widespread belief, it's not the most naturally gifted individuals who excel in Navy SEAL training. Rather, it's those who can maintain a positive mindset amidst the challenges and hardships of rigorous training who ultimately succeed.

According to Andrew, various stimuli such as emotional news, movies, intense video games, and stimulants can trigger fluctuations in neurochemical levels, leading to the opening of neural plasticity. These experiences, whether intensely positive or negative, can cause dopamine levels to soar. Putting things into perspective, emotional anger increases dopamine by 250% while cocaine and caffeine only give rise to 200%, even chocolate can boost the mesocorticolimbic pathway (major dopamine reward pathway) by 150%.[143] What's intriguing is that these behaviors, activities, and substances can compound on one another, a phenomenon referred to as dopamine layering or chemical stacking. Now, how about one of those **shiny** bags of Flamin' Hot Cheetos?

Certain of the most effective social media platforms have mastered the art of creating divisions by exploiting chemical triggers and inundating users with tailored frictionless content. This content is designed to capitalize on short time windows, effortlessly drawing individuals deeper, over and over just like **milking**, into specific narratives or directions without their conscious awareness in a **blink**. Leaving users craving more with each interaction. Gradually, over time, these platforms subtly alter neural connections, rewiring (**milking**) them in their favor. By targeting core belief **systems**, amplifying narratives, and evoking emotional responses, they unleash a potent neurochemical cocktail that keeps users hooked.

At the core, we must grasp that everything, whether a tool or a temptation, possesses the potential for both light and darkness, especially within ourselves. The goal isn't to eradicate emotions but to discern when they or when the external **shiny** influences hold sway over us. By reclaiming control over our reactions and impulses, we safeguard our autonomy and preserve our capacity for choice—**true power**. It's essential to refrain from using manipulation for self-serving ends, whether in business or personal interactions. Whether the worker striving to earn a livelihood or the provider meeting a customer's **wants-needs**, your **little ol' register** actions should always prioritize nobility and mutual benefit—a genuine win-win scenario for all involved.

A counter-intuitive thought, the journey toward a goal often holds more joy than the actual achievement itself. As dopamine floods our **system** in anticipation of success, we experience a sense of euphoria that sustains us through the effort. However, once the goal is reached, dopamine levels plummet, leaving us vulnerable to the "Arrival Fallacy"—the realization that the destination wasn't as fulfilling as anticipated in our minds. This phenomenon underscores the importance of maintaining a balance in our pursuit of rewards, as excessive dopamine spikes can skew (**milk**) our perception of risk and reward.

In the sphere of customer service, understanding these nuances can inform strategies for delighting customers and exceeding their expectations, all while fostering a sense of satisfaction and accomplishment in your staff and yourself. Yet, for those with lower dopamine levels (cough, cough), a boost in this neurotransmitter can tip the scales in favor by pursuing more challenging tasks, fostering a greater willingness to tackle new obstacles head-on.[8, 144]

Let's clarify, this value of intrinsic motivation and drive becomes even more pronounced when tasks slightly exceed one's perceived ability by a margin of around 10%.[143] This slight increase in difficulty triggers a significant boost in dopamine levels, propelling individuals to tackle challenges with heightened enthusiasm and determination.[8] Back in the bubble of customer service, leveraging this understanding can revolutionize how businesses and their agents approach interactions with clients. By strategically calibrating the difficulty of tasks to stimulate this dopamine surge, organizations can inspire their teams to go above and beyond in delivering exceptional service, surpassing customer expectations, and fostering a deeper sense of fulfillment and achievement among employees.

In the cat-and-mouse game of business, where every decision feels like tiptoeing through a minefield, risk aversion reigns supreme. Picture this: one misstep, one tiny hiccup, and suddenly, it's panic stations everywhere! Like that time Karen accidentally hit "reply all" on the office-wide email announcing the surprise birthday party for the boss. Cue frantic backpedaling and damage control, as everyone scrambles to salvage the situation and avoid the impending disaster. It's a classic case of risk aversion at its finest, with everyone on high alert and ready to pounce at the slightest hint of trouble. Businesses often operate in an environment where risk aversion is prevalent. A single negative incident may be perceived as a potential risk or threat, causing individuals to pay more attention to it and take corrective actions to mitigate the perceived risk.

Did you know that unhappy customers are more likely to share their experiences than satisfied ones? Negative reviews or feedback tend to be more vocal

10% Boost

and spread more quickly, maybe it's because we all love to complain. This potentially can reach a larger audience and influence public perception as a whole. Reputation, once tarnished, is challenging to restore, and people may be more sensitive to negative information harming your **little ol' register's** image.

A negative experience can erode trust quickly, while positive experiences may take longer to build trust. Think of it as an emotional bank account.[7] You make small deposits of goodwill over time, but those deposits can be completely wiped out and your account can go negative, quite quickly, not only by excessive withdrawals but compounded by the outraged overdraft fees.

The human brain's inclination to prioritize negative information for memory and recall stems from its evolutionary roots in survival. In a world fraught with dangers, this protective mechanism has enabled our species to navigate threats and ensure our continued existence. This bias toward negativity means that individuals often remember and emphasize negative experiences more than positive ones, shaping their decision-making and behavior in various contexts.

When it comes to customer service, this tendency becomes particularly relevant. Customers typically have grand expectations when engaging with a business, anticipating positive outcomes and experiences. However, when these expectations are not met, regardless of validity, it can lead to disappointment and dissatisfaction. Negative experiences tend to stand out more prominently in the customer's mind, especially when they deviate from the perceived and expected positive outcomes. As a result, businesses must prioritize meeting or exceeding customer expectations to avoid negative experiences that could tarnish their reputation and impact customer loyalty.

True power emanates from within, rooted in the ability to navigate the intricate landscape of one's mind. It's a dance between the intricate neurotransmitters, such as dopamine, and the profound capacity to control oneself. Jordan, in "12 Rules for Life: An Antidote to Chaos," delves into the essence of **true power**. It's not about dominating others or succumbing to base desires; instead, it resides in the mastery of one's reactions and the disciplined governance of the self. A physically strong individual may possess the potential to inflict harm, yet the real power lies in choosing peace and exercising restraint.[51] This concept underscores the profound truth that genuine power is not external but an internal force—one that can guide individuals toward wisdom, resilience, and the capacity to flourish amidst the chaos of life.

In the intricate world of humanity's mind, the **true power** is that from the power within. Just as we are learning to control and master the intricate workings of your **little ol' register**, **true power** unfolds in our ability to govern the inner workings of our minds. The principles of customer service, echoed in our interactions with ourselves, teach us that real strength lies in choosing peace over conflict, in guiding our reactions, and in wielding the power of self-control. So, as we tread through the unpredictable terrain of entrepreneurship, may we embrace the **true power** within, much like your **little ol' register** faithfully recording every transaction with precision and purpose. In this dance with chaos, let the melody of self-mastery and customer-centric principles guide us toward a symphony of success.

THE SWEETEST THING

Going over the demographics for the company may reveal the "who" of your audience, but now they have been brought into the family. Teach your **little ol' register** good manners. A famous quote from Dale's book "How to Win Friends" is, "A person's name is to him or her the sweetest and most important sound in any language." This is a powerful reminder of the importance of using people's names. When we hear our name, it triggers emotions and memories that **sound good** and are associated with how we feel about ourselves.

Similarly, when we use other people's names, it shows that we value and respect them. What about seeing the value in using another person's name? When people hear your name, they automatically have emotions and memories that are brought to the surface that are associated with how they feel about you. As much as we like to be recognized and called by our name, it's important we use others' names as much as possible too.

Using people's names is especially important in business, as it helps to build strong relationships with customers and colleagues. This means your **little ol' register** is going to have to learn a cacophony (a lot) of names. One way to remember people's names is to use an Autistic flashcard **system**, or what others might call it, a Customer Relationship Management tool (CRM). People want to know they are special. Engaging with your customers in this manner can help you create a more personalized experience for them and make them feel special and important, which they are.

In addition to using people's names, there are other ways to engage with your customers and show them that you care. For example, your **little ol' register** can send thank you cards, thinking of you, or remembering your customers' birthdays are wonderful ways to show them how much you care. Another is branded swag (stuff). It helps in recalling and reminiscing on those little unannounced tokens of appreciation and exceptional experiences. Yes, they are all technically **milking**, but "improving customer interactions" **sounds good**.

Ultimately, it is crucial to harness the power of your corporate brand to craft a consistent and unforgettable experience for your customers. This involves prominently featuring your brand name on all marketing materials and developing a distinctive, easily recognizable logo. Notably, certain brands have even cultivated such strong associations that customers willingly purchase items adorned with their coveted logos, exemplified by iconic names like Nike, Polo, Gucci, Louis Vuitton, and Saint Laurent.

Utilize the strength of your brand name and leverage the heuristic power of priming and consensus, as we have touched on before. This is often referred to as "Bandwagoning" and is deployed in various forms on a near-daily basis. By consistently showcasing your brand and associating it with positive elements, you can prime customers to think favorably about your **little ol' register's** products or services. Got **Milk**?

Additionally, tapping into the consensus effect—where people are influenced by the actions and opinions of others—can further bolster your brand's appeal. This might involve highlighting customer testimonials, positive reviews, or demonstrating the popularity of your offerings, creating a sense of belonging and trust among your target audience—**Think Customer**.

Furthermore, understanding the power of **milking** extends to thoughtful gestures that enhance the overall customer and stakeholder experience. Distributing cards and gifts on local holidays is a prudent decision, demonstrating appreciation and fostering a sense of connection. Whether it's expressing gratitude to customers through thank-you cards, extending thoughtful gifts to vendors, or surprising staff with unexpected bonuses, these actions go beyond transactions. They contribute to building relationships, making individuals feel valued and integral to the collective success of the enterprise—depositing into that emotional bank account.[7] Such gestures not only align with the heuristic of reciprocity but also create positive associations that influence perceptions and decisions in the long run.[140]

Brand identification plays a pivotal role in the success and recognition of your **little ol' register**. It goes beyond just a logo; it's about creating a distinct identity that resonates with your **little ol' register's** audience. When customers see your brand name consistently across marketing materials, products, and services, it becomes imprinted in their minds. This repetition contributes to the psychological concept of priming, where exposure to a stimulus influences subsequent behavior.

Imagine the iconic swoosh of Nike or the interlocking C's of Chanel—these symbols are instantly associated with the respective brands, evoking emotions, memories, and perceptions. This powerful form of **milking** sets the stage for positive customer experiences and influences purchasing decisions. The familiar becomes trustworthy, and trust is the bedrock of any successful business.

Consistency in branding is not just about visuals; it's about the promises your brand makes and the experiences it delivers. A strong brand identity sets expectations and builds anticipation. Customers should be able to recognize your brand, trust it, and understand what it stands for. This identification is your ticket to a lasting impression and customer loyalty.

In the business landscape, especially when competing against other companies vying for attention, your brand **wants-needs** to stand out. It's not merely a name; it's a representation of your *values*, quality, and commitment. When people see your brand, they should associate it with positive experiences, reliability, and a distinct identity that separates your **little ol' register** from the competition.

The psychological impact of consistent branding, coupled with strategic **milking**, fosters a sense of trust and reliability. It transforms your **little ol' register** from a mere entity into a familiar and respected presence in the minds of your audience. And in the grand scheme of business, this recognition is invaluable.

To enhance customer interactions and fortify your brand identity, consider incorporating these strategies:

■ **Personalization**: Tailor your interactions to individual customers. Use their names, remember their preferences, and offer personalized recommendations. This not only shows that you value their business but also creates a more memorable experience.

■ **Consistent Messaging**: Ensure that your brand's voice and messaging are consistent across all platforms. Whether it's social media, email communication, or face-to-face interactions, a unified message reinforces your brand identity.

■ **Engaging Content**: Develop content that aligns with your brand values and resonates with your target audience. Engaging content, be it press releases, blogs, videos, or social media posts, helps keep your brand in the spotlight and maintains a connection with your customers.

■ **Quality Products/Services**: The best branding efforts can be undermined by subpar products or services. Ensure that the quality of what you offer matches or exceeds the expectations set by your brand. Consistency in delivering value builds trust.

■ **Feedback Mechanism**: Establish a feedback loop with your customers. Encourage them to share their experiences and actively listen to their suggestions or concerns. This not only shows that you care but also provides valuable insights for continuous improvement.

■ **Community Engagement**: Participate in community events, support local causes, and engage with your community both online and offline. This creates a positive association with your brand and fosters a sense of community.

Remember, **the sweetest things** your **little ol' register** can offer are soundful delights and consistent experiences that customers associate with your brand. This sweet connection goes beyond transactions; it's about building relationships. By leveraging your brand effectively, you create a lasting impression that keeps customers coming back, ultimately contributing to the growth and success of your **little ol' register**. Now don't forget to write that thank you note, telling them they are special, and put that **little ol'** message in their lunch pail.

PEANUT BUTTER

One thing horses adore nearly as much as molasses-covered feed is peanut butter. Even the famous Mr. Ed, the talking horse, relied on peanut butter to coax his mouth into action. It's the classic example of giving something to get the desired result.

In the heart of Costa Rica, far from the well-trodden tourist paths, nestled a butterfly museum waiting for its story to unfold. Within its humble walls, a dedicated researcher, fueled by a passion for Lepidopterology, was on a relentless quest for knowledge to enrich a prestigious university back in the United States. [145] Wilbur had stumbled upon the hidden gem of a museum, a repository of the most exquisite butterflies one could ever imagine.

As he marveled at room after room adorned with the vibrant hues of fluttering wings, Wilbur struck up a conversation with the museum's curator, the researcher. Starving but undeterred, the conversation veered towards the researcher's longing for the comforts of home, particularly a simple peanut butter and jelly sandwich. The following day, fueled by empathy and a jar of peanut butter and jelly in hand, Wilbur was welcomed by the researcher for another round of exploration.

Touched by this thoughtful gesture, tears of happiness welled up in the researcher's eyes as he savored the taste of home in a foreign land. The jar of peanut butter became a bridge between worlds, connecting the mundane with the extraordinary. But the story didn't end there. In a gesture of profound gratitude, the researcher, overwhelmed by the beauty around him, decided to reciprocate Wilbur's kindness.

He carefully removed extinct frames of butterflies from the museum's walls, each a delicate masterpiece frozen in time. Placing these wonders of the world in Wilbur's arms, the researcher transformed a $2 jar of peanut butter into a priceless exchange of beauty and appreciation. In this poignant moment, the "Give to Get" principle echoed through the halls of the butterfly museum, reminding us that sometimes, it's the smallest gestures that yield the most profound rewards in both life and business.

Traversing the maze-like dominion of customs agents, a saga rife with its unique blend of hurdles, deserves a story of its own—one filled with **kings** reigning over **their domains** and their majestic **high horses**. The escapades with inept customs agents merely added another amusing twist to the elaborate tango of regulations and characters.

Returning to the crux of the matter, the essence of consistent relationship, business, and personal growth lies in the timeless principle: Give as much as you get. It's a delicate equilibrium, a dance of reciprocity where the ebb and flow of generosity and exchange determine the rhythm of success.[146]

On our quest of life and business, the bonds we forge are threads in a tapestry of shared experiences. By contributing, whether it be knowledge, support, or kindness, we enrich the fabric of our relationships. Simultaneously, we open ourselves to receiving the abundance that flows back—lessons, opportunities, and camaraderie.

The principle encapsulated in "Give as much as you get" isn't just a transactional mantra; it's a philosophy that transcends the boundaries of business into the sphere of personal development. The symphony of growth is harmonized when each note of giving is met with a chord of receiving.

So, in the grand orchestration of life, let the melodic exchange of generosity and reciprocity guide your journey.[147] It is through this dance that relationships flourish, businesses thrive, and personal growth becomes an ever-evolving melody echoing through the corridors of time.

The principle of "Give to Get" is a fundamental aspect of effective negotiation. It operates on a straightforward premise: if you expect something from me, I should receive something in return.[148] This principle becomes particularly relevant when addressing customer requests. It forms the basis of a reciprocal relationship where both parties benefit.

This concept of **peanut butter**, embedded in the Integrated Interrogation Technique employed by intelligence service agencies worldwide, illustrates the power of giving to influence others.[149] A small favor, coupled with some skillful priming and a warm smile, can create a sense of obligation, making people more amenable to your requests. This psychological dynamic is potent and can be harnessed to achieve desired outcomes.

In negotiation, the "Give to Get" principle contributes to a win-win solution. By offering something valuable to the other party, you encourage them to reciprocate, fostering a collaborative atmosphere. This strategy isn't just about making concessions; it's a strategic move aimed at building rapport and trust.

Furthermore, employing **peanut butter** involves proactively providing something that stimulates conversation and engagement. It's about getting the other party invested in the interaction. By giving them a reason to open up, share, or contribute, you set the stage for a more productive exchange, where both sides feel they are gaining something meaningful.

There is no magic **system** for closing more deals, building a customer base, or boosting revenue. Even my learned friends on the other side say there's no formula for it. These formulas are specific to each **register,** each type of business, each market and must be tailored accordingly. Nevertheless, know that growth starts with a **little ol'** bit of **peanut butter** a little give to get. If that's not top of mind, you'll either be living in perpetual imbalance (and stagnate or fall backward), or you'll find momentary wins that quickly slip away.

In the world of marketing and sales, the principle takes center stage as a potent strategy for creating win-win scenarios. As you craft your **shiny** marketing and **sounds good** sales plans, consider incorporating a dash of **Kool-Aid** to complement the **peanut butter** approach.

The essence of a win-win situation in marketing lies in offering value to your audience. Whether it's through compelling content, exclusive deals, or personalized experiences, providing something of significance creates a positive exchange. Your customers feel they are gaining something valuable, establishing a sense of reciprocity that can lead to brand loyalty.

By strategically integrating some **peanut butter** into your **little ol'** marketing campaigns, you not only attract potential customers but also nurture existing relationships. For instance, offering informative and engaging content on your website, social media, or through email marketing serves as a giving gesture. In return, your audience is more likely to engage with your brand, share your content, and eventually become loyal customers.

Consider the scenario of a company providing insightful industry reports, webinars, or whitepapers. These offerings serve as a valuable resource for their target audience. In return, customers may be more inclined to purchase products or services from this company, knowing they consistently receive valuable information.

Adding a touch of **Kool-Aid** to your marketing efforts involves infusing your brand with a sense of identity and community. When customers feel connected to a brand, they are not just buying a product; they are becoming part of a larger narrative. This emotional connection enhances the perceived value of your **little ol' register's** offerings, fostering a win-win situation where customers receive more than just a product—they become part of something meaningful.

So, as you spread the **peanut butter** of value in your marketing, don't forget to wash it down with the refreshing **Kool-Aid** of **shiny** brand identity and community building, creating a perfect recipe for success.

CHECKING IN: MONITORING AND EVALUATION

Grow strong, **little ol'**. Your **little ol' register** needs its annual checkup from the doctors and progress reports from the "School of Hard Knocks." In the intricate dance of business, it's crucial to ensure that your venture is not only surviving but thriving. Picture it as an annual doctor's exam for your business health, complete with gold stars for achievements and valuable lessons learned from navigating the occasional **landmine**.

In this section, we delve into the significance of regular assessments and reviews, drawing parallels between performance evaluations and maintaining optimal health for your **little ol' register**. So, tighten your business shoelaces, and let's start to stretch, ready for some physical training, medical check-ups, and self-reflection therapy to keep your entrepreneurial mind, body, and spirit in prime condition.

COUNT YOUR STEPS!

You have been playing the **sim** for a few minutes now, haven't you already found improvement in your gameplay? Consider this scenario: if, throughout your day, you find yourself repeatedly trekking across the room to reach the trash can, perhaps it's time to reconsider its placement and bring it a little closer to your workspace. **Counting your steps** isn't just a fitness mantra; it's a practical principle in the world of business efficiency.

Reducing your pedometer count in the office may give your feet a break but there is something even more process than your energy, your time! In the opposite direction moving the trashcan may just increase time and steps or be such a friction point that the trash piles up right at the start.

These steps aren't only measured in physical distance but also in time. Think about McDonald's innovative move to automate the fry basket, preventing employees from burning the fries and significantly reducing the time spent on this task. Similarly, the once time-consuming process of manually filling up large sodas has been streamlined by machines and soon, the burger building to be totally automated.[150] It's a lesson in recognizing the value of optimizing your surroundings and processes to save both physical and temporal steps, contributing to enhanced productivity and operational efficiency.

For the kingdom of business, where survival hinges on constant adaptation and innovation, providing tools for evaluating performance becomes paramount. Key Performance Indicators (KPIs) act as the heartbeat monitor for your **little ol'**

register. One thing we learned going to the aquarium as a child is that if a shark dies if it stops swimming, your business, too, can stagnate without continuous movement and evolution. The classic "Who Moved My Cheese?"[45] analogy is a daily reminder to stay nimble, anticipating shifts in the market and proactively considering the next move. Just as a shark keeps swimming to breathe and survive, your business must consistently assess its performance, linking it directly to the health of the cash register.

Through KPIs and strategic foresight, you not only ensure the survival of your **little ol' register** but also empower it to thrive and grow in the ever-changing tides of the business landscape.

When constructing your **system**, it's crucial to break it down into distinct parts, each station and workflow accounting for every step, regardless of how seemingly small. In the initial stages, all tasks might converge on the same desk, station, or work area but understanding the unique flow for each role is essential. Whether it's slicing through the workflow of someone handling payroll and bill payments or navigating the intricacies of customer calls, order checking, and inventory management, recognizing the diversity and building the **system** for each of these processes is key.

Cross-functional teams, often steered by a seasoned business manager, bring together diverse expertise and viewpoints to tackle multifaceted challenges. Their collective insight spans beyond the traditional realms of direct sales, finance, or operations, delving into areas such as marketing strategy, product development, customer experience, and beyond. By integrating specialists from various disciplines, these teams foster collaboration, innovation, and holistic problem-solving approaches, ensuring that all aspects of a business are considered and optimized for success. Additionally, their interdisciplinary nature allows for a more nuanced understanding of market dynamics, consumer behavior, and industry trends, enabling organizations to adapt swiftly to changing landscapes and capitalize on emerging opportunities.

This vertical slice for your **little ol' register** mirrors the meticulous floor plan design, whether for a new high-rise office, a 50,000-square-foot logistics center, or a humble garage startup. The methodology remains consistent, emphasizing that if it works seamlessly at a smaller scale, it's poised to scale up effectively across the broader spectrum of operations.

Checking In: Monitoring and Evaluation

During the deliberation of implementing a new **system**, it's common to hear the refrain, "We don't need that right now." However, a prudent double take is warranted when those two seemingly innocuous words, "right now," are spoken. It prompts a series of crucial inquiries: How imminent is "right now?" **Why** doesn't it need to be immediate? What risks might we incur by delaying its implementation? It's essential, in the early times, to scrutinize the reasons larger companies adopt such **systems**. Are they privy to insights or challenges that elude us? These questions become a necessary internal dialogue whenever the notion of "right now" is contemplated. The urgency of these decisions often reveals the latent potential for improved efficiency and strategic positioning, challenging the assumptions about what is truly essential and when it should be integrated into the operational framework.

Start envisioning the intricate choreography of your **little ol' register's hats** as they seamlessly transition from one role to another, ensuring each task is completed efficiently and effectively. Anticipate the natural progression of responsibilities, foreseeing the handoff between **hats** as they navigate through the various stages of the job process. Just like understanding that **chicken is chicken**, grasp the inherent flow between each stage, preemptively preparing the next station based on the logical sequence of events. By predicting the movements of your **hats** and proactively orchestrating their interactions, you can streamline operations, minimize bottlenecks, and optimize productivity across your entire business ecosystem.

This in turn requires patients. How long does it take to learn patience; one may ask. Mastering time management is a journey of continuous improvement, characterized by progress rather than perfection. It's about honing your skills, refining your strategies, and adapting to the ever-changing demands of life and work.

At the outset, it's essential to recognize that effective time management is not an innate talent but a learned skill that develops over time. As with any skill, it requires patience, practice, and persistence to cultivate. You may encounter setbacks and challenges along the way, but, as we know, each obstacle presents an opportunity for growth and learning.

Learning to manage your time effectively involves understanding your priorities, setting clear goals, and implementing strategies to allocate your time wisely. It requires self-awareness to recognize your strengths and weaknesses, as well as the discipline to make conscious choices about how you spend your time.

It's important to approach time management as a process of experimentation and adaptation, rather than expecting instant success. Be willing to try new techniques, evaluate their effectiveness, and make adjustments as needed. What works for one person may not work for another, so it's essential to find methods that resonate with your unique preferences and circumstances.

Remember that progress is incremental, and small changes can yield significant results over time. Celebrate your successes, no matter how small, and use setbacks as opportunities to learn and grow. With dedication and perseverance, you can gradually improve your time management skills and achieve greater efficiency, productivity, and satisfaction in all areas of your life.

In the intricate dance of time management, understanding the nuances of our neurobiology can be the key to unlocking peak performance and productivity. From the moment we wake up, our bodies and brains undergo a series of chemical changes that influence our energy levels, focus, and creativity throughout the day. By aligning our activities with these natural rhythms, we can optimize our cognitive functions and achieve greater success in our personal and professional endeavors. From the reflexive tasks of the early morning to the creative bursts of the afternoon, each hour presents an opportunity to harness our neurochemistry and maximize our potential. So, let's jump off the synaptic cleft into the fascinating world of effective time management and neurobiology, exploring how we can leverage the **true power** of our brain's innate capabilities to conquer the challenges of modern life.

■ **Early Morning Symphony (Gamma Rest Cycle)**: Ah, the mysterious night gamma rest cycle. Imagine it as a cosmic DJ spinning chill-out tunes for your neurons. During this cycle, your brain resets, tidies up, and whispers, "Hey, buddy, let's start fresh." So when you wake up, you're primed for action. It's like slipping into a comfy pair of sneakers—you're ready to get in the zone. So, during the first hour or two after waking, when adrenaline and alertness levels are at their lowest—like a cat that just woke up from a nap, stretching, yawning, and rubbing its eyes. This is **why**, reflexive and light activities are the name of the game. Think of it as a warm-up jog for your brain.

Complex Thinking: Nope, not yet! Your mind is still in its cozy beta state, not quite ready for the mental gymnastics of quantum physics or existential philosophy. Instead, embrace the mundane. Boring tasks become your secret weapon. Organize your sock drawer, alphabetize your spice rack, or sort your email inbox. It's like a gentle nudge to wake up your cognitive gears. This period is not ideal for complex thinking tasks, so focusing on boring or mundane tasks can be most productive.[143]

To jumpstart your **system** and increase energy levels, incorporate movement into your morning routine. Whether it's yoga, fitness exercises, cleaning, or simply going for a walk, physical activity helps generate energy and primes the body for the day ahead. Additionally, fasting during this time can be beneficial, as it stimulates the production of adrenaline, which enhances learning and motivation.

Turning back to the wisdom of the **Warrior**, in Japanese work culture, there's a practice known as "group workout" or "rajio taiso," where employees participate in light exercise routines together at the start of the workday. This not only promotes physical health but also fosters camaraderie and teamwork among colleagues. Similarly, incorporating movement into your morning routine can set a positive tone for the day and improve overall productivity and well-being.

■ **Mid-Morning Crescendo (Adrenaline Peak):** During the next 2 to 7 hours after waking, characterized by intense focus and peak adrenaline levels, it's crucial to tackle tasks that demand the utmost concentration.[143] This period is ideal for linear tasks and learning endeavors, as adrenaline levels are at their peak, optimizing cognitive function. To maximize productivity, it's recommended to engage in focused activities for no more than 90 minutes at a time, aligning with the body's ultradian rhythm. Lunch, typically consumed between 11 am and 1 pm, should consist primarily of protein and fats to boost dopamine levels while avoiding carbohydrates that can elevate serotonin. Conversely, dinner consumed 2 to 3 hours before bedtime, should prioritize carbohydrates. By strategically managing our behaviors and nutrition to modulate adrenaline and dopamine levels, we can optimize our performance throughout the day.

■ **Afternoon Interlude (Adrenaline Decline):** As time moves toward hours 6 to 9, as adrenaline levels start to lower, it's time to shift focus to tasks that require less intense concentration, such as answering emails or responding to texts.[143] These activities demand small amounts of time and focus, making them more reflexive than the tasks tackled during prime time earlier in the day. It's important to avoid caffeine consumption after 2 pm, particularly around 4 pm, as it can significantly disrupt the transition to sleep and overall sleep quality. Caffeine affects adenosine receptors, which regulate sleep drive, for approximately 8 hours, prolonging wakefulness and hindering the ability to fall asleep. Instead, this period is ideal for engaging in creative pursuits.

Creativity thrives in a relaxed state when serotonin levels are elevated, facilitating calmness and relaxation. By deactivating and raising serotonin levels, we can effectively prime our minds for innovative thinking and generate truly novel ideas.

Why did the procrastinator break up with time management? Because they couldn't commit to a schedule—they were always "just five more minutes" away from getting started!

One of the other critical facets, particularly in the early stages of business, revolves around personal productivity and related topics like time management and self-management. Distinguishing between important and urgent matters is pivotal in this context. It's a strategic exercise in allocating time and resources effectively, ensuring that crucial tasks take precedence over merely pressing ones. Prioritizing based on importance rather than urgency lays the foundation for long-term success.

As your **little ol' register** embarks on its journey, mastering the art of personal productivity becomes a cornerstone in navigating the intricate landscape of entrepreneurship. I have two kinds of problems: the urgent and the important. The urgent are not important, and the important are never urgent. –Dwight D. Eisenhower

Effective time management is the cornerstone of productivity and efficiency. Therefore, prioritizing tasks and responsibilities is essential for ensuring that valuable time and energy are allocated to activities that contribute most to our goals and objectives in both personal and professional life. To effectively manage time, it's crucial to categorize tasks based on their urgency and importance.[7] [151] Tasks that are both urgent and important should be addressed first, as they require immediate attention to prevent crises or address pressing issues. These may include deadlines, emergencies, or critical projects that cannot be delayed.

Next, tasks that are important but not urgent should be prioritized. These activities contribute to long-term goals, personal development, and strategic planning. By dedicating time to these tasks, individuals can proactively prevent crises and make progress towards their objectives. Tasks that are urgent but not important should be carefully evaluated to determine if they can be delegated, postponed, or eliminated altogether.[7]

Finally, tasks that are neither urgent nor important should be minimized or eliminated to avoid wasting valuable time and resources. By prioritizing tasks and responsibilities based on their urgency and importance, individuals can optimize their time management, increase productivity, and achieve greater success in both their personal and professional endeavors.

President Eisenhower was not alone: In their work lives people routinely feel pulled between tasks that demand immediate attention and tasks that are important, the ones that bring them closer to achieving their long-term goals. [151] Unfortunately, research shows that people have a natural tendency to overly focus on the former (such as responding to mundane emails) at the expense of the latter.

Checking In: Monitoring and Evaluation

One of the main reasons this happens is that human brains are wired to seek completion and the pleasure it brings—a tendency we term "completion bias."[133, 152] Completing simple tasks, such as answering emails or posting updates on your **little ol' register's** Twitter account, takes little time and allows you to check off items on your to-do list. Ongoing research (not yet published) has found that checking off items is psychologically rewarding: After you complete a task, being able to literally check a box makes you happier than when you are not given a box to check.

Complicating matters, finishing immediate, mundane tasks actually improves your ability to tackle tougher, important things. Not only does your brain release dopamine when you achieve goals but frees the mind of the thoughts of these actions that linger while unfinished. [152]

The concept of "Big Banana, Little Banana," similar to the **shiny** "little Big principle, emphasizes the importance of breaking down larger tasks or projects into smaller, more manageable components.[153] When faced with a daunting or complex task, such as completing a monthly report, it's easy to feel overwhelmed and procrastinate until the deadline looms large.

However, by adopting the "Big Banana, Little Banana" approach, your **little ol' register** can enhance productivity and alleviate stress by dividing the task into smaller intermediate goals or milestones. Rather than the team tackling the entire report at once, you can set achievable objectives to be completed over the course of several weeks.

Breaking the task into smaller increments offers several advantages. First, it makes the overall project feel less daunting and more manageable. Instead of focusing on the enormity of the entire report, the team can concentrate on completing one section or aspect at a time.[154] When we observe in the wild, a trend emerges more effort is always performed as the deadline looms closer. [153]

Second, dividing the task into smaller goals provides a sense of progress and accomplishment as you work through each step.[155] Each completed milestone serves as a motivator, releasing that little dopamine reward, reinforcing your momentum, and spurring you onward toward the ultimate goal of completing the report.

Additionally, breaking the task into smaller components allows for greater flexibility and adaptability. If unexpected challenges or obstacles (**sh*t happens**) arise along the way, you can adjust your approach and prioritize the most critical aspects of the report while still making progress on other elements.

Moreover, the "Big Banana, Little Banana" approach to time management promotes efficiency and effectiveness by encouraging focused attention on specific tasks or objectives. By concentrating your efforts on one aspect of the report at a time, you can devote your full energy and concentration to each task, leading to higher-quality results.[153] By breaking larger tasks into smaller, more manageable components, you can make steady progress toward your goals and achieve greater success in your endeavors.

And since dopamine improves attention, memory, and motivation, even achieving a small goal can result in a positive feedback loop that makes you more motivated to work harder going forward.[143, 156] Blending this as a **game** and throwing some brownie points or gold stars in, staff can be even more effective at their monotonous and repetitive tasks. Sidework disguised as a group relay race or customer email reaction time–**sounds** pretty **good**.

The danger, of course, is devoting too much time to the mundane and too little to important projects. How can you ensure that you are not succumbing to the completion bias, striking a balance between easier short-term efforts and tougher long-term goals? One way is to audit how you structure your workday and, if necessary, change how you plan your daily tasks.

This is where an operating plan, sometimes reflected in a Gantt chart, serves as a roadmap for achieving the objectives outlined in your **little ol' register's** strategic plan. It provides a detailed outline of the actions and initiatives that need to be undertaken within a specific timeframe to execute the strategic *vision* effectively. By breaking down long-term goals into actionable steps, an operating plan helps ensure that resources are allocated efficiently and that progress can be monitored and evaluated regularly.

One of the key benefits of an operating plan is its role in enhancing efficiency. By clearly defining **hats**, responsibilities, and timelines for each task or initiative, an operating plan minimizes confusion and duplication of efforts. Team members know exactly what is expected of them and can focus their time and energy on activities that contribute directly to the achievement of organizational goals. Additionally, an operating plan allows for the identification of potential bottlenecks or obstacles early on, enabling initiative-taking problem-solving and resource reallocation to maintain productivity—a proactive approach.

Effective time management is another critical aspect facilitated by an operating plan. With a well-defined plan in place, individuals and teams can prioritize tasks based on their importance and deadlines. This helps prevent procrastination and ensures that critical activities are completed on time. Moreover, by scheduling regular checkpoints and milestones (**little bananas**), an operating plan provides opportunities for reflection and adjustment, allowing for continuous improvement and adaptation to changing circumstances.[141] Ultimately, by providing a structured framework for goal-setting, task execution, and progress monitoring, an operating plan empowers organizations to achieve greater efficiency, productivity, and success.

When **counting our steps**, we often seek to streamline processes and eliminate barriers to facilitate sales and productivity. However, there are instances where adding friction intentionally can serve as a powerful tool for addressing undesirable habits or behaviors, both in ourselves and in our employees.

Consider this: just as a well-oiled machine operates smoothly with minimal resistance, individuals within your **little ol' register** may fall into patterns of behavior that are counterproductive or even detrimental. These could range from procrastination and time-wasting activities to neglecting essential tasks or failing to adhere to company policies.

In such cases, introducing friction—creating obstacles or hurdles that impede the execution of these behaviors—can be an effective strategy for encouraging change and promoting accountability. This could involve implementing additional approval processes, instituting checklists or protocols, or imposing consequences for non-compliance.

By intentionally increasing the effort required to engage in undesirable behaviors, individuals are prompted to pause, reflect, and reconsider their actions. The introduction of friction serves as a reminder of the importance of adhering to your **little ol' register's** standards and fosters a culture of responsibility and discipline within the organization.

Moreover, adding friction can also be utilized as a means of training and skill development. For instance, employees may encounter friction in the form of structured training programs or mandatory compliance modules designed to enhance their proficiency and knowledge in specific areas, **warrior** training.

Ultimately, while the goal of business operations is often to minimize friction and maximize efficiency, strategically adding friction in certain contexts can be a valuable tool for promoting positive behavioral change, reinforcing organizational *values*, and driving continuous improvement.

An additional improvement can be found simply by identifying your peak productivity hours and optimal work environment. This can significantly enhance your effectiveness and efficiency. For some, the late hours of the night, when the household is quiet and distractions are minimal, provide the perfect setting for deep focus and uninterrupted workflow. Others thrive in the early hours of the morning, harnessing the fresh energy of a new day before the hustle and bustle begins.

Understanding when you are most productive or following your biological clock allows you to capitalize on these periods of heightened focus and mental clarity, enabling you to tackle tasks with greater speed and precision. Incorporate short breaks into your schedule to recharge and avoid burnout. By aligning your work schedule with your natural rhythms and energy levels, you can optimize your output and achieve more in less time.

Likewise, identifying your ideal work environment is equally crucial. Whether it's the quiet excluded corner of your home office, a bustling café, or a serene outdoor setting, finding a space that fosters concentration and creativity can elevate your productivity to new heights. Experimenting with different environments and observing how they impact your focus and motivation can help you pinpoint the settings where you thrive the most.

By tailoring your work schedule and environment to suit your individual preferences and tendencies, you can maximize your effectiveness and put a spring in your step as you tackle your daily tasks and projects. Don't overcommit yourself; learn to decline tasks or activities that don't align with your prior. Whether you're burning the midnight oil or seizing the dawn, knowing when and where you work best is the key to unlocking your full potential.

As you immerse yourself in the intricacies of business efficiency, it's evident that time management is at the crux of success. Just as **counting your physical steps** can lead to greater fitness, counting your time spent on various tasks can lead to enhanced productivity and effectiveness. By identifying areas where you can streamline processes, eliminate waste, and prioritize tasks, you can optimize your workflow and achieve greater results with less effort. Embrace the principles of strategic planning, incremental progress, and continuous improvement as you navigate the complexities of entrepreneurship.[7, 141] With dedication and perseverance, you can master the art of time management and unlock your full potential, propelling your **little ol' register** toward success in the ever-evolving landscape of business.

Checking In: Monitoring and Evaluation

STICKERS

Ah, the humble **sticker**—how it adorns our world with color and character. From childhood to adulthood, we find joy in affixing them to everything from our belongings to our surroundings. It's as if they're ingrained in our DNA, signaling our sense of belonging and identity. Whether it's a mark of status or a badge of camaraderie, **stickers** speak volumes about who we are and what we represent. And so, it's only natural that we've begun to amass a collection, adorning your **little ol' register** with these small but significant symbols.

Indeed, **stickers** come in myriad forms, each with their own unique power. From the coveted gold star to the reassuring checkmark and the ever-friendly smiley face, these symbols hold sway over both children and adults alike. They serve as potent tools for motivation, boosting self-esteem, and reinforcing positive behavior. With just a glance, these visual cues offer immediate feedback, affirming one's efforts and accomplishments. The simple act of receiving a sticker creates a **shiny** sense of achievement, recognition, and validation, igniting intrinsic motivation and a desire for further success. It's no wonder they become so addictive—we're tapping into a deep-seated engagement **paradigm** that transcends age and circumstance.

The simplicity and clarity of these symbols make them universally comprehensible, even for the youngest learners. Whether it's a gold star, a checkmark, or a smiley face, these visuals serve as tangible markers of achievement, reinforcing positive behavior and instilling a sense of pride in children. As they accumulate stickers, they begin to associate these emotions and values with the symbols themselves, creating a powerful link between effort and reward. Moreover, the visual representation of success through stars or checkmarks can contribute to the cultivation of a growth mindset—a belief that abilities can be developed through dedication and hard work. By framing challenges as opportunities for growth rather than obstacles to be avoided, **stickers** help foster resilience and perseverance in the face of adversity. Ultimately, these symbols play a vital role in creating a nurturing learning environment where individuals feel motivated, supported, and confident in their abilities.

Nevertheless, **stickers** are not just for individuals—they can also serve as powerful branding tools for businesses. Imagine covering your **little ol' register** in **stickers**, adorning everything from the storefront to the packaging with these vibrant symbols. **Stickers** have the potential to convey a wide range of emotions and messages to customers, whether it's promoting a sense of safety and security to lower insurance premiums or inviting people to join a movement or cause. In fact, **stickers** can become a symbolic representation for your

Part 4: Working the Register

little ol' register to express its values and affiliations, whether it's supporting a political party, championing environmental causes, or gaining approval from governmental organizations. Your **little ol' register** can develop its own collective attitude and identity, using **stickers** to communicate its ethos and connect with customers on a deeper level. Whether it's sporting the logo of a reputable organization or proudly displaying its accomplishments, **stickers** offer a versatile and insightful way for your **little ol' register** to make its mark in the world.

Stickers aren't limited to just your **little ol' register**—they can also be applied to products themselves. Imagine your products adorned with **shiny stickers** boasting credentials like "Non-GMO," "Doctor Approved," "Happily Raised," or "Heart Healthy," among others. These **stickers** serve as powerful signals to customers, tapping into their instinctual emotions and conveying important information about the product's qualities and benefits. **Sounds good**, right? Whether it's assuring customers of the product's safety and health benefits or highlighting its ethical sourcing and production practices, these stickers play a crucial role in building trust and loyalty among consumers.

And if none of the existing stickers quite fit the bill, **why** not create your own? Your **little ol' register** can even create its own **sticker**, crafting a catchy phrase that **sounds good,** and gleams **shiny** and brightly. The aim is to convey to the customer the instinctual emotions tied to that thought, influencing their perception and decision-making. Designing custom **stickers** allows you to tailor your messaging precisely to your brand and product, ensuring that every **sticker** serves as a compelling and persuasive touchpoint for your customers.

As we have seen, **stickers** serve as a metaphorical badge of belonging and accomplishment. Much like earning a medal or certificate, receiving a **sticker** signifies inclusion in a group or achievement of a milestone. Whether it's a **sticker** denoting membership in a club or association, showcasing academic or professional credentials, or displaying participation in a noteworthy **warrior** event, **stickers** carry symbolic meaning that extends beyond their adhesive backing.

In the context of business, **stickers** can be likened to accolades or certifications that demonstrate competence, quality, or adherence to specific standards. For example, your **little ol' register** might proudly display stickers showing compliance with industry regulations, endorsements from reputable organizations, or recognition for outstanding service or product excellence. These

stickers not only validate the business's credentials but also instill confidence in customers and stakeholders.

Additionally, **stickers** serve as a form of self-expression and identity projection. Individuals and businesses alike use **stickers** to convey their *values*, interests, and affiliations. By carefully selecting and displaying **stickers** that resonate with your **little ol' register's** beliefs or aspirations, they signal their alignment with certain ideologies, causes, or communities. This act of **sticker** placement becomes a visual representation of identity and belonging, allowing individuals and businesses to showcase their personality and ethos to the world.

In essence, **stickers** are more than just adhesive labels—they are symbolic artifacts that communicate a sense of belonging, achievement, and identity. Whether proudly displayed on a laptop, water bottle, or storefront window, **stickers** serve as tangible reminders of one's journey, affiliations, and aspirations.

Be proud of your **stickers**. **Stickers** are not merely trivial adornments but powerful symbols of identity, achievement, and affiliation. As you adorn your **little ol' register** with these emblematic decals, remember the significance they hold. Let them inspire your employees, serving as visual reminders of their accomplishments and contributions. Display them proudly to signal to your customers the *values*, standards, and commitments you uphold. Collect them as tokens of your journey, each **sticker** representing a milestone, a triumph, or a cherished memory. Embrace the power of **stickers** as a source of pride and joy for your **little ol' register**, and let them serve as beacons of inspiration, unity, and authenticity in your business journey.

LANDMINES

The gentle, flickering glow of candlelight casts a warm ambiance upon the parchment spread across the desk, where the quill, dipped in red ink, dances with purpose. The mind races with thoughts of adequacy, the weight of conveying knowledge leaving traces of red marks on the pristine white surface. As the fatigue of a long day takes its toll, the head gradually descends, finding respite on the smooth surface of the desk.

Suddenly, the weary eyes snap open, greeted by the dawn of a new day—already? For certain youthful pupils, propelled by the desire for acceptance and validation, their focus narrows, seemingly blinded by the quest for peer approval. The Latin lesson from the previous day now fades into obscurity, overshadowed by the relentless pursuit of external validation. No better reward for the one who bled all night working. The toll of burning the midnight oil becomes clear: "We

Part 4: Working the Register

spend our mid-day sweat or midnight oil; We tire the night in thought; the day in toil."

When we are **counting our steps**, sometimes under the influence of burning a candle at both ends, we can fail even to see the **landmines** lying right in front of our **little ol' register's** feet. A hidden pothole that can derail your progress, trowing off the whole alignment in your **vehicle**. The speed bumps through the parking lots take you down to a crawl, of course, the worst are the ones that blow up and take out more than you have planned for. A seemingly insignificant issue, like a supply chain disruption or a sudden drop in sales, can quickly escalate into a major problem. That's why it's crucial to stay vigilant and address potential issues before they escalate. Remember, even the simplest task, like changing a lightbulb, can become a complex and time-consuming process if not approached with careful planning and execution.

How many safety officers does it take to change a light bulb? Well, it requires a team of at least ten, a comprehensive risk assessment, a safety permit, and a weeklong safety training course. Then, add three days of work, a 50-page report on the best practices for lightbulb replacement, a feasibility study, and the implementation of a new lighting management system.

Jokes aside, there are plenty of benefits that come from having a healthy and safe workplace and protection of the environment where we all live. With OSHA regulations in place, most employers are not only required to provide a safe working environment for their employees but is a wise and prudent business decision regardless.[157] If anyone gets hurt the ultimate bearer of responsibility is your **little ol' register**. This is **why** pragmatic thinking includes ensuring that all equipment is up to date and meets safety standards, providing proper safety training, and investigating any accidents that may occur. Yet some regulations can be **landmines** within themselves.

As the film crew embarked on the ambitious venture of capturing the opulence and grandeur of a new 52-store luxury hotel and casino, little did they anticipate the unexpected twist that awaited them—a twist dictated not by the script, but by the ever-evolving realm of aviation regulations.[158, 159]

In a curious turn of events, the Federal Aviation Administration (FAA) decided to redefine the rules of the sky, perhaps prompted by the airborne antics witnessed during the Hoover Dam episode (or at least that's what the crew humorously speculated). The new FAA mandate dictated that, under a low-flying helicopter, all individuals had to be restricted from entering the airspace below. Cue the need for an unconventional solution to solve to keep the production on track.

In an effort to comply with the newfound regulations, the ingenious minds behind the commercial **solved the solution** and transformed the production crew into a fleet of human hazard cones. Clad in vibrant orange shirts and strategically placed around the flight area like a living perimeter, the crew members took on the role of real-life safety markers, ensuring that no unwitting pedestrian ventured into the restricted zone.

As the crew donned their eye-catching ensembles and assumed their positions, the once glamorous production scene morphed into a whimsical display of brightly colored individuals creating a protective barrier for the hovering helicopter. Passersby were left bewildered, and onlookers couldn't help but chuckle at the sight of a human hazard cone brigade choreographed by the aerial cinematography.

In the end, what began as an attempt to capture the allure of a luxury casino unfolded into a lighthearted tale of adaptation and creativity in the face of unexpected regulatory hurdles. The crew, now adorned in their unmistakable orange attire, became an unwitting ensemble of on-set superheroes, bravely safeguarding the airspace below from any unsuspecting interlopers. In the unpredictable world of filmmaking, where **landmines** take on unexpected forms, a splash of humor and a touch of improvisation can turn regulatory challenges into memorable anecdotes.

However, not all **landmines** are confined to the visible surface; some lurk beneath the ground, waiting to detonate at the slightest misstep. Enter the EPA, or as some humorously dub it, the "employment prevention agency"—no, scratch that, it's the Environmental Protection Agency. In the course of navigating the complex terrains of business, many **little ol' registers** have had encounters with this regulatory force that felt almost as unpredictable as stepping on hidden **landmines**.

In the vast expanse of the Las Vegas desert, where water is as precious as gold, attempting to quell the ever-present dust devil ballet can inadvertently lead to environmental missteps. In one instance, the EPA took issue with something as seemingly innocent as treading on endangered soil, yes endangered dirt, in the heart of the Nevada desert. It doesn't stop there. Another incident involved the act of spraying plain water over the trucks returning to the yard, an earnest attempt to mitigate the encroaching sandy dust. Little did they know that in the eyes of the EPA, this well-intentioned dust control measure amounted to a crime of contaminating rainwater with dirt.

Part 4: Working the Register

The desert, with its paradoxical need for water, becomes a battleground where the line between environmental stewardship and unwitting transgressions blurs. The lesson learned. Even in the quest to preserve the delicate balance of nature, navigating the regulatory landscape can be as treacherous as a minefield—each step carrying the potential for unexpected explosions of consequences.

In the treacherous scene of on-location filmmaking, unforeseen **landmines** can detonate even in the most well-intentioned endeavors. Picture this: a scorching summer day on location, with the film crew diligently loading up ice chests brimming with extra water bottles—a thoughtful gesture to combat the relentless heat and ensure the well-being of the team. A commendable move for customer service and OSHA protections, right? Little did they know that in the world of film production, Murphy sometimes has a mischievous sense of humor.

As the crew rolled through North Las Vegas with their mobile oasis of hydration, their well-meaning intentions collided with the suspicions of one of the city's finest. The police, perhaps fueled by an unquenchable thirst for law enforcement, decided to pull over the production rig under the suspicion of excess weight. Curbside anticipation ensued until, lo and behold, a colossal tow truck materialized, ready to transport the crew a staggering 300 feet away to the scales.

Ordinarily equipped with a weight class buffer, the crew found their safety margin obliterated by the innocent-looking ice chests. It turns out that 240 pounds of well-intentioned refreshment exceeded the permissible limit by a mere 1 extra ice chest. The **little ol' register** of the police officer began churning out violations like an overzealous carnival ticket dispenser: "No CDL, no fuel tags, no weight inspection," and the list went on. The grand total for this unwitting cinematic escapade? A jaw-dropping $15,000—a hefty price tag for the crime of carrying too much hydration in the scorching Nevada sun. In the world of filmmaking, where even the most virtuous deeds can trigger unexpected consequences, this episode stands as a cautionary tale of the high costs that can accompany a well-chilled heart.

Certain regulations impose significant burdens on your **little ol' register**, serving as formidable barriers to entry. These hurdles can effectively deter smaller, agile competitors or emerging startups from entering the market. They act as protective shields for larger, well-established companies, shielding them from ankle-biting rivals. To overcome these barriers and establish a significant presence, one must adopt a bold, expansive approach. Embrace the ethos of playing big to break through the constraints and assert dominance in the market landscape.

We know **sh*t happens**! There are a few ways to deal with them, one of them is not putting your head in the sand but how you play the game. The other, the easiest, way to eliminate some of the risk is through insurance but that can only take you so far. Most speed bumps potholes and **landmines** our lessons to be learned ways to improve your **system** and **why** franchises exist today. With a franchise you've already bought the roadmap, the **system**, which has been taken and perfected before by someone else.

Landmines, like ourselves, don't discriminate; they lie in wait for businesses of all sizes, from small startups to corporate giants. And as the days go by, the target on your **little ol' register**' back doesn't diminish; it expands as your company grows, even if your primary offering is something as seemingly innocuous as water or in this case a cup of hot coffee.

The infamous "McDonald's coffee case" starring Stella is a classic cautionary tale. Picture Stella, innocently trying to secure her cup of joe between her knees while wrangling the lid off, only for disaster to strike as the coffee spills, scalding her in the process.[160] Oh, the audacity of that steaming hot coffee! At the time of the incident, all McDonald's restaurants were required to serve coffee between 180 and 190 degrees. At this temperature, spilled coffee causes third-degree burns in less than 3 seconds. While the media hypes up Stella's hefty $3 million settlement, let's not forget to keep things in perspective. In the 90s, you would have to pay around $0.75 for a cup of coffee, McDonald's roasts around 1 million coffees sold every single day. Did this coffee giant learn anything from Stella's misadventure, or are they still playing with fire?[161]

Well, in a recent legal tango, a plaintiff made waves by alleging that hot coffee, improperly contained by a lid, had cascaded over her, resulting in "severe burns." McDonald's lawyers fired back, claiming that the potential for coffee to burn doesn't make it faulty by design. But the plaintiff's attorney had a steamy rebuttal, blaming the mishap on the negligent lid-securing skills of the staff. Ah, the perils of a piping hot brew! Who knew a simple cup of joe could brew up such a legal storm? This underscores how seemingly routine aspects of business, like serving cold water or hot coffee, can turn into legal **landmines** with far-reaching consequences.

These **landmines** can show up even without the direct action of your **little ol' register**. Another unexpected voyage comes from GEICO when it was ordered to pay $5.2 million in a settlement to a woman who got an STD in an insured car. [162] Because the car was covered by GEICO at the time, she says the company is obligated to compensate her for contracting HPV from its owner in the **vehicle**, citing medical expenses and her pain and suffering.

This may be a suitable time to advocate for the assignment of risk, AKA insurance. This philosophy started with two rafts trying to cross the river. The first raft was filled with chickens, the other filled up with feed. Knowing that the river can be volatile the two men looked at each other curiously and pondered their losses if one would tip. If both didn't make it each would be a loss and a deterrent to the other for chicken without feed nor the reciprocal is futile. They both came up with the idea that they would share half of the other's cargo, ensuring that no matter what each would double their chances and share in the loss of the other if things did go awry.[163]

This principle of sharing risk fueled the origin of insurance and can be traced back to English bars in the 17th century, where the concept evolved from maritime risk management practices. Ship owners and merchants would frequent these establishments, and in a bid to mitigate the uncertainties associated with maritime trade, a **system** of bets or wagers emerged.[163] Bar patrons would place bets on the safe arrival of ships and their cargoes, essentially wagering on whether a particular voyage would be successful or end in disaster. Insert joke here. Over time, this informal betting practice transformed into a more structured arrangement, laying the groundwork for the formalized insurance industry we recognize today. The idea was to distribute the risk among multiple parties, ensuring that the financial burden of a shipwreck or loss of cargo didn't fall solely on one individual or business. This innovative approach eventually led to the establishment of insurance policies and companies, marking a pivotal moment in the history of risk management.

Similar to a casino managing bets, insurance offers a safeguard for a myriad of risks and valuable assets. The insurance landscape spans various types, from General Liability (GL) and Umbrella, Worker's Compensation and Health to Errors & Omissions and professional insurance. In the vast sea of possibilities, there's even missile insurance, as Ned found out, highlighting the diverse nature of risk mitigation.

Navigating the intricacies of insurance can be comparable to deciphering a complex legal landscape, especially for those unfamiliar with the nuances, just ask the guru Ned. For instance, distinguishing between Auto and Marine insurance becomes crucial; while the former covers the **vehicle**, like SUVs, the latter protects goods in transit in the SUV.

This insurance web serves as a buffer against potential blows to your **little ol' register** or the individual **hats** and **warriors** it encompasses. As long as there are

Checking In: Monitoring and Evaluation

no malevolent actions or breaches of duties, the corporate shield stands strong. It doesn't, however, eliminate the challenges posed by lawsuits or potential public relations crises. Instead, it acts as a protective barrier for the primary company assets, ensuring that the **landmines** encountered along the way don't obliterate the entire venture. While insurance doesn't eradicate the hassles that may arise, it offers a strategic layer of defense, allowing the journey to continue despite the occasional explosions.

In this rendition of The Whipping Boy, the **landmine** of oneself is a story that illustrates the true prince. In the hushed shadows of a quaint little town, there lived a young boy with a spirit as mischievous as the flickering flames of a secret adventure. The town itself whispered tales of a newly bloomed family venture; a culinary endeavor set in motion by the tireless efforts of the boy's parents. The father, a seasoned food & beverage director of the hotels of the world, and the mother, a triumphant contract winner for the parochial school food program, collectively steered the ship of their newfound family business—feeding the minds and hearts of youth.

It was within the walls of this academic sanctuary that the mischievous spirit of the young boy, still in the tender years of kindergarten, found an outlet. An after-school program unfolded in the school gym, an innocent canvas for the boy's playful antics. He, like any other child, reveled in the simple joy of turning off the lights, playfully frightening his fellow students.

However, in the sanctity of their home, the father, bearing the responsibility of securing the family's livelihood, took a decisive stand. The spanking that followed was not a result of the lights flickering into darkness but a stern response to the potential jeopardizing of the delicate family enterprise. The leather belt, once a symbol of discipline, etched an indelible impression deeper than its physical sting—a mark of the unspoken gravity attached to the family's **little ol' register**. At that moment, the boy learned that even in the sphere of innocence, there lay a responsibility not just to oneself but to your **little ol' register** and the fragile dreams of a family navigating uncharted waters. The prince and the whipping boy, intertwined in the intricate dance of the **little ol' register**, both understood that each action held consequences far beyond the span of childhood years.

Improve your **system** daily with the knowledge and experiences you have learned from **counting your steps**, and the stories of others. No matter what **chess** piece or **hats** you're working with, run the **Sim** over and over to see the faults and try to reduce the risks or bet on sharing it. Use the wonderful burdensome regulations as a template to build your **system** in raising your **little**

ol' register, so adapting to them as it grows up isn't so painful or preventive, and as a bonus (as long as you don't shoot yourself in the foot) you'll get an extra **shiny sticker**. Yay!

It's imperative to find innovative ways in what is already being conditioned by our everyday lives. Achieving our goals and knowing the difficulties of keeping everything balanced while we are walking down this unseen path, there is still hope. Just remember, As the candle goes out, we turn on the light switch, and spark that internal flame in all of us: Alere Flammam Veritatis.

Part 5: Counting the Register

"I do not think that there is any other quality so essential to success of any kind as the quality of perseverance. It overcomes almost everything, even nature."

– John D. Rockefeller,
Founder and CEO of Standard Oil Company

LEARNING OBJECTIVES, THE FINANCIAL PERSPECTIVE

In the financial battleground, prepare to embark on a financial odyssey these learning objectives stand as strategic maneuvers, you'll navigate the treacherous waters of fiscal responsibility with the finesse of a seasoned captain, steering your **little ol' register** towards the shores of profitability and prosperity. With each objective, you're orchestrating a masterful campaign to conquer the monetary challenges and emerge victorious in the relentless pursuit of financial supremacy. So, as we hoist the sails of our final mission, sharpen your accounting acumen, and let's set sail on this exhilarating voyage to fiscal enlightenment!

■ **Financial Planning and Budgeting:** Understand the importance of financial planning and budgeting in managing business finances effectively, and learn how to create comprehensive financial plans and budgets to guide decision-making and resource allocation. Develop skills in analyzing financial statements such as income statements, balance sheets, and cash flow statements to assess the financial health and performance of your business.

■ **Cost Management and Control:** Explore techniques for managing and controlling costs to improve profitability, including cost reduction strategies, cost-volume-profit analysis, and activity-based costing.

■ **Capital Budgeting and Investment Analysis:** Learn how to evaluate investment opportunities and make informed decisions about capital allocation through techniques such as net present value (NPV), internal rate of return (IRR), and payback period analysis.

■ **Financial Risk Management:** Understand the concept of financial risk and learn how to identify, assess, and manage various types of financial risks, including market risk, credit risk, and liquidity risk.

■ **Debt Financing and Equity Financing:** Explore different sources of financing for businesses, including debt financing (such as loans and bonds) and equity financing (such as issuing shares), and learn how to evaluate the advantages and disadvantages of each.

■ **Financial Forecasting and Planning:** Develop skills in financial forecasting and planning to predict future financial performance and identify potential areas of concern or opportunity for your business.

■ **Tax Planning and Compliance:** Understand the basics of tax planning and compliance, including tax obligations for businesses and strategies for minimizing tax liabilities while remaining compliant with tax laws and regulations.

■ **Financial Reporting and Compliance:** Learn about financial reporting requirements for businesses, including Generally Accepted Accounting Principles (GAAP) and International Financial Reporting Standards (IFRS), and develop an understanding of compliance obligations.

■ **Corporate Finance Strategies:** Explore advanced topics in corporate finance, such as mergers and acquisitions, capital structure optimization, dividend policy, and corporate restructuring, to enhance shareholder value and achieve long-term financial goals.

Notes:

COUNTING THE DRAWER: FINANCIAL MANAGEMENT

And in the grand scheme of business ownership, financial management is no different than the careful guardianship of your **little ol' register's** piggy bank. Just as a piggy bank holds the treasures and savings of a child, your business's financial health holds the key to its stability, growth, and success.

Imagine your **little ol' register's** piggy bank as the repository of all its resources—cash flow, revenues, investments, and expenses. Every decision you make regarding these financial aspects determines what goes into the piggy bank and what comes out. Just as a child learns to save pennies for a rainy day, your business must manage its finances to weather economic storms and capitalize on opportunities.

Financial management involves not only keeping track of the money coming in and going out but also making strategic decisions to allocate resources effectively. Just as a child might carefully plan how to spend their allowance, you must prioritize spending and investments to support your business objectives and long-term growth.

Furthermore, just as a child's piggy bank needs occasional shaking to ensure all the coins are counted, your financial management practices should include regular reviews, audits, and assessments to maintain accuracy and transparency. This ensures that you have a clear understanding of your financial standing and can make informed decisions to steer your business in the right direction.

Ultimately, the importance of financial management in business cannot be overstated. Just as a child's piggy bank represents their financial security and future aspirations, your **little ol' register's** financial health determines its ability to thrive and prosper in the competitive marketplace. So, be diligent in managing what goes into your piggy bank, and watch as your business grows and flourishes with sound financial management at its core.

Even when filming with high-dollar budgets, mostly all in petty cash for several different departments, devising ways to maintain the equilibrium of control and function can be challenging. In dynamic economic frameworks, implementing an adaptive **system** of checks and balances is crucial. Subsequently, to ensure the longevity of the company and fulfill fiduciary responsibilities to stakeholders, the need to audit effectively becomes key. The numbers are vital. Even so, the implementation of a robust information technology **system** to relatively examine the data for any regulatory agency or committee becomes prudent.

100 PENCILS

Let's explore the philosophy of business within economies of scale, and in a paternal voice, "you'd rather sell **100 pencils** at a penny than 1 at a dollar." This adage encapsulates the essence of maximizing efficiency and reaching broader markets. This principle highlights the power of volume and mass production. When your **little ol' register** focuses on selling a large quantity of a low-priced item, it taps into the unsharpened benefits of scale.

The cost per unit decreases as production increases, making each sale contribute incrementally to covering fixed costs and generating profit. This approach embraces the idea that catering to a larger customer base, even with lower-priced goods, can lead to substantial revenue.

Moreover, this philosophy extends beyond the internal workings of a business and spills over into the external marketplace. The principle of buying power emphasizes the reciprocal relationship between businesses and consumers. As businesses leverage economies of scale to reduce production costs, consumers, in turn, enjoy the fruits of these cost efficiencies through lower prices. This dynamic not only makes products more accessible to a broader audience but also enhances the overall economic landscape by fostering affordability and accessibility. The idea is simple yet transformative: by embracing volume and efficiency, businesses create a win-win scenario where both the producer and the consumer benefit from the advantages of scale.

Yet scale extends far beyond the manufacturing domain; it applies to various aspects of business operations. From marketing and distribution to technology and customer service, the philosophy underscores the advantages gained by increasing the scale of activities. By adopting this perspective, your **little ol' register** positions itself to thrive in competitive markets, providing affordable products to a wide audience while simultaneously optimizing its own efficiency and profitability. The philosophy of selling in volume at lower prices reflects a strategic understanding of how to leverage economies of scale for sustained success in the business landscape.

Within the scope of economies of scale and equity in business ownership, there is a **little ol'** adage "A slice of pie is nice, but a piece of everyone else's is better." This simple **paradigm** underscores the mutual dependencies and shared prosperity inherent in broad participation. While the conventional idea of receiving a "slice of the pie" conveys obtaining a portion of a finite resource, this alternative perspective highlights the potential for greater advantages by actively engaging and empowering everyone within the **system**, or many **systems** collectively. The emphasis shifts from individual gains to collective benefits, emphasizing the interconnectedness and collaborative nature of success in a business context.

Continuing with this notion, actively participating in everyone else's endeavors not only diversifies economic risk but also serves as a prudent strategy in the face of downturns in specific business sectors. By having a stake in various areas, the impact of a downturn in one sector is mitigated by the resilience of others. This approach represents a more balanced and resilient investment portfolio within the business landscape—"Don't put all your eggs in one basket."

Nevertheless, even with adding some grass-feed cheddar, the concept of taking a "piece of everyone else's slice," advocates for a cooperative model where collaboration and shared success prevail. Rather than seeking an oversized portion for oneself, contributing modestly to various ventures ensures that the collective benefits outweigh individual gains.

This economic strategy encourages a healthy and sustainable business ecosystem, leaving ample room for future growth and innovation. Think of it as a business potluck, where everyone brings a dish to share, rather than one person making off with the entire smorgasbord. It reinforces the idea that a thriving and interconnected network is more robust than relying solely on individual slices or the whole pie. As the old Latin proverb wisely reminds us, "Qui totum vult, totum perdit." Or, as your grandma might say, "Greed is a hungry beast that can devour everything in its path." Remember, a rising tide lifts all boats, so let's work together to create a thriving business ecosystem. Let's all get a taste and keep the buffet going strong!

Economies of scale often thrive when various components within a **system** contribute collaboratively. In a business context, this could mean encouraging widespread participation, input, and collaboration among employees, stakeholders, and partners. Rather than focusing solely on individual gains or isolated slices of the business process, the emphasis shifts toward the collective well-being and success of the entire ecosystem.

In this collaborative approach, profit-sharing becomes a powerful tool for the empowerment of employees, aligning their interests with the overall success of the company. All helping to build the **pyramid**. The infusion of the company **Kool-Aid**, representing shared values and a common *vision*, fosters a sense of camaraderie and collective purpose. As employees become stakeholders in the broader business ecosystem, there's an inherent understanding that individual success is intertwined with the prosperity of the entire **little ol' register**. This interconnected mindset cultivates a culture of mutual support and accountability. In the face of challenges or setbacks, collective resilience prevails, providing a safety net and shared responsibility. Ultimately, the success or failure of any given endeavor is viewed as a collective outcome, reinforcing the notion that the whole is greater than the sum of its parts.

The philosophy behind "piece for everyone'" aligns with principles of fairness, inclusivity, and recognizing that, in a thriving **system**, everyone's contribution adds value. By fostering a culture of shared participation, businesses can harness the diverse strengths and perspectives of their workforce, leading to increased efficiency, innovation, and overall success. The expression encourages a holistic approach, where each individual's "piece" contributes to a more prosperous and equitable whole. However, it's crucial to acknowledge that the pursuit of economies of scale involves a trade-off, and this brings us to the concept of opportunity cost. While focusing on producing a large quantity of a low-priced item can lead to cost efficiencies and increased sales, it also means allocating resources away from other potential ventures. The resources, whether financial, human, or time-related, are finite, and choosing one path inherently means forgoing other opportunities.

From the vantage point of a **chess** master in the realm of business strategy, the concept of "opportunity cost" emerges as a pivotal piece on the board. Every move, every decision—a delicate dance between competing alternatives.

Imagine business as a grand chessboard, where each square represents a choice. The pawn advances, the knight gallops, and the queen surveys the horizon. But behind each move lies a shadow—the road not taken. The unexplored squares whisper of untapped potential, of paths diverging into the unknown.

Consider this: Your **little ol' register**, like a seasoned player, contemplates its next move. It invests heavily in mass production—a bold gambit. Yet, in doing so, it sacrifices other avenues—the uncharted territories of new markets, the alchemical laboratories of innovation, the branching tree of product diversification.

The road not taken becomes a phantom adversary. It beckons with promises—benefits unclaimed, profits unrealized. The mass-produced product thrives, but what of the roads forsaken? Could they have led to greater conquests, richer spoils?

Counting the Drawer: Financial Management

In this intricate game, the business strategist weighs the cost of each choice. The ledger balances not only in dollars but in foresight. The opportunity cost—the hidden currency—measures the forfeited gains, the alternate destinies.

And so, the chess master contemplates. The rook maneuvers, the bishop calculates, and the king guards the kingdom. Each move echoes across the board, shaping the narrative. The road taken, the road left behind—they intertwine, defining the game.

In this grand strategy, the business thrives not by chasing every pawn but by orchestrating a symphony of choices. The sacrifice of one piece fuels the advance of another. The collective harmony—the crescendo of shared success—becomes the ultimate endgame.

So, fellow strategist, ponder your moves. Survey the board, anticipate the rival's gambits, and embrace the dance of opportunity and cost. For in this intricate ballet, the business unfolds—a masterpiece painted stroke by stroke, choice by choice.

Opportunity cost, therefore, is not just a financial concept; it's a strategic mindset. Business leaders must weigh the potential gains and losses associated with each decision, considering both short-term and long-term implications. This nuanced understanding allows companies to navigate the complex panorama of choices, making informed decisions that align with your **little ol' register's** overarching goals and *vision*.

Furthermore, the concept of opportunity cost extends beyond individual businesses and permeates economic **systems**. Governments, investors, and entrepreneurs, each faced with limited resources, must grapple with the trade-offs inherent in their choices as we know as the **wants-needs** problem. By embracing the principle of opportunity cost, businesses can make more deliberate and strategic decisions, ultimately maximizing their potential for success in an ever-evolving marketplace.

Once upon a time in a small town, there lived a bright and imaginative adolescent named Alex. Despite his tender age, Alex had a passion for inventing things that could make the world a better place. One day, he came up with a revolutionary idea—a device that remote pack that could power any shop tool, without plugging it into the wall, making it accessible to even the most distant job sites.

Excited about his invention, Alex decided to take a bold step and file for a patent. With his humble prototype in hand, he set out to share his idea with companies that could bring it to life. His target? A renowned American chemical corporation, known for its innovation and commitment to positive change.

Walking into this multinational chemical company's headquarters with his patent in hand, Alex's youthful exuberance caught the attention of the receptionist. Intrigued, she arranged for a meeting with the president of the company. Alex, unfazed by the grandeur of the corporate office, confidently presented his idea.

To his surprise, the president loved the simplicity and potential impact of Alex's invention. Instead of treating him like a mere child, he recognized the value in his creation. Determined to help, he personally called Alex's mother to negotiate terms. During this call, a wise rule of thumb passed on—each level of the supply chain increases the end price, adding a fivefold cost—was immortalized. [164] The sincerity of Alex's passion and the potential for positive change won the president and the company over.

This chemical company, fueled by the spirit of innovation, assigned its best engineers to work on transforming Alex's basic prototype into a sophisticated, scalable product. The collaboration between a young inventor and a corporate giant became an inspiring tale of mentorship and shared purpose.

As the engineers refined the design, Alex learned valuable lessons from the chemical company experts, and his invention began taking shape on a grander scale. The battery device was no longer a simple prototype; it had evolved into a powerful tool that could change lives.

In the end, the product was manufactured, distributed, and made available at an affordable price to the mass market. The collaboration between Alex, his mother, and the company had defied the norm, making a profound impact on the world, and proving that innovation knows no age. The story of Alex and the company became a beacon of hope, inspiring future generations to dream big and collaborate for a better tomorrow.

Back in the world of business, the need for prospective and sales projections is as necessary as having a map and compass in uncharted waters. It's about charting a course for the future, anticipating obstacles, and setting ambitious yet attainable goals. Imagine having a fresh box of 100 pencils at the start of a journey, each pencil representing a potential sale or transaction. The challenge lies in knowing how many of those pencils will be used, how quickly they'll be sharpened, and when you'll need to restock.

Prospective and sales projections serve as the blueprint for navigating the unpredictable terrain of the market. By analyzing historical data, market trends, and consumer behavior, businesses can forecast future sales volumes, revenue streams, and growth opportunities. This allows companies to allocate resources efficiently, identify potential bottlenecks, and capitalize on emerging market trends.

The value of prospective and sales projections extends far beyond mere number-crunching. It's about strategic foresight and informed decision-making. For startups and small businesses, accurate projections can mean the difference between survival and failure. They provide a roadmap for resource allocation, investment planning, and strategic initiatives.

What's more, prospective and sales projections play a crucial role in attracting investors, securing financing, and building confidence among stakeholders. Investors want to see a clear path to profitability and a realistic assessment of growth potential. By presenting well-researched projections, businesses can instill trust and credibility, paving the way for strategic partnerships and long-term success.

In essence, prospective and sales projections are more than just numbers on a spreadsheet; they're a compass for navigating the turbulent seas of the market. They provide direction, clarity, and confidence in an uncertain world, guiding businesses toward their ultimate destination of sustainable growth and prosperity. We will see more of this in **knowing your numbers.**

Now for the hard part, in the **paradigm** of accounting, the choice between cash and accrual methods is akin to selecting the lens through which you view your financial landscape. It's about deciding whether to count the cash in hand or the sales that have been made but not yet received. Each method offers its own set of advantages and considerations, influencing how businesses track revenue, expenses, and overall financial health.

Cash accounting, much like its name suggests, revolves around the actual flow of cash in and out of your **little ol' register.** Under this method, revenue is recognized only when payment is received, and expenses are recorded when they are paid. It provides a clear, straightforward picture of a company's current cash position and liquidity. For small businesses and startups, cash accounting offers simplicity and ease of use, making it a popular choice among entrepreneurs.

On the other hand, accrual accounting takes a more holistic approach, recognizing revenue and expenses when they are incurred, regardless of when cash actually changes hands. This method provides a more accurate representation of a company's financial performance over a given period, matching revenues with the expenses they generate. Accrual accounting offers insights into long-term trends, profitability, and the overall health of a business.

The decision between cash and accrual accounting hinges on factors such as the size of your **little ol' register**, its industry, and regulatory requirements. Cash accounting is suitable for small **little ol' registers** with straightforward financial transactions and minimal inventory. In contrast, accrual accounting is preferred by larger enterprises with complex operations, as well as those seeking a more comprehensive view of their financial position.

Similarly, the choice between cash and accrual accounting methods has implications for tax reporting, financial planning, compliance with accounting standards, and even motivation.[165] It's essential for businesses to weigh the pros and cons of each approach carefully and consult with accounting professionals to determine the best fit for their **wants-needs**.

Ultimately, whether you opt to count the cash or the sale, the goal remains the same: to maintain accurate, transparent financial records that support informed decision-making and drive business growth. By selecting the accounting method that aligns with your objectives and circumstances, you can effectively manage your finances and position your company for long-term success.

In the vast bean-counting world of accounting, the choices between cash and accrual methods, opportunity cost, or economies of scale, are not just about numbers—it's about the very foundation upon which financial decisions are made. Whether you count the cash or the sale, the importance lies in having a clear understanding of your business's financial position and performance and a sharp pencil. By carefully considering the advantages and considerations of each method, and by seeking guidance from financial "experts" when needed, your **little ol' register** can wield the power of accounting to navigate challenges, seize opportunities, and chart a course toward prosperity. In the end, it's not just about the pencils you use to tally the numbers—it's about the story those numbers tell and the insights they provide into the journey of your business.

COUNT YOUR PENNIES!

In the bustling city, beneath the neon glow of streetlights and amidst the rhythmic hum of urban life, there lived a young boy named Jake. His parents, the proud owners of various small businesses scattered across the city, would often gather at their separate desks snuggled against the walls of the office off the kitchen after the day's work was done and dinner was finished. It was a nightly ritual—a symphony of counting, rolling pennies, banding dollars, and poring over usage reports all while the maid reset the home for the day to come. Jake, with wide-eyed curiosity, observed as his parents meticulously tallied the

Counting the Drawer: Financial Management

earnings from each location, audited expenses, and calculated profits. Intrigued by the jingle of coins and the crispness of bills, Jake couldn't resist being drawn into the world of financial stewardship that unfolded before him.

As the evening progressed, Jake's parents transformed their home into a makeshift headquarters, reviewing the day's transactions and meticulously documenting every detail. Jake, a budding learner, found himself immersed in the art of counting pennies and understanding the intricacies of business finances, all while the subtle echoes of Zig Ziglar, preaching, reverberated off the walls, making a profound impact on his malleable mind. The office transformed into an impromptu classroom, and the nightly routine became a lesson in fiscal responsibility and prudent management. Little did Jake know that these early experiences would shape his foundational understanding of money, planting the groundwork for his own financial acumen in the years to come.

Early the next morning, fueled by curiosity and a longing for a taste of forbidden sweetness, Jake embarked on a daring mission. With determination in his eyes, he climbed the pantry shelves, reaching for a **shiny** box that held his favorite cereal—a treasure he was not allowed to have due to its sugary contents. As he precariously balanced on the shelf, the coveted box tipped over, cascading to the floor. To Jake's surprise, instead of cereal, the box revealed bundles of money, some familiar from the night before all neatly stacked within.

A mixture of excitement and disappointment coursed through Jake as he gazed upon the unexpected misfortune. The tear that escaped his eye wasn't one of joy but rather a reflection of the disappointment that the pot of gold at the end of this particular rainbow was not a box of Lucky Charms but, quite literally, a hidden stash of money. Little did Jake realize that this unexpected encounter would further deepen his understanding of the value of money and the surprises that financial exploration could unveil.

Counting pennies instead of dollars may seem trivial, but as they say, 'A penny saved is a penny earned.' In fact, sometimes that single cent can make all the difference, potentially leading to the loss of millions. Now, let's dive into the legendary tale of McDonald's and its humble ketchup packets. Imagine this: for every customer, at every store, day after day, in a single year, if just one extra ketchup packet were distributed, how much would it cost? Now, here's the kicker: what if all the packets cost just a single penny more? In the 1980s, McDonald's underwent a major transformation in its ketchup distribution strategy.

Out went the traditional glass bottles, and in came the revolutionary packets. No, they were not green. This seemingly minor change allowed McDonald's to meticulously control portion sizes and drastically reduce waste. Not only did this shift cut costs, but it also boosted operational efficiency—a win-win situation, wouldn't you agree?

Now, let's add a bit of humor to the mix. You might say McDonald's took the "saucy" route to savings! And indeed, they've continued to spice up their packaging game over the years. From tweaking packet sizes to optimizing designs, McDonald's has demonstrated a commitment to both cost-effectiveness and sustainability. After all, when it comes to condiments, every drop—and every cent—counts! So, the next time you reach for that ketchup packet, remember: behind its humble exterior lies a tale of strategic decision-making and financial savvy that's worth its weight in gold...or should I say, "cents"?

Humans have a tendency to waste a lot, in the spotlight of cost management, and understanding the psychology of consumer behavior is paramount. One intriguing phenomenon that your **little ol' register** can leverage is the concept of friction points—the subtle yet impactful obstacles that influence purchasing decisions and spending habits.

Consider, for instance, the ubiquitous paper towel machine, hanging there staring back at you with dripping hands. How often have we found ourselves frustrated by its sluggish dispensing speed or the paltry size of each piece? Have you noticed, while eating, that you only take about three napkins out of that dispenser?[166] This is a prime example of how friction points can manifest in everyday scenarios, subtly nudging consumers towards behaviors that reduce costs. Left to our own demise, in moments of impatience, or perceived necessity, we may resort to pulling chunks multiple times, each pull contributing to incremental waste and unnecessary expense.

However, savvy **little ol' registers** can turn this phenomenon to their advantage by strategically introducing friction points to mitigate expenses or removing them to facilitate a different desired result. By deliberately designing **systems** or processes that impose minor inconveniences or delays, organizations can encourage more mindful consumption and curb unnecessary spending.

An example could be, in a retail environment, eliminating even the slightest delay in the checkout process or removing an extra step to online purchases, such as requiring a correct credit card number or authorization, can ensure that customers' carts are swiftly ordered, minimizing the chance of them rethinking their purchasing decisions. On the flip side, within a corporate framework, instituting approval workflows or review procedures for expense reimbursements can act as a deterrent against frivolous spending, fostering a culture of fiscal prudence and accountability among employees.

By recognizing and capitalizing on friction points, your **little ol' register** can effectively manage costs without sacrificing customer satisfaction or operational efficiency. It's a subtle yet powerful strategy that highlights the intricate interplay between psychology and economics in the scope of financial management. After all, in the game of counting pennies, every friction point counts.

Can we be too focused on the penny? Indeed, the adage of being "penny wise and pound foolish" is a cautionary tale that extends far beyond mere purchasing decisions. It serves as a poignant reminder and the protagonist to "count your pennies," that focusing too intently on small savings in the short term can lead to greater losses or missed opportunities in the long run.

Consider the scenario of driving miles out of the way to save a few cents per gallon on gas, only to realize that the time and fuel spent on the detour far outweigh any potential savings. Similarly, in driving business success, obsessing over minor cost reductions without considering the broader implications can ultimately prove detrimental to the bottom line. It's often wiser to consolidate your vendors, even if it means paying slightly higher prices for some items, rather than dealing with numerous vendors, each supplying only one item. While it may seem that you're paying more for certain products, the overall efficiency and cost-effectiveness of streamlining your supply chain can outweigh the apparent savings from seeking out cheaper individual items. Additionally, working closely with a select group of vendors fosters better relationships, streamlines communication, and allows for more effective negotiation of prices and terms. So, while the costs may vary across a diverse item list, the benefits of vendor consolidation can lead to greater savings and operational efficiency in the long run.

Another example, cutting corners on employee training or skimping on investments in technology may yield immediate cost savings, but it can result in decreased productivity, lower morale, and diminished competitiveness over time. Likewise, neglecting preventive maintenance on equipment or infrastructure to save money in the short term can lead to costly breakdowns and repairs down the line, not to mention the loss of productivity and revenue when your **little ol' register** is forced to unexpectedly shutdown because of repairs.[7]

In essence, being penny-wise and dollar-foolish is about failing to recognize the bigger picture and the true cost-benefit analysis of a decision. It's about prioritizing small savings at the expense of larger, more significant gains or efficiencies—instant or delayed gratification. By adopting a more holistic approach to financial management and weighing the potential long-term consequences of each choice, individuals and businesses can avoid the pitfalls of shortsightedness and make more informed, strategic decisions. After all, in the grand scheme of things, a penny saved may not always be a dollar earned—it could be a dollar lost in disguise.

This can be seen even when transitioning from manual labor to machinery involves the classic debate of man versus machine. When considering the adoption of machines to replace human workers, it's essential to evaluate the costs associated. The investment in machinery should align with the time and money spent on human employees performing the same tasks, ultimately ensuring that the assets (man or machine) contribute to revenue generation—one of the truest metrics of value to your **little ol' register**. This shift underscores the economic balance between workforce and technology in the pursuit of efficient and cost-effective operations.

Let's view a real-world example of man (woman) vs machine. In the heart of the bustling Las Vegas Strip, amidst the glitz and glamour, lay a hidden gem—a club like no other, pulsating with vibrant themes and electric energy. However, behind the façade of excitement, whispers of financial woes loomed, threatening to extinguish the club's spark forever.

Enter the intrepid line producer, armed with a keen eye for opportunity and a determination to turn the tide. Amidst the chaos of a low-budget horror movie at the club location, a revelation struck—a simple yet transformative idea that would breathe new life into the struggling establishment.

The club's five silent sentinels, the Coca-Cola vending machines, stood as both a symbol of convenience and a drain on resources. With each sale, a significant portion of profits evaporated into the coffers of Coca-Cola Bottling Co., helping to drive the teetering club closer to the brink of collapse.

But fortune favors the bold, and with a stroke of inspiration, the line producer saw a path to salvation. In one of many bold moves, the vending machines were replaced with a live bartender—a living, breathing embodiment of customer engagement. The switch not only eliminated the need for costly electricity but also ushered in a new era of profitability.

Now, patrons were greeted by a friendly face, a bartender who not only served identical drinks, for the identical price, but also became a cornerstone of the club's ambiance. With each conversation and interaction, the bartender cultivated connections, ensuring patrons were entertained and engaged. What's more, the beauty of it all was that the bartender didn't need to remain tethered and plugged in around the clock, even during quieter moments or when the club was closed.

As these and other **systems** were revamped throughout the club, the results were nothing short of remarkable. By embracing change and daring to challenge the status quo, the club not only survived but thrived. The once-struggling establishment now buzzed with renewed vitality, its coffers filled with pennies saved from the jaws of financial ruin.

In this tale of triumph, the lesson rings clear: sometimes, the smallest adjustments yield the greatest rewards. By shunning the allure of convenience and embracing innovation, businesses can defy the odds and emerge stronger than ever before. After all, in the world of finance, it's not just about counting pennies—it's about making every dollar count.

Indeed, the rapidly evolving landscape of technology and industry presents a formidable challenge for both employers and employees alike. As we find ourselves in an era where jobs are constantly being reshaped by automation, artificial intelligence, and other emerging technologies, the traditional model of education and workforce preparation is struggling to keep pace.

For years, we've been striving to equip students with the skills and knowledge needed for jobs that haven't even been conceived yet, using tools and technologies that haven't been invented, all in anticipation of solving problems we may not even be aware of.[14] This forward-thinking approach has undoubtedly fueled innovation and progress, but it has also created a disconnect between the skills individuals possess and the demands of the modern workforce.

Employers are faced with the daunting task of adapting to rapidly changing technology and market dynamics, often requiring them to retrain their workforce on a regular basis to remain competitive. Meanwhile, employees may find themselves feeling disillusioned or overwhelmed by the constant need to learn new skills and adapt to new technologies.

Amidst the uncertainties of our rapidly changing world, we find a unique opportunity to leverage technology to foster continuous learning and adaptation. By instilling a growth mindset and fostering resilience, providing ample resources for professional development, and creating an environment where mistakes are embraced as learning opportunities, we can empower individuals to acquire new skills and remain relevant in an ever-evolving job market. Facilitating knowledge sharing and collaboration, exploring innovative ideas and technologies, and implementing dynamic training programs, workshops, and courses further enhance our capacity for growth and adaptation. With these strategies in place, your **little ol' register** can navigate the challenges of today's landscape with confidence and agility.

Additionally, organizations that prioritize employee development and invest in training initiatives are better positioned to attract warriors and retain top talent, foster a culture of innovation, and drive sustainable growth in the long term. Rather than viewing technological advancement as a threat, we must embrace it as an opportunity to redefine the way we learn, work, and thrive beyond the digital age.

Ultimately, the key to navigating this ever-changing landscape lies in our ability to remain agile, resilient, and open to new possibilities. By embracing change and adapting to the demands of the present moment, we can chart a course toward a future where technology serves as a catalyst for progress and prosperity for all.

In the intricate dance of financial transactions, the concept of time holds a profound significance, especially when it comes to the value of money. In essence, money is most valuable in the present compared to its future worth. This principle forms the cornerstone of borrowing, where obtaining money entails certain costs the same as acquiring a commodity.

Consider this scenario: if it takes five units of a commodity, let's say chicken, along with an additional one dollar in interest until the investment matures and is ready for the market, the total cost becomes six units. However, in the grand scheme of things, the market may yield a return of ten units. Here lies the essence of strategic scaling—it's like pressing down on the gas pedal, aiming to maximize returns relative to the initial investment.

Moreover, there are tactical maneuvers that savvy investors and businesses employ to optimize their financial position. For instance, strategically timing purchases toward the end of the tax year can have significant implications. Even if the payment for a purchase is deferred to the following year, the deduction can still be claimed in the current tax year, effectively reducing taxable income, and maximizing tax benefits.

In essence, mastering the art of financial management involves understanding the nuances of time and leveraging them to one's advantage. Whether it's optimizing borrowing costs, maximizing investment returns, or strategically timing purchases for tax purposes, every decision carries the potential to shape the financial landscape and pave the way for long-term success.

Let's take a trip down memory lane to the ancient Sumerians, those ingenious folks who used clay tablets to track the sale orders of rice and wheat

Counting the Drawer: Financial Management

some 3,000 years ago.[167] While we may have swapped clay for spreadsheets, the essence remains the same: meticulous record-keeping is the bedrock of sound financial management.

Yet, amidst the hustle and bustle of business, it's crucial not to overlook those flashing red and blue lights behind you—taxation. Navigating the labyrinth of tax laws is equivalent to walking a tightrope; one misstep can have dire consequences. Just ask Al Capone, whose notorious reign came crashing down not due to his criminal exploits, but rather his failure to pay taxes.[168] It's a stark reminder that even the most formidable figures can't evade the long arm of the taxman.

In today's treacherous regulatory landscape, staying abreast of tax laws is non-negotiable. Whether it's changes in deductions, credits, or reporting requirements, ignorance is no excuse. "**Sh*t**," the ever-elusive "middle-of-the-night filled loophole"! You know, the one that politicians always seem to close right when they're burning the midnight oil? It's like they have a sixth sense for sniffing out those sneaky little gaps in the law when the rest of us are counting sheep. But fear not, dear citizens, for with each passing bill, we can rest assured that another one of those pesky loopholes bites the dust, leaving us all to marvel at the wonders of democracy...or at least its uncanny ability to keep us on our toes, even in our sleepiest state! That's where a seasoned CPA and Tax Attorney become invaluable allies, guiding your **little ol' register** through the intricate multicursal maze of tax compliance.

And let's not forget the importance of documentation. Whether you prefer old-school grid paper or state-of-the-art digital platforms, maintaining detailed records is your best defense against **landmines** and tax woes. Every transaction, every receipt—they all play a pivotal role in ensuring smooth financial operations and safeguarding your business against any unforeseen liabilities—remember **sh*t happens**!

Ah, the allure of expenses—the golden ticket to minimizing taxable income and maximizing profits. In the world of business, almost anything can be justified as a legitimate expense if it's deemed necessary for the operation or promotion of your enterprise. From office supplies to client entertainment, the possibilities are endless.

But here's where things get dicey. While it may be tempting to write off every dinner, gadget, or getaway as a business expense, tread carefully. Using your startup as your personal piggy bank isn't just unethical; it's a recipe for disaster. Not only does it blur the lines between personal and business finances, peaking through the veil, but it also opens the door to potential legal and financial repercussions.

And let's not forget about your fellow shareholders–the individuals who've invested their hard-earned money and time in your *vision*–willing to believe and take a chance in you. They're not just silent partners; they're stakeholders with a vested interest in the success and integrity of the business. Cheating them out of their fair share isn't just bad business; it's a betrayal of trust that can irreparably damage relationships and reputations.

So, before you start treating your **little ol' register** like a personal slush fund, pause and consider the long-term consequences. Remember, building wealth isn't about cutting corners or exploiting loopholes; it's about creating value, fostering trust, and upholding integrity every step of the way.

In the ever-evolving scenery of entrepreneurship, the ancient wisdom of the Sumerians still rings true today. Keep those receipts close, for they are the breadcrumbs that lead to financial clarity and compliance. Stay vigilant, navigating the maze of tax codes like a seasoned sailor charting turbulent waters.

Remember, time is money, and the tax code is a relentless game of whack-a-mole, constantly shifting and evolving. But with meticulous record-keeping, informed decision-making, and the guidance of seasoned professionals, you can navigate these choppy waters with confidence.

So, **count your pennies**, but don't overlook the value of a well-placed dollar. By embracing financial prudence and maintaining unwavering integrity, you'll steer your **little ol' register** toward success, one expense report at a time.

KNOW YOUR NUMBERS

Knowing **your numbers** is not just about tallying up figures on a spreadsheet; it's about gaining insight, making informed decisions, and steering your ship towards success. Just like the US Department of Defense invests billions in asset management software to ensure operational efficiency and strategic planning, businesses must also prioritize knowing their numbers. Winston Churchill's famous quote underscores the importance of historical data—it allows you to gain perspective, anticipate trends, and plan for the future.

By **knowing your numbers**, you gain a clear picture of your **little ol' register's** financial health, operational efficiency, and growth trajectory. You can track revenue, expenses, profit margins, and cash flow to understand how your business is performing. This insight enables you to identify areas of strength and areas that require improvement. For example, if you notice declining profit margins, you can investigate the root causes and take corrective action before it impacts your bottom line.

Moreover, **knowing your numbers** empowers you to make strategic decisions with confidence in a **blink**. Whether it's setting prices, allocating resources, or expanding into new markets, having accurate and up-to-date data allows you to assess risks and opportunities effectively. You can identify trends, forecast future performance, and devise strategies to capitalize on market opportunities.

Additionally, **knowing your numbers** is essential for financial management and compliance. It enables you to meet regulatory requirements, file taxes accurately, and secure financing from investors or lenders. When you can demonstrate a deep understanding of your financial position and performance, you instill trust and confidence in stakeholders, fostering stronger relationships and opportunities for growth.

Ultimately, **knowing your numbers** is not just a matter of arithmetic—it's a strategic imperative for business success. Whether you're a small startup or a multinational corporation, the ability to track, analyze, and leverage data is paramount in today's competitive landscape. So, heed Winston Churchill's wisdom, and dive deep into **your numbers** to chart a course for long-term prosperity. Imagine you're in the shoes of...

Once upon a time in a small town, there lived a quirky accountant named Bob. Bob's accounting skills were top-notch, but his luck with the IRS was anything but ordinary.

One sunny morning, as Bob was crunching numbers in his cozy office, he received a knock on the door. To his surprise, standing before him was Mr. Smith, a peculiar IRS agent known for his unorthodox methods and overburdensome attention to detail.

"Good morning, Mr. Smith! To what do I owe the pleasure of this unexpected visit?" Bob greeted him with a polite smile.

Mr. Smith adjusted his thick-rimmed glasses and replied, "Ah, Mr. Bob, I'm here to conduct a routine audit of your **little ol' register's** financial records. Just a formality, you know."

Bob nodded apprehensively, leading Mr. Smith to his cluttered desk. As they began reviewing the millions of documents, Mr. Smith's curiosity seemed to pique beyond the usual tax-related inquiries.

"Now, Mr. Bob, this expense here for 'business lunches' seems quite intriguing. Tell me, where exactly did you dine, and what was on the menu?" Mr. Smith inquired; his eyes gleaming with curiosity.

Bob blinked in confusion but decided to play along. "Oh, well, we often frequent a quaint little diner down the street. The meatloaf special is simply divine!"

Mr. Smith scribbled notes furiously, his interest seemingly more personal than professional. "And what about this 'office supplies' expense? I'm quite curious about the brand of pens and paper you prefer," he pressed on, his tone unusually enthusiastic.

Bob couldn't help but chuckle nervously at Mr. Smith's peculiar line of questioning. "Well, we only use the finest ink pens and recycled paper, of course. It's all about quality and sustainability!"

As the audit progressed, Mr. Smith's inquiries became increasingly absurd. From the type of coffee beans Bob purchased to the brand of toilet paper stocked in the office restroom, nothing seemed off-limits to the curious IRS agent.

In the end, Bob couldn't help but wonder if Mr. Smith was conducting the audit for the IRS or simply satisfying his own quirky curiosity. Nevertheless, amidst the absurdity, Bob managed to navigate the Fourth Annual Department-Wide Audit with humor and a touch of bemusement, earning him a newfound reputation as the accountant who survived the most peculiar IRS auditor in town.

Quirky or not, understanding the causes and numbers that drive your **little ol' register** and the levers that can produce results is essential for sustainable growth. Investors and banks are not likely to invest in a business that is struggling to survive or lacks a clear plan for profitability. Therefore, it's crucial to have a firm grasp of **your numbers** and the factors influencing them.

Today's costs are tomorrow's income, and every decision you make affects your bottom line. By analyzing **your numbers**, you can identify areas where you can cut costs, improve efficiency, or capitalize on opportunities to increase revenue. This might involve renegotiating contracts with suppliers, streamlining operations, or investing in marketing initiatives to attract new customers.

However, it's equally important to watch out for red flags that could indicate trouble ahead. Running too hot for too long—expanding too quickly without the necessary infrastructure or resources—can lead to burnout and financial strain. Similarly, neglecting key aspects of your business, such as customer service or quality control, can damage your reputation and erode trust among stakeholders.

By staying vigilant and proactive in monitoring **your numbers**, you can steer your business toward sustainable growth while mitigating risks and maximizing opportunities. Whether it's through regular financial reporting, performance metrics, or feedback from customers and employees, having a finger on the pulse of your **little ol' register** allows you to make informed decisions and adapt to changing circumstances effectively.

Ever wondered about the extensive details on those seemingly endless pesky receipts? Even if some items lack specific amounts, a line item showing a cost of $0 on them or in your financial statements can still hold significant importance. It serves as a crucial tool for tracking performance metrics, managing inventory, or adhering to regulatory procedures. Surprisingly, the absence of a cost can often indicate efficiency or optimization in certain areas of your business operations. For example, a $0 cost for customer complaints or returns might suggest that your products or services are meeting or exceeding customer expectations, resulting in fewer issues that require resolution. Similarly, a $0 cost for employee turnover could indicate a positive work environment and effective retention strategies.

Tracking these metrics can provide valuable insights into the health of your business and help you identify areas of strength and areas for improvement. By monitoring performance indicators closely, you can make informed decisions to capitalize on successes and address challenges before they escalate.

Furthermore, certain line items with a $0 cost may still have non-financial implications that are important to track. For instance, while a marketing campaign might not incur direct costs, its impact on brand awareness, customer engagement, or lead generation could be significant for the overall success of your business.

In essence, every line item in your financial statements, regardless of its cost, contributes to the larger picture of your business's performance and effectiveness. By paying attention to these details and leveraging them as performance indicators, you can gain valuable insights and make strategic decisions to drive growth and success.

Let us venture forth into these uncharted lands, where numbers hold secrets and fortunes unfold. Understanding **your numbers**, my fellow traveler, is akin to gripping that trusty machete. Each swing reveals pathways—the financial arteries of your enterprise. Expenditures today ripple through time, shaping the contours of tomorrow's revenue. The jungle breathes, and so does your balance sheet.

In your mind's eye: You stand at the crossroads, surrounded by three levers—each a compass point. Cost of goods sold (COGS)—the raw materials, the alchemical transformations. Labor—the beating heart of your workforce, their sweat and skill. Profit—the elusive treasure, glinting in the dappled sunlight.

Now, heed the ancient wisdom—the "third, third, and third equilibrium." It's no rigid formula etched in stone; rather, a dance—a waltz of interconnectedness. Imagine dividing your resources into thirds, like a cosmic pie:

■ **COGS**: The raw materials, representing the direct costs associated with producing goods or services, the forge fires, the sweat of artisans. A third of your energy flows here. It's the alchemy—the transmutation of base elements into marketable gold. Analyzing and optimizing this aspect involves scrutinizing factors like raw materials, production costs (overhead), and manufacturing efficiency.[169]

■ **LABOR**: The beating heart, the hands that shape destiny. Another third—dedicated to wages, benefits, and the symphony of human effort. For every dollar spent, a life touched. This encapsulates the human force driving your business. Beyond wages (indirect cost), it encompasses the efficiency, productivity, and overall well-being of your workforce.[170]

■ **PROFIT**: Ah, the elusive prize—the final third. It beckons from the canopy. But beware! It's not just about hoarding gold; it's about reinvestment, growth, and resilience. The jungle rewards those who plant seeds. It is the lifeblood of sustainability and growth. It encapsulates not only revenue but also factors in the costs and expenses associated with running the business (general & administrative costs).[171] Effective management of this lever requires strategic decision-making, pricing optimization, and constant vigilance over expenses. Oh, and let's not forget our favorite, Taxes!

Yet, my friend, this equilibrium is no static tableau. It shifts with seasons, market tides, and lunar cycles. The machete must adapt—sometimes hacking through thickets, sometimes tracing delicate ferns.

And so, you wield **your numbers**—the compass, the sextant. You navigate by starlight, recalibrating as you go. The jungle murmurs its secrets—the whispers of opportunity cost, the rustle of risk.

Remember: The machete is not just a weapon; it's a tool for survival. The "third, third, and third" principle—etched not in stone but in the very fabric of commerce—guides your steps. Balance, my friend, balance.

As you forge ahead, may your ledger be clear, your compass true, and your machete ever sharp. For in these vast lands, where numbers intertwine with fate, you carve your legacy—one swing at a time.

Furthermore, realistic assumptions and accurate forecasting are essential in navigating this financial journey. Understanding the uncertainties inherent in business, meticulous scenario planning is crucial for anticipating and addressing potential challenges. By analyzing historical patterns, market trends, and external factors, businesses can develop a robust financial strategy. Whether it's knowing the true expenses or making estimations, most costs can be calculated and validated based on standard assumptions such as electricity, rent, or employee costs.

Researching other buildings in the area of similar size can provide insight into nominal expenses for these line items. Incorporating these numbers into simulations offers a more precise depiction of the **system**, not only ensuring sound decision-making but also demonstrating to lenders or investors the competency of your **little ol' register**.

Wait, **why** did the accountant break up with their pencil? Because it wouldn't stop drawing conclusions! Making up stuff, assumptions and forecasting are essential components of financial projections, especially when starting a new venture or expanding to a new location. Running simulations repeatedly allows you to refine your projections and identify potential blind spots or overlooked factors, much like ensuring all necessary elements, like bathrooms or water, are accounted for on a film set in the desert.

By continuously revisiting and adjusting your assumptions, you can improve the accuracy of your financial forecasts and better prepare for various scenarios. This iterative process enables you to test different strategies, assess their potential outcomes, and make informed decisions based on the results.

Just as in the **Sim's game** where players strive to build and manage successful virtual worlds, business owners and managers can use financial simulations to anticipate challenges, optimize resource allocation, and mitigate risks. Whether it's estimating revenue growth, projecting expenses, or forecasting cash flow, the ability to model different scenarios empowers you to make proactive choices and adapt to changing circumstances.

Likewise, financial projections serve as a roadmap for your business, guiding decision-making and resource allocation to align with your long-term goals. By incorporating realistic assumptions and leveraging forecasting tools, you can navigate uncertainties more effectively and position your **little ol' register** for sustainable growth and success.

Fundamentally, never underestimate the importance of assumptions and forecasting in financial planning. Just as a director meticulously plans every aspect of film production, from script to set design, attention to detail and continuous refinement of financial projections are crucial for the success of your business venture. Keep running those **sims**, refining your assumptions, and preparing for the unexpected to ensure your business thrives in any scenario.

Ultimately, **knowing your numbers is** not merely a matter of computation or regurgitation; it's an art of balancing, predicting, and adapting. Regularly monitoring the dashboard of your financial metrics ensures you stay on course, avoiding the pitfalls of running too hot or letting the red line approach. These financial insights are the collective efforts of the various **hats** worn in your business **system**, reflecting the symbiotic dance of cost, labor, and profit.

The financial insights gleaned from your **little ol' register's** operations are a culmination of the diverse roles played within your organizational framework, epitomizing the interconnected relationship between income and expenses. While capitalization tables are typically associated with startups and nascent ventures, their utility extends across various business models and stages of development. Essentially, a capitalization table serves as a comprehensive delineation of a company's shareholders' equity, offering invaluable insights into the composition of the company's balance sheets and its overall financial health.[172] By meticulously dissecting ownership structures and equity distributions, businesses can gain a deeper understanding of their capital resources and strategic positioning within the market landscape.

At its core, accounting is the same as managing **water** in your bucket collected **from the river**. Picture your financial transactions as cups of water out of one bucket into another, each representing income, expenses, investments, and debts. Now, imagine your bucket as your financial **system**, where you store and track every drop of water that flows in and out.

However, not all buckets are created equal. Some may have tiny leaks, symbolizing expenses or losses eating away at your resources. Others might not even belong to you, reflecting shared financial responsibilities or investments in partnerships. Then there are the buckets that showcase efficiency, like modern toilets conserving water, highlighting smart financial practices that maximize resources.

Despite the variations, all the water in these buckets originates from the same source—the river of your financial transactions. Accounting ensures that you manage this flow effectively, plugging leaks, optimizing usage, and ensuring that every drop serves its purpose in achieving your financial goals. So, whether your bucket is pristine or peppered with holes, the essence of accounting lies in mastering the art of managing the water within, harnessing its potential to sustain and nourish your financial well-being.

Understanding **your numbers** transcends mere financial accounting; it permeates every facet of your business strategy, from bidding on projects to pricing your products or services within a specific market or demographic. Whether you're grappling with the decision to wholesale or retail, rent or sell, or navigating the intricacies of different contract types, **knowing your numbers** is paramount. For instance, when bidding on a job, the approach can vary depending on the type of contract—fixed-price bids typically entails higher pricing than cost-plus contracts due to the increased risk undertaken by the contractor. Understanding the intricacies of different contract types is crucial to grasp their value and significance fully. With the nuances within each arrangement, you can gain a comprehensive understanding of their structures and leverage them to your advantage. Take firm-fixed-price contracts, they necessitate clear delineation of unit prices and total prices, whereas cost-type contracts eschew unit prices in favor of incorporating relevant elements (all direct & indirect costs) as per regulatory guidelines.[173]

Finally, let's visualize the "Time-Money-Quality Pyramid", a fundamental **paradigm** when looking at **your numbers**. Imagine it as a three-sided pyramid, each side representing one of the critical factors: time, money, and quality.

■ **Time:** This refers to the available time to complete a project. It's the ticking clock that influences deadlines and project schedules.

■ **Money:** Representing the budget or resources allocated for the project. Financial constraints impact decisions and resource allocation.

■ **Quality:** The fit-to-purpose that the project must achieve to be successful. Quality encompasses meeting or exceeding customer expectations.

Now, let's explore the trade-offs within this pyramid. You can only prioritize two sides while the third adjusts accordingly. Choose Two, Sacrifice One!

■ **Time and Money:** If you prioritize completing the project quickly (time) and within budget (money), you might compromise on quality. Rushing can lead to errors or shortcuts.

■ **Quality and Time:** Focusing on delivering high-quality results within a tight deadline may require additional resources (money). Quality takes time and effort.

■ **Money and Quality:** Investing more resources (money) to ensure top-notch quality often extends the project's timeline. High-quality outcomes come at a cost.

Striking a delicate balance involves skillfully handling three critical factors, keep the following principles in mind:

■ **Efficient Operations:** Streamline processes to save time and resources without compromising quality. Look for opportunities to automate repetitive tasks and eliminate bottlenecks. **Count your steps!**

■ **Financial Sustainability:** Allocate budgets judiciously. Avoid overspending while ensuring that quality remains uncompromised. Regularly assess your financial health and adjust your strategies accordingly. **Count your pennies!**

■ **Customer Expectations:** Deliver exceptional products or services that not only meet but exceed customer expectations. Understand your target audience, actively seek feedback, and continuously improve. **Think customer!**

In essence, **knowing your numbers** entails not only comprehending the figures themselves but also understanding the methodologies and rationales behind them, ensuring informed decision-making and strategic planning in every aspect of your **little ol' register**—the bedrock of successful endeavors.

SIDE WORK: GENERAL & ADMINISTRATIVE

Achieve a white glove system. Even your **little ol' register** requires its version of a housekeeper to assist with the daily chores. Within every organization, there exists a category of work that often goes uncelebrated—the less glamorous tasks, often dubbed "crappie work." These are the assignments that nobody genuinely enjoys doing, yet they are essential for keeping the machinery of a company well-oiled. While they may not directly contribute to the bottom line, in fact mostly take away from it, they play a vital role in maintaining order and averting chaos.

One often overlooked aspect that plays a pivotal role is the nuanced understanding of costs. Noticing the different subtle flavors requires discerning between direct and indirect costs, as well as overhead versus general and administrative costs. Direct costs are the expenses directly tied to the production of goods or services, such as raw materials or labor. On the other side, indirect costs are more elusive, encompassing overhead expenses that contribute to the overall functioning of the business but aren't explicitly linked to a specific product or service.

In parallel, we encounter the distinction between overhead costs, which include expenses essential for the day-to-day running of the business, and general and administrative costs (G&A), which are associated with the management and support functions. Recognizing these nuances is paramount for effective economic management, as it enables businesses to allocate resources strategically, minimize unnecessary expenditures, and optimize their overall operational efficiency. Unraveling the complexities of these cost categories is comparable to decoding the language of business, offering valuable insights that can shape informed decision-making and foster sustainable growth.

Imagine your business as a bustling kitchen, where you're whipping up delicious financial recipes!

- **Direct Job Costs:** When you prepare a specific dish, the ingredients you use directly contribute to that dish. These ingredients are your direct job costs. They can be traced directly to the dish you're cooking. For example, if you're making a pasta dish, the direct materials are the penne noodles—the juicy tomatoes, the succulent **chicken** breasts, and the aromatic herbs and fromage. You can easily trace them to specific dishes. Direct labor is your skilled sous chef—the one who meticulously seasons the steak or crafts the delicate pastries. Their efforts directly contribute to the final product.

■ **Indirect Job Costs:** The salt and pepper on the table—the small but necessary elements that enhance every dish. Think of it as the kitchen's heartbeat—essential for flavor but not explicitly listed on the menu. Now, consider the kitchen equipment and utilities, these include the electricity used to power the stovetop, and the salaries of kitchen staff who work on multiple dishes. They're essential for the kitchen's existence but only helped to create the dinner plate. These are indirectly necessary for running the kitchen, but they're not tied to any specific dish. These all are the essential ingredients that make your dishes possible.

■ **Direct Overhead:** Picture the managing chef's office. The chefs oversee the entire kitchen operation, but they don't directly cook any dishes. Their salary, training, repairs to the flurry ice cream machine, and other costs related to managing the kitchen are considered direct overhead. These costs contribute to the overall functioning of the kitchen but aren't directly served on the plate.

■ **Indirect Overhead:** Now, think about the restaurant as a whole. The lights, air conditioning, and paper towels in the bathrooms benefit the entire establishment, not just the kitchen. These costs are indirect overhead they also include expenses like building maintenance, insurance, and the rent for the kitchen space. Each plays a crucial role behind the scenes.

■ **General and Administrative Costs:** Finally, let's step out of the kitchen and into the restaurant's front office. Here, you have the district manager, the accountant's coffee, office supplies, filing cabinets, and administrative staff. They're the unsung heroes who maintain order behind the swinging kitchen doors. They ensure the kitchen's overall well-being. Their salaries, office rent, and other costs related to running the entire restaurant fall under G&A costs. G&A costs cover everything needed to keep the restaurant operational, from bookkeeping to marketing. The costs of doing business.

So, next time you're cooking up financial success, remember: Overhead costs are the hidden spices, and G&A costs are the kitchen's administrative magic! Mastering this distinction allows your **little ol' register** to craft a recipe for success, allocating resources with precision and maximizing operational efficiency. The secret sauce—where every ingredient counts towards creating a sustainable and thriving enterprise. As we navigate through the nuances of "side work", we uncover its significance in covering one's proverbial backside, ensuring the wheels keep turning even when the financial gains might not be immediately apparent. Join us on this exploration through the unsung heroes of business operations—the side work that quietly keeps the wheels turning.

PUSHING PAPER

Have you ever pondered **why**, in nearly every interaction, people attempt to hand you a piece of paper? And have you ever questioned **why** some individuals choose to preserve these seemingly insignificant scraps? No, they are not used as baby wipes.

Each cash **register** generates a receipt that itemizes purchases, delineating between items such as burgers, fries, and happy meals. This breakdown involves categorizing various components into specific line items. In today's context, nearly everything is considered a line item, transforming transactions into a detailed list of individual elements.

The exchange becomes a simple principle: <u>provide a piece of paper, receive a piece of paper</u> in return, encapsulating the details of the transaction, immortalizing the meeting of the minds, in a clear and organized manner. Right?

Once upon a time in the whimsical world of accounting, there was a kingdom ruled by a meticulous monarch named King Ledger. The kingdom's accountants were known far and wide for their ability to turn chaos into order with nothing more than a quill and an abacus.

One fine day, Sir Spreadsheet, the bravest accountant in the land, found himself knee-deep in paperwork. The royal printer, a mischievous contraption, had decided to go on strike, spewing out endless reams of paper in protest. Sir Spreadsheet, undeterred by this rebellion of machinery, grabbed his sword—which suspiciously resembled a calculator—and set forth on a quest to tame the unruly paper.

As he waded through the sea of invoices and receipts, Sir Spreadsheet encountered the formidable Paper Dragon. This mythical creature had the power to turn even the most organized ledger into a chaotic mess. With a twirl of his mighty spreadsheet, Sir Spreadsheet engaged in an epic battle of number-crunching with the Paper Dragon.

The kingdom's accountants gathered around, cheering for their valiant hero as he skillfully dodged paper cuts and vanquished the Paper Dragon with the magical formula of balance. The defeated dragon transformed into a pile of meticulously organized files, surrendering to the indomitable power of accounting.

The victory was celebrated with a grand feast, where spreadsheets were toasted, and calculators were raised high. Sir Spreadsheet, hailed as the Paper Slayer, became a legend in the kingdom, forever remembered for his daring exploits in the perilous dominion of paperwork.

And so, in the enchanted world of accounting, where every debit has its credit and every ledger tells a tale, the tale of Sir Spreadsheet's triumph became a cherished bedtime story for number-crunchers across the land.

People are often surprised to learn that the earliest piece of writing we have on record is not a piece of poetry or even a letter. The earliest written documentation ever found takes the form of—you guessed it—a shopping receipt! Mesopotamia was the site of the very first international cities, and thus its people may have created the written form as a way to manage trade and land. Some of the earliest pieces of writing procured from Mesopotamia include shopping lists, lists of wages, and documentation of rations set aside for temple workers. [167] And let's not forget most importantly that report from the human resource manager who took that important survey at the **pyramids**.

In the intricate web of transactions that define the lifeblood of your **little ol' register**, every line item holds significance—even the $0 ones. Whether it's for chicken pieces, grilled chicken, or a whole case of poultry, each transaction represents a tangible exchange of goods or services. It's the very essence of what your **little ol' register** rings up, capturing the essence of your business dealings.

But let's not overlook the broader landscape of **pushing paper**. Look around, and you'll find a myriad of examples—from health statements to utility bills and even the layout of your local grocery store's receipts—all offering inspiration for structuring your own line items and service offerings.

Yet, amidst this discussion, it's surprising we haven't delved into the core of it all—the product itself. Understanding what your **little ol' register** buys and sells is fundamental to shaping the how and what of your business operations.

While the advent of technology has streamlined many processes, the importance of processing paper remains paramount. It's not just about acquiring the documentation; it's about the ability to retrieve and utilize it efficiently when needed—a challenge that many businesses grapple with.

Consider the standardized practices of accounting, such as GAAP, which serve as the backbone for businesses across industries. Whether you're dining at a restaurant, calling a plumber, or shopping at a big-box store, the principles of invoicing, accounts payable, and accounts receivable remain consistent. **Chicken is chicken**, after all, and the paperwork involved in business transactions follows a universal protocol.

As your business grows, leveraging technology becomes increasingly vital. Fortunately, there's a plethora of apps available—from text messaging and voice recording to date and time logging—that streamline administrative tasks and

Side work: General & Administrative

facilitate auditing processes. Any method will suffice: a screenshot of the online form submission, photocopy of a fading receipt, or writing down a tracking number for important snail mail delivery. However, in the interim, it's prudent to stick to the basics—utilizing readily available tools like ink sticks and paper to create a paper trail that keeps your business operations running smoothly.

In the intricate dance of business operations, the seemingly mundane act of "**pushing paper**" holds profound significance. A well-organized filing **system** serves as the backbone of efficient management, providing a structured repository for the wealth of documents that accompany the journey of your **little ol' register.** The decision to embrace or forgo those little colorful file folders is emblematic of the nuanced choices that can impact your day-to-day operations.

At the heart of this organizational symphony lies the customer/vendor folder, a repository that mirrors the timeline of your incoming and outgoing interactions. Adopting a reverse chronological order places the oldest documents at the back, with the freshest papers sitting atop the stack. This simple strategy not only aids in locating historical records but also aligns seamlessly with the natural flow of business transactions. The division between correspondence and transactional papers within the folder brings clarity to the multifaceted facets of your business relationships.

To enhance navigability and offer a swift overview, introducing a top-sheet summary on the left side of the folder acts as a compass for anyone delving into the contents. This strategic placement allows for a quick grasp of the folder's context and contents. As you traverse the realm of paper management, consider the handy companions—the two-hole punch and brads. These unassuming tools transform disparate sheets into a cohesive unit, reinforcing the organizational structure of your filing **system**.

In essence, **pushing paper** is not just about the physical act of managing documents; it's a symphony of choices that shape the efficiency and accessibility of your business archives. The meticulous arrangement of files is a silent conductor orchestrating the harmonious flow of information, ensuring that your **little ol' register's** transactions are preserved and readily accessible in the grand historical scrolls of business operations.

In the meticulous art of **pushing paper**, every detail holds significance, and each choice echoes in the corridors of organizational efficiency. Extending the saga, consider the role of receipts in this symphony of documentation. A pragmatic approach suggests taping every receipt to its dedicated 8 x 11 standard copy paper, a canvas for financial journeys that transcends the limitations of mere transaction records. Embracing the golden rule of never writing directly

Part 5: Counting the Register

on a receipt, this blank canvas becomes a playground for the liberation of notes— a mishmash of scribbles, doodles, and reflections—that breathe life into the transactional past. Circling dates and final amounts is a subtle yet effective ritual that eases the subsequent data-entry process. The ceremonial act might seem contradictory at first glance (aren't we not supposed to write on them?), but hey, rules are made to be creatively bent, right? It's like saying never use a highlighter—next thing you know, it's all blacked out by the end of the week!

Venturing into the scope of petty cash management, the strategic numbering of receipts corresponds harmoniously with the **register** log housed on the envelope. This numerical alignment forms a cohesive link, intertwining the narrative of financial transactions in a structured dance of numbers.

Zooming out to the broader spectrum of communication, summarizing meetings and immortalizing discussions through email follow-ups becomes a key practice. A fusion of the spoken and written word, these digital missives serve as historical markers, documenting the nuances of interactions. A note to file becomes a treasure trove of observations—capturing nuances, deciphering nervous energy, or noting a pushy demeanor. This annotated trail paints a vivid picture in the mosaic of business relationships.

And so, from hand-dawned papers to meticulously tagged and colored folders, each action is a stroke in the evolving canvas of your **little ol' register's** journey. The transition from abacas to a dynamic **system** encapsulates not just an evolution in tools but a profound metamorphosis in the very nature of documentation. In the end, **pushing paper** transcends the mundane—it becomes an art, a science, and a living chronicle of your business's odyssey.

Why did the bookkeeper meticulously make copies of every transaction? So, they could exclaim, "I'll let the CPA and attorneys untangle this financial spaghetti later—I'm just here for the paper chase, chasing that elusive Dragon!"

In the labyrinthine realm of paperwork, a single misstep can trigger significant consequences, particularly concerning tax liabilities. Ensuring compliance with meeting minutes, adhering to regulatory guidelines, and assigning the right **hats** to the right **warriors** are all crucial steps in safeguarding against potential **landmines**. The distinction between various forms of paperwork, such as the 1099 and W-2 employee status, can have profound implications for both individuals and businesses alike. While some may perceive being classified as a 1099 contractor as advantageous, as it may seem simpler and more flexible, it's crucial to consider the broader financial circumstances.

For the company, opting for independent contractors can mean avoiding additional expenses like workers' compensation and federal and state employment taxes, shifting the hefty self-employment tax, which hovers around 15.3% to the individual. In contrast, traditional employees entail a split responsibility between the employee and employer, each bearing a ~7.65% tax burden. However, determining the appropriate classification involves navigating a series of criteria, such as control over working hours, provision of necessary tools, and the level of independence in performing tasks.

While gig workers may prefer the flexibility of contract labor, the distinction between employee and contractor ultimately boils down to the level of control exerted by the hiring entity. Whether it's specifying work hours or providing detailed instructions, these factors play a pivotal role in determining the appropriate classification and associated tax liabilities. One slip-up could cause your **little ol' register** to cough up every matching dollar due to an incorrect classification regardless of the original intention.

Indeed, the devil is often in the details, especially when it comes to tracking expenses like that **little ol'** gas receipt. The seemingly mundane task of retrieving a receipt can quickly become a headache, particularly when the method of payment isn't crystal clear or the pump is out of paper. Whether the gas was pumped at the moment or prepaid beforehand can make a significant difference, especially when it's your **little ol' register** footing the bill. This distinction becomes particularly crucial in business scenarios where multiple individuals may be reimbursed by company funds for various transactions.

Without clear documentation and verification of each expense, reconciling accounts and ensuring accurate financial records can become a daunting challenge. Therefore, establishing clear protocols for expense reporting and documentation is essential to avoid misunderstandings and discrepancies down the line. By implementing standardized procedures for capturing and categorizing expenses, businesses can streamline their accounting processes and ensure transparency and accuracy in financial reporting.

After getting a handle on the normal paper flow, exploring avenues for tax rebates and credits can definitely be a savvy financial strategy for businesses, particularly when it comes to offsetting upfront costs and generating additional income. Tax incentives offered by both state and federal governments can provide significant financial relief, especially for initiatives like internship education credits. By leveraging these credits, businesses not only benefit from the valuable contributions of interns but also stand to gain financially. Every dollar spent in eligible categories can translate into tax savings or even refunds (credits), effectively reducing the overall cost of operations and increasing profitability. So, what is the catch? You guessed it more **paper pushing**!

Likewise, the process of navigating tax incentives and rebates involves **pushing paper**, generating documentation that not only ensures compliance with regulatory requirements but also serves as evidence for claiming these benefits. Therefore, **pushing paper** in this context becomes more than just administrative work—it becomes a strategic financial maneuver that can yield tangible returns for the business. As such, your **little ol' register** should actively explore and capitalize on available tax incentives to optimize their financial performance and maximize their bottom line.

In reality, the art of **pushing paper** extends beyond mere documentation—it encompasses the meticulous organization and categorization of financial records, especially during the end-of-year reporting period. From determining which receipts belong to which expense category (bucket) to understanding the nuances of tax regulations regarding deductibles and credits, there is a delicate balance to be struck.

While most mortals curl up with novels or cinematic delights, our business owners—like seasoned bibliophiles—snuggle by the hearth. Their furry companions, wide-eyed and curious, join them on this nocturnal odyssey. But what do they read? Not tales of dragons or star-crossed lovers, but a saga more riveting: tax regulations. Ah, the Federal Register—a bedtime companion for the intrepid souls who dare to dream in legalese!

Fear not, weary traveler, for within this labyrinth of clauses and numerals, a hero emerges—the CPA and Tax Attorney. These financial wizards don their robes, summon their quills, and set sail upon the stormy sea of tax laws. Their compass? Not North or South, but the elusive Section 162(a)(1) and the enigmatic Form 1120.

The camera comes into focus: The tempest rages—the winds of deductions, the tides of credits. Our navigators steer their vessels—the SS Schedule C and the SS Schedule E—through treacherous waters. They decipher the runes of Section 179, unravel the cryptic Schedule A, and fend off the sirens of AMT.

Their mission? Not gold doubloons or ancient artifacts, but something equally precious: compliance. They ensure we dance within the chalked lines—the tax tango of legality. But wait, there's more! These sorcerers wield a second wand—the wand of optimization. They conjure deductions from thin air, spin credits like silk, and reveal hidden treasures—the Holy Grail of Tax Savings.

And what of audits? Ah, the krakens of bureaucracy! Our heroes—armed with spreadsheets and caffeinated scrolls—stand firm. They ward off the IRS's probing tentacles, invoking the sacred mantra: "Substantiation, substantiation, substantiation!"

So here's to the unsung champions—the midnight readers, the code-crackers, the guardians of balance sheets. They make tax season bearable—one regulation at a time.

Next time you cozy up with your ledger, raise a quill in their honor. For they sail where others fear to tread—the uncharted waters of Form 4562 and Schedule D. And as the fire crackles, remember: Behind every deduction lies a tale, and behind every credit, a whispered incantation. To the CPAs, Tax Attorneys, and all financial wayfarers—may your spreadsheets be error-free, your audits swift, and your deductions abundant.

Moreover, their guidance extends beyond mere compliance; they serve as trusted advisors, offering insights and recommendations tailored to the unique requirements and goals of the business. In essence, partnering with a proficient CPA (Certified Pain in the Arse, okay Certified Public Accountant) or Tax Attorney is like having a seasoned navigator guiding the ship through turbulent financial waters, not the ones rowing the boat of paper but steering it towards prosperity and stability. Therefore, investing in expert assistance to **push paper** effectively is not just prudent—it's essential for the long-term success and sustainability of the business.

The importance of documentation cannot be overstated in the dominion of **pushing paper**. Without proper receipts and records to substantiate expenses, the risk of overpaying or underpaying taxes looms large. Either way, it's going to cost you. Each transaction, each expense, represents an opportunity to reduce taxable income and minimize the tax burden on your **little ol' register** and yourself. However, without the necessary documentation, these expenses may be overlooked or disregarded during tax preparation, resulting in higher tax liabilities. This not only erodes profitability but also distorts financial performance metrics, painting an inaccurate picture of the company's financial health.

Here's a fun little mental exercise: imagine it as a fee for every receipt you misplace or forget, you magically end up paying, out of your pocket, an extra 25% to your Uncle Sam for whatever it was you bought. Suddenly, that missing receipt doesn't seem so insignificant anymore, does it? It's like a sneaky little tax on forgetfulness, reminding us all to keep better track of our expenses. Unless, of course, you enjoy donating extra cash to the National forgetfulness fund!

Essentially, the lack of proper documentation doesn't just affect tax obligations; it also erodes financial transparency and accountability. Without clear records, tracking spending patterns becomes a puzzle, identifying inefficiencies feels like searching for a needle in a haystack, and spotting "inadvertent" misappropriations—well, that's like chasing shadows. And let's not forget the trio of troublemakers: fraud, theft, and embezzlement.

Therefore, the act of **pushing paper** serves not only as a means of fulfilling regulatory requirements but also as a safeguard against unnecessary tax liabilities and financial inaccuracies. In essence, while **pushing paper** may consume its fair share of trees, the benefits of meticulous documentation far outweigh the environmental costs, ensuring fiscal prudence and regulatory compliance for your **little ol' register**.

KILLING A TREE

From the cloud-touching buildings of business, the size of your file and how well you can **push paper** can often be seen as a badge of honor, a symbol of your endurance in the face of challenges. However, this pursuit of voluminous documentation can sometimes lead to what is colloquially known as "**killing a tree**." A notable example of this phenomenon occurred in a clash between commercial titans, where a class of merchants led by Wal-Mart engaged in extensive legal battles. Their discovery process alone involved reviewing approximately five million pages of documents, conducting nearly 400 depositions, and gathering information from around 200 non-parties. The sheer magnitude of paperwork generated during this seven-year ordeal underscores the burdensome nature of legal proceedings and the toll they can take on both time and resources.

Governmental regulatory agencies also have a penchant for "**killing trees**" through their rigorous demands for documentation and compliance. Failure to meet these requirements can result in hefty fines and penalties, adding further financial strain to businesses already grappling with the burdens of bureaucracy and endangered dirt. For instance, neglecting to file W-2, and 1099 contract labor reports, or failing to maintain accurate financial records can lead to significant tax liabilities, fines, penalties, interest, and legal repercussions, exacerbating the already daunting challenges of regulatory compliance.[174] Last but not least—literally—are the penalties charges for intentional disregard, which is a fancy way of saying that filing is being ignored. At this point in time, for example, minimum fees are $630 per report or 10% of the purported income, whichever is greater, and you guessed it, there's no maximum penalty limit.[175]

Thanks to our pals over at Enron, Sarbanes-Oxley is infamous for its strict demands on CEOs when it comes to filing accuracy.[176] It's like having a financial watchdog breathing down your neck, making sure every number is in its right place.[177] So, if you're the CEO, you better have your paperwork game on point, or you might find yourself in hot water faster than you can say "audit" or "hand-cuffs." Just imagine them as an additional boss always looming over your shoulder, making sure you **know your numbers** inside and out.
And let's not forget their knack for "killing trees" with all the paperwork they require. It's like they have a personal vendetta against forests! But hey, if you want to stay on the right side of the law and avoid any regulatory headaches, you'd better get cozy with your spreadsheets and filing cabinets.

In the scope of accounting, the value of receipts as records of expenses cannot be overstated. Proper documentation not only ensures compliance with tax laws but also strengthens the corporate shield against potential legal disputes or audits. However, the proliferation of paperwork also invites the risk of "lawfare" and "paper warfare," where adversaries use the legal and regulatory systems as a battleground to overwhelm opponents with mountains of documentation and procedural hurdles.

Moreover, the cost of processing and managing extensive paperwork can be substantial, both in terms of time and financial resources. For instance, the average reading speed for technical material is significantly slower than that for standard literature, with students typically reading around 11 pages per hour. [178] This means that deciphering a dense legal document or regulatory notice can consume valuable hours and incur significant advisory costs. As your **little ol' register** grapples with the challenges of navigating complex regulations and legal proceedings, the need to streamline documentation processes and mitigate the burdens of paperwork becomes increasingly imperative.

Record keeping is not just about complying with regulations or covering your assets; it's about having the necessary backup for when a metaphorical **landmine** inevitably hits. In this side to the beautiful world of business, where reality is often stranger than fiction, unforeseen legal disputes or regulatory audits can arise at any moment, and having meticulously maintained records can mean the difference between weathering the storm or facing significant legal and financial consequences. Whether it's corporate governance paperwork, meeting minutes, or documentation of financial transactions, thorough record-keeping practices serve as a vital shield against potential liabilities and disputes.

Let's look at another example, corporate governance paperwork, such as articles of incorporation, bylaws, and shareholder agreements, lays the foundation for the structure and operation of a company. These documents not only establish the rights and responsibilities of shareholders and directors but also serve as a roadmap for decision-making and accountability within the organization. Similarly, maintaining accurate minutes of meetings ensures transparency and accountability in corporate decision-making processes, providing a clear record of discussions, resolutions, and actions taken by the board of directors or executive leadership.

In the event of a legal dispute or regulatory inquiry, these records serve as critical de jure evidence to support the company's position and defend against allegations of misconduct or negligence. They provide a comprehensive paper trail that can corroborate the company's compliance with laws and regulations, adherence to corporate governance best practices, and adherence to ethical standards. Moreover, well-documented records can help demonstrate diligence and due diligence on the part of company management, mitigating the risk of personal liability for directors and officers in the event of litigation or regulatory enforcement actions.

In essence, effective record-keeping practices are essential for ensuring corporate transparency, accountability, and legal compliance. By maintaining accurate and thorough documentation of corporate activities and decisions, businesses can protect themselves against legal and financial risks, uphold the principles of good governance, and safeguard the interests of shareholders, stakeholders, and employees alike.

It's a world where the pursuit of success is as relentless as the Monday morning alarm clock, and where the phrase "work-life balance" is uttered with a knowing smirk. So, grab your coffee (extra strong, of course), be rest assured knowing that your **little ol' register** is armed with the necessary paperwork to navigate any legal challenges that may come its way.

THE BAR

3 Lawyers walk into **the bar**, no matter what optimistic thoughts you initially had, let's be honest, somewhere deep down, a tiny voice was whispering, "Brace yourself, this is going to hurt." The general consensus? "It's going to cost me." Whether they're batting for your team or playing for the opposition, the legal arena has this uncanny ability to deliver a sting that transcends allegiances. We can collectively acknowledge that they have mastered the art of **arboreal**

destruction and are unparalleled in their ability to engage in the ancient ritual of **paper pushing**, all with a certain finesse. Legal matters seem to have mastered the art of impartial discomfort.

As the lawyers walk into **the bar**, and suddenly the atmosphere is charged with the cost of doing business. Legal minds engage in spirited conversations, discussing contracts, litigation strategies, and the intricacies of the latest cases. The bar becomes a makeshift courtroom, where billable hours are calculated with each exchanged idea. The clinking of glasses harmonizes with the rhythm of legal jargon, creating a unique symphony of business and law. In this impromptu legal forum, **the bar** patrons unwittingly become the jury, and the cost of doing business manifests not only in the drinks ordered but in the intellectual currency of legal discourse.

Don't fool yourself into thinking that the unexpected won't happen to you; it's the unavoidable whispers of Murphy, **sh*t happens,** a factor that lurks in every business venture. Much like a plot twist in a novel, unforeseen challenges can emerge when least expected. It might be a sudden economic downturn, a shift in consumer behavior, or a global crisis. Acknowledging this reality is not about dwelling on negativity but preparing for resilience. Businesses that navigate through the unpredictable storms with adaptability and a strategic mindset are the ones that not only survive but often emerge stronger. So, embrace the mantra that "**sh*t happens**," and equip your **little ol' register** with the flexibility to weather whatever surprises the business world throws your way.

The cost of legal matters can indeed be exorbitant, a very high **bar**, and the financial implications can be daunting. Whether you're faced with a legal dispute, intellectual property issues, or any other legal challenge, the reality is that navigating the legal world comes with a price tag.[179] It's a harsh truth that without sufficient resources to mount a legal offense or defense, you may find yourself at a significant disadvantage. The legal battlefield often favors those with the financial means to sustain a prolonged fight. To safeguard your **little ol' register**, it's crucial to factor legal expenses into your business strategy and financial planning. This proactive approach not only prepares you for potential legal challenges but also ensures that you have the means to protect your business interests when needed.

Certainly at times, the saying "you can't get blood from a turnip" encapsulates the financial crux in the reality of legal battles. Whether you find yourself pursuing legal action or being targeted with a lawsuit, the costs involved can be substantial. Legal proceedings often demand a significant investment of both time and money. Even if you emerge victorious in a lawsuit, the expenses incurred during the process can be substantial, potentially leaving both parties financially strained. You can either be right or be married underscores the emotional toll to be paid along with the health of your **little ol' register**. It underscores the importance of seeking alternative dispute resolution methods, such as mediation or negotiation, whenever possible. Proactively addressing conflicts and potential legal issues can help mitigate the financial burden associated with legal proceedings, allowing you to protect your **little ol' register** without bleeding your resources dry.

According to a blog by renowned penny stock investor Timothy, the average millionaire goes bankrupt at least 3.5 times. While bankruptcy can offer a protective shield for your **little ol' register**, there are instances when the best course of action is to dissolve and start anew. Bankruptcy, while providing a legal framework for financial recovery, may not always be the ideal solution for every business circumstance. Dissolving a business, though a difficult decision, can be a strategic move to shed financial burdens, liabilities, and pave the way for a fresh start. It allows for a clean slate, giving you the opportunity to learn from past mistakes, reassess your business model, and embark on a new entrepreneurial journey. Recognizing the signs and making the tough decision to dissolve can be a courageous act, ensuring the long-term well-being of your **little ol' register'** dreams rather than persisting in a **vehicle** that may no longer be viable.

A tale of such dreams being washed away began with a single phone call. Engaging with a contractor bidding on FEMA's disaster relief efforts seemed like an excellent opportunity for this **little ol' register**, with the potential for revenue in the millions. The prospect of uplifting the entire crew and donning multiple **hats** and **warriors** in a monumental task for months, or even years, was both exhilarating and financially promising. However, cautionary tales often lurk behind glittering opportunities. The critical need to ensure timely payments to all involved parties loomed large considering the operation's scale and the financial stakes. Yet, in the pursuit of this colossal contract, the little ol' register risked neglecting other potential clients and diversified revenue streams, placing all its eggs in one precarious basket.

After signing the contract and getting the green light for the crews, warning signs became glaring. The contractor proposed charging FEMA extra, displaying a willingness to exploit the situation. This approach, comparable to a smaller fish attempting to manipulate a much larger one, raised red flags about the contractor's ethics and integrity. Adding to the precarious situation, the contractor couldn't secure a surety bond, a fundamental safety net that would have mitigated most of the financial risks for the **little ol' register's** crew.

As fate would have it, the contract with FEMA was abruptly canceled. The crews, geared up for a significant venture, were forced to return to their regular operations. However, the aftermath was far from business as usual. A week later, the ominous clouds of a lawsuit gathered, illustrating the perils of navigating a high-stakes venture without due diligence and a diversified risk management strategy. [180] This cautionary tale serves as a poignant reminder for your **little ol' register** and others to tread carefully when enticed by seemingly lucrative opportunities and to safeguard against potential pitfalls that can jeopardize a business's very essence.

Something else your **little ol' register** will learn that truly a contract is only there to give the lawyers something to fight over. Your **little ol' register**, in its journey of growth and maturity, will come to understand a peculiar truth about contracts—they often serve as fodder for legal battles. While contracts are designed to delineate agreements, expectations, responsibilities, and solidify the meeting of the minds, they seem to possess a mystical ability to attract lawyers like moths to a flame.

Rather than being pristine instruments of clarity, contracts sometimes transform into battlegrounds where legal minds engage in skirmishes over interpretations, loopholes, and the ever-elusive "fine print." It's as if contracts have a secret pact with the legal realm, providing a constant supply of contentious material to keep lawyers on their toes. So, your **little ol' register** will soon realize that in the grand theater of business, contracts aren't just documents; they're potential plot twists in the ongoing drama of legal wrangling.

The intricate dance between business and the legal jurisdiction, the importance of coloring within the lines cannot be overstated. It's a delicate ballet, snuggling comfortably within the defined boundaries, rubbing shoulders with the established norms, and laying one's actions right up to the edges but never daring to cross or color outside. The lines, like the boundaries of legality and compliance, serve as a structured canvas upon which your **little ol' register** paints its operations.

Straying beyond these lines can lead to a cacophony of legal issues, coloring outside the lines and creating a messy, uncoordinated masterpiece. In the business and legal world, precision is key, and the artistry lies in navigating the established boundaries with finesse, ensuring harmony and compliance in every stroke. It's a dance where adherence to rules is not just a suggestion but a fundamental choreography that determines the success and sustainability of the performance. The lines are our friends.

Ah, the enchanting world of business! Where dreams come to be meticulously analyzed, strategies concocted, and fortunes gambled on a daily basis. In the end, the three lawyers sauntered out of **the bar**, perhaps a little wiser, a tad more cautious, and with legal fees still looming in the air. As they parted ways, they couldn't help but chuckle at the absurdity of their own legal banter in a place where cases were made but never settled, and repercussions were discussed but never finalized.

It was just another night for these legal jesters, navigating the complex maze of legalese with a shot of humor and a twist of irony. And so, the tale of the three lawyers walking into **the bar** ended not in a courtroom but in the laughter-filled echoes of a legal punchline—costs. After all, when lawyers walk into **the bar**, you can bet there's a joke in the mix and the punchline is always delivered with a side of legal wit and a sprinkle of lightheartedness.

Dreams don't require you to tap into and drain the college fund of your **little ol'**, do they? Expanding your business is a significant step, and it's crucial to do so without jeopardizing the financial stability of your **little ol' register**. One strategy to consider is putting the customer first. Building a strong customer base is the foundation of any successful business. Once you have a solid customer pool, you can then strategize and plan how to efficiently meet their **wants-needs**.

Step right in, folks, to witness the spectacle of profit margins, corporate jargon, and power plays galore; financial concepts like budgeting, cash flow, and profit are essential. Budgeting helps you allocate resources wisely, ensuring you can cover your expenses while leaving room for growth. Understanding your cash flow is crucial for managing day-to-day operations and planning for the future. Profit, of course, is the ultimate goal, and careful financial management will help you achieve it.

When considering expansion, keep in mind that banks prefer lending to financially stable companies. Building a strong financial foundation by demonstrating responsible budgeting and positive cash flow will make your business more attractive to potential lenders.

Remember, growing your business should be a strategic and thoughtful process, ensuring a sustainable and prosperous future for your **little ol' register**.

BROKE TIL' MIDNIGHT

Many claim that they can't secure contracts without prior financial backing, but this assertion is unfounded. In reality, the key is to initiate the process by engaging with potential customers and understanding their requirements before determining the financial means. While costs may be higher, such as renting equipment instead of purchasing or outsourcing certain requests, the focus should be on finding innovative solutions to meet customer demands. The primary objective is to set the **register** in motion, even if some aspects involve initial expenses, with the ultimate goal of building momentum and generating positive outcomes.

Imagine your business, your **little ol' register**, as a ship and captain navigating the vast seas of commerce. Cash flow is the wind in your sails, propelling your vessel forward. It's not just about the grandiose concept of profit; it's about the tangible, day-to-day liquidity that keeps your enterprise afloat.

Cash flow management is the vigilant captaincy required to ensure your ship doesn't run aground or, in this case, go broke before the clock strikes midnight. It involves the delicate balance of inflows and outflows, meticulously tracking the currents of revenue and expenditures. Without this steady financial breeze, even the mightiest vessels can find themselves stranded.

There are many strategies and tactics necessary to master the art of maintaining a healthy cash flow. From optimizing billing and collections to prudent expense management, each action serves as a rudder to steer your business away from the treacherous shoals of insolvency. In essence, it's a guide on how to keep the lights on, the doors open, and the ship sailing smoothly into the midnight seas of financial viability.

As a small business proprietor, one keenly understands the cautious nature of banks, particularly in the early stages of the banking relationship. Banks tend to be conservative, especially when it comes to releasing funds that haven't completed the clearance process. While a modest sum, usually under a couple of hundred dollars, is promptly made available from a deposit, the remainder might be held until the bank deems it fit (a 3-day hold) or until the conclusion of the banking cycle, typically around midnight. This specific timeframe can induce stress for a fledgling business owner who has diligently managed all payments, bringing everything down to the last penny to successfully complete a project. The final payment represents the company's profits and the much-needed shareholder draw. However, depositing funds and the actual availability of those funds are distinct and crucial aspects of financial banking debauchery. In their defense, most tellers nor management are taught the intricacy of the banking rules and regulations that we all must follow.

In the thrilling chronicles of financial fiascos, Patty Cakes Co. once found itself navigating the labyrinth of international and local banks' idiocracy in a quest for a smoother transaction. Picture this: a hefty deposit for a demanding project graced their investment and trust account at an international bank with global reach. Eager to transfer this imperative resource to the local operating account for immediate use on the client project, the team led by Frank embarked on a banking odyssey.

The morning sun bore witness as this financial triumvirate confidently marched into the well-known international bank, requesting a cashier's check for a cool half-million dollars. This move seemed a much better option than trying to stuff all the bills into his briefcase. Moreover, it changed the remitting party from Patty Cakes Co. to the international bank itself. Armed with the certified funds, Frank triumphantly sauntered into the company's local bank, visions of expeditious transactions dancing in the team's heads. However, reality proved more obstinate than their dreams.

The local branch manager, donning an expression of bureaucratic stoicism, explained the dreaded three-day hold on the funds, even though they were certified and guaranteed by the renowned international bank. A wire transfer, he suggested, would be the swift alternative, allowing immediate access to the funds. Crestfallen but undeterred, the team retraced their steps, returning to the international bank across the street to revoke the five-minute-old cashier's check and wire the funds.

Here, the plot thickened. In a Shakespearean twist, the international bank decided to impose a week-long hold on the funds, which essentially were cash not minutes before. Frank proclaimed loudly to the branch manager: "A bank is NOT allowed to put a hold on an 'on-us' check!" which only caused postures to become more defensive. Agitations reached their zenith, tempers teetered on the brink of legality and flirted with arrest-worthy territory, and kings of domains shattered. Yet, Frank remained resolute until the funds were begrudgingly released and transferred across the street, thus restoring financial harmony. Ergo, a tale of cashiers' checks, wire transfers, and the capricious whims of banking institutions unfolded, leaving the team with a hearty laugh and a lesson that **sh*t happens** even in the unpredictable rumble of finance and the tender aspect of liquidity.

In times of financial strain, the need to borrow money quickly, even for short durations, can be crucial for the survival of your **little ol' register**. Fortunately, there are tools and strategies available to assist in such situations. One option is to leverage your purchase orders, essentially turning them into a form of short-term financing resembling a payday loan. Additionally, tapping into lines of credit, such as those offered by credit cards, can provide immediate access to funds when needed most. These credit lines act as a safety net, allowing you to bridge temporary cash flow gaps and keep your business afloat.

However, it's important to understand that when buying and selling paper—essentially trading financial instruments or agreements—you're not just exchanging money but also time. Valuable time itself becomes the true commodity that can be bought and sold. For instance, consider the concept of purchasing a spot in line, as seen in the aircraft manufacturing industry. Aircraft orders often come with lead times of several months or even years. In such cases, the ability to secure a position in the production queue can be more valuable than the aircraft itself, reflecting the premium placed on time.

Another example of buying and selling paper is through the trading of notes or loan obligations. Servicing companies may sell off portions of loans, such as future payments, to investors. For instance, if a loan is structured to be repaid over a year with monthly installments, the servicing company may sell the rights to receive the 12th payment to another party. In this scenario, the purchaser of the note collects the first 11 payments, while the final installment goes to the new owner of the note rather than the original lender. This practice allows for the monetization of future cash flows and can provide immediate liquidity to the seller.

In a nutshell, buying and selling paper offers a flexible and efficient means of managing cash flow and accessing capital when needed. By leveraging these financial instruments effectively, your **little ol' register** can navigate through periods of financial uncertainty and emerge stronger on the other side.

Is there a caveat? Indeed, while the options for accessing quick capital may seem enticing, it's essential to recognize the importance of financial stability and creditworthiness for your **little ol' register**. Banks and financial institutions typically prefer to lend money to companies that demonstrate a solid financial standing and a clear path to achieving their goals, rather than those teetering on the brink of survival. This underscores the necessity of employing sound accounting principles, such as GAAP, in preparing profit and loss statements and cash flow projections. These standardized practices not only ensure accuracy and transparency but also enhance the credibility of your financial statements in the eyes of lenders and investors.

Enterprises like Dun & Bradstreet (D&B) play a pivotal role in assessing the financial health and creditworthiness of businesses, they are de facto auditors of your CPA's work. Much like how consumer credit bureaus like Equifax, Experian, and TransUnion evaluate individuals' credit scores, D&B specializes in providing commercial data and analytics insights about companies. Their comprehensive assessments, including the D&B Credit Rating, offer valuable insights into a company's creditworthiness and financial stability. This business credit score serves as a critical tool for businesses and financial institutions alike, enabling them to make well-informed decisions about extending credit, forming partnerships, or engaging in other financial transactions with a specific company. By maintaining a strong credit rating and adhering to sound financial practices, your **little ol' register** can instill confidence in potential lenders and partners, paving the way for sustainable growth and success.

In the labyrinth of financial management, where the ebb and flow of cash can determine the fate of your **little ol' register**, one must tread carefully, armed with knowledge and resourcefulness. As we've journeyed through the intricate dance of cash flow management, from leveraging purchase orders to navigating the capricious whims of banking institutions, it becomes abundantly clear that resilience and adaptability are essential traits for survival in the tumultuous seas of commerce.

The tale of cashiers' checks, wire transfers, and the tender dance of liquidity serves as a poignant reminder that, despite our best-laid plans, unforeseen obstacles can test our mettle and resilience. Yet, in the face of adversity, there is opportunity—opportunity to innovate, to seek alternative solutions, and to emerge stronger on the other side. So, as you navigate the midnight waters of financial uncertainty, remember the lessons learned, the tools at your disposal, and the unwavering resolve to steer your **little ol' register** toward prosperity and success.

And in this quest for financial stability and growth, the importance of financial constancy and creditworthiness cannot be overstated. By adhering to sound accounting principles and leveraging resources like your local bank or Dun & Bradstreet for accessing credit, your **little ol' register** can not only weather the storms but also thrive in the competitive landscape of business. So, let us chart our course with confidence, guided by the principles of prudence, perseverance, and prudent stewardship, as we sail toward the horizon of opportunity and prosperity.

MORE MONEY MORE PROBLEMS

The dichotomy between big businesses and sole proprietors lies at the heart of the strategic landscape in the business world. When you're a lone entrepreneur or a sole proprietor, you possess unique agility and flexibility. You can pivot swiftly, adapting to changes in the market or industry. It's likened to being able to march twenty miles and sleep in a tree—a dynamic and adaptive approach that allows for quick decision-making and responsiveness to challenges.

However, as a business grows into a larger entity, especially a big corporation, the dynamics change significantly. With increased size comes increased visibility and influence, but it also brings a more fixed position and a larger target. A big business operates more like a fortified structure—a complex **system** with various departments, hierarchies, and established procedures. While this structure offers stability, protection, and resources, it also becomes a more prominent target for scrutiny, competition, and regulatory oversight. The bigger you are the bigger the target on your **little ol' register** is.

In the grand scheme, the stakes rise in the playground of big businesses. They have a more significant impact on the economy, more employees relying on them, and often, more extensive legal and compliance considerations. Conversely, sole proprietors enjoy a certain level of independence and maneuverability. Each business model has its strengths and weaknesses, and the choice between the two depends on factors such as the nature of the industry, personal preferences, risk tolerance, and long-term objectives.

One of the targets that grows pervasively is paying the babysitter. When a business owner or founder opts not to pay themselves a salary and operates in the business, it may seem on the surface that costs are reduced, as the owner foregoes a regular paycheck. However, this decision has nuanced implications for the overall financial health of your **little ol' register**.

Firstly, while it may appear that the business is saving money on employee wages, there is an opportunity cost associated with the owner's time and effort. Operating a business requires significant dedication, and the value of the owner's labor should be accounted for, even if not in the form of a traditional salary. This becomes particularly relevant when considering the potential growth and expansion of the business—a one-man band often juggles various responsibilities, limiting the time and energy available for strategic planning, innovation, and business development.

The intricacies of this failure become glaringly evident in the realm of the self-employed. The assertion that they would earn the same amount of money at double their current output is both true and false—a paradox shaped by perspective. Yet they have not embraced the philosophy of **the system** to generate passive income, **rich thinking**, making your **little ol' register** do the work, receiving a piece of the pie, instead of the individual.

One significant financial pitfall for business owners is the tendency to forgo a regular salary. Failing to pay oneself a regular salary can have serious financial implications for a business. Not only does it distort the true profitability of the business, but it can also hinder reinvestment and growth. In traditional accounting terms, profits are calculated after deducting costs and expenses, including management salaries. When an owner who also works within the business chooses not to draw a salary, it may artificially inflate the apparent profitability of the business. By neglecting to pay yourself, you may find it difficult to secure loans, attract investors, or plan for your own financial future. Remember, a healthy business owner is essential for a healthy business.

Furthermore, not paying oneself as an employee will also hinder the ability to reinvest in the business. Without a structured compensation plan, adapting to the cost of the hat at hand, your **little ol' register** may struggle to allocate funds for growth, marketing, and operational improvements. This, in turn, can limit the company's capacity to scale and compete effectively in the market.

While the decision not to pay oneself a salary might seem like a cost-saving measure, it's essential to recognize the broader impact on the business's financial performance and long-term sustainability. Striking the right balance between personal compensation and business reinvestment is crucial for achieving both short-term stability and long-term growth. So, pay yourself a fair salary, if and when you can, until some **warrior** can **take your job,** yet never truly take your eyes off the game; trust but verify.

Human culture, science, and the arts have thrived on the practice of keen observation of the world (**looking up**), including the intricacies of human society. It involves understanding the nuances by absorbing information, replicating it, refining it, and striving for continual improvement. Throughout pages of business past, this philosophy is exemplified by the renowned quote often attributed to Steve, although we really know who said, "Lesser artists borrow; great artists steal."

The concept of borrowing, stealing, or innovating, whichever **sounds good**, is particularly evident in the wild cut-throat country club of business, where companies often draw inspiration from successful strategies and ideas. However, amidst the pursuit of innovation, the need to safeguard trade secrets becomes paramount. In the race to get new products to market, **little ol' registers** sometimes neglect their critically important intangible assets—their valuable trade secrets.[181] In the highly competitive realm of the food industry, for instance, companies invest significant resources in protecting their unique recipes, processing techniques, and other confidential information that give them a competitive edge.

Beyond intellectual property protection, businesses also grapple with the imperative to establish robust security protocols and risk management mechanisms. This is crucial to shield against potential disruptions, ranging from cyber threats to natural disasters, that could jeopardize operations and financial stability. As the saying goes, **more money, more problems,** and with increased financial success comes the responsibility to fortify the foundations of a business against potential risks and challenges.

Around the inner rings of business, the adage "**More Money, More Problems**" takes on added significance when considering the need for counterintelligence.

The quote by Douglas MacArthur, expressing concern for the security of the nation from insidious forces within, resonates similarly in the corporate arena. Counterintelligence in business involves protecting against internal threats that could compromise the integrity, assets, and confidential information of a company.

As businesses and your **little ol' register** accumulate wealth and success, they become more attractive targets for various forms of internal threats, including corporate espionage, employee misconduct, and sabotage. Counterintelligence measures aim to identify, assess, and mitigate these risks, ensuring the sustained security and resilience of the organization. Just as nations deploy counterintelligence to safeguard their interests, businesses must adopt strategies and protocols to protect against internal vulnerabilities that could undermine their operations—protect your **system**.[181]

In essence, the pursuit of financial prosperity necessitates a concurrent commitment to maintaining a secure and resilient business environment. By embracing counterintelligence practices, companies can fortify their defenses, thwart potential internal threats, and uphold the values and success that define them.

In a twist of irony and humor, the scrappy crew, led by the notorious Brett, found themselves transformed from potential liabilities into essential assets for the company. Tasked with penetration testing and secret shopping within their own ranks, this team of once sticky-fingered individuals embraced their new roles with gusto. The directive was clear: try to steal from the company, but this time, with official approval.

The crew, armed with their mischievous ingenuity, embarked on a mission to outsmart their own security measures. They became the corporate equivalent of undercover agents, blending into the daily operations while testing the organization's vulnerabilities. Their exploits turned the workplace into a comedy of errors and cunning schemes, highlighting the need for heightened security awareness.

As Brett and his crew danced through the elaborate choreography of their staged heists, the company's security protocols faced the ultimate stress test. Each successful attempt at "stealing" exposed areas for improvement, leading to a robust revamping of security measures. The once mischievous crew, now armed with a newfound sense of responsibility, became the unsung heroes of the company's counterintelligence efforts.

This amusing tale underscores the importance of embracing humor and creativity in addressing serious issues. By turning potential threats into a source of entertainment and education, the company not only strengthened its security but also fostered a culture of vigilance and camaraderie among its employees.

In the vast landscape of business decisions, your **little ol' register** will find itself amidst a cacophony of voices—a multitude of opinions, perspectives, and influences vying for attention. As the roster of stakeholders grows, so does the complexity of discerning whose advice to heed. Investors bring financial acumen and strategic insight, partners contribute diverse expertise, **blind men** offer varied experiences, and the **Kool-Aid** drunken **warriors** passionately advocate for a shared *vision*.

Navigating this chorus of voices requires a delicate balance, which is the same in orchestrating a symphony where each instrument contributes to the harmonious whole. Investors may bring a keen eye for financial viability, partners offer specialized knowledge, blindmen provide practical wisdom, and the fervent **Kool-Aid warriors** infuse the enterprise with shared passion. The challenge lies in orchestrating these diverse elements into a coherent and effective strategy.

As more individuals become part of the business family, it becomes crucial for your **little ol' register** to develop a discerning ear—one attuned to the nuances of each voice. Seeking a harmonious blend of insights, embracing the wisdom of experience, and channeling the collective energy of passionate advocates can transform the discordant noise into a symphony of success. It's not just about hearing more voices; it's about cultivating the wisdom to listen, filter, and integrate the right notes into the grand composition of your business journey.

Embarking on the journey to the **river for water** (building **the system**), becomes an even more daunting task when the pace of progress is hindered. Accelerating the development process emerges as a pivotal strategy, allowing every piece of the puzzle to be secured in advance, mitigating the challenges of a slow and cumbersome journey.

The ability to prepay for essential components not only expedites the overall plan but also plays a crucial role in managing the burn rate—the rate at which resources are expended. It's colloquially known as "extending the runway," determining how much time remains until the critical "game over" moment, providing the necessary leeway for effective navigation and strategic decision-making. In the intricate fashion of business, the acceleration of foundational elements becomes a key determinant of sustained momentum and a prolonged runway for success.

Securing additional funding through the sale of company stock aligns with the fundamental concept of raising capital for a longer runway. **Chicken is chicken** selling a product—in this case, the product being a stake in the business is the

same. Much like selling chicken, where the quality and quantity of the product determine its market value, the sale of company shares involves careful consideration of the remaining portions of the business pie.

The critical question arises: How much of your **little ol' register** are you willing to relinquish in exchange for the financial infusion needed to fuel growth and development? Are you willing to have shared custody?

Balancing the equation between obtaining the necessary resources and retaining a substantial ownership stake becomes a delicate art, requiring astute calculation and strategic negotiation to ensure that the core essence of your **little ol' register** remains firmly in your hands. It's a dance between expansion and preservation, with each decision impacting the overall flavor and longevity of your entrepreneurial journey.

You take fire when you're over the target and in the intricate explosions of business, where success amplifies both opportunities and challenges, the journey towards prosperity is marked by resilience, agility, and strategic foresight. As companies navigate the complexities of growth, they must remain steadfast in their commitment to safeguarding their interests, fostering a culture of vigilance, and embracing creativity and innovation in addressing serious issues. By integrating diverse perspectives, embracing humor, and cultivating a harmonious blend of insights, businesses can transform discordant noise into a symphony of success. In this ever-evolving fashion show, where **more money** inevitably brings **more problems**, it is the ability to adapt, innovate, and persevere that ultimately defines the trajectory of success for your **little ol' register** and its journey towards excellence.

GOING VERTICAL

When considering the strategic direction for business growth, the concepts of vertical and horizontal expansion emerge as intriguing prospects. Going vertical involves expanding within the existing industry supply chain, capturing various stages of production or distribution. On the other hand, horizontal expansion involves diversifying into related or unrelated industries, broadening the scope of products or services offered.

Reflecting on history, during the construction of the Hoover Dam, an industry tycoon contemplated similar ideas. The notion of owning the store where his employees made purchases or even the housing, they rented crossed his mind.[182] This echoes the historical phrase, "I owe my soul to the company store," capturing the potential interconnectedness of various facets of employees' lives under one ownership umbrella. This tycoon's visionary thinking serves as a reminder that both vertical and horizontal expansion strategies can hold significant promise, each presenting unique opportunities and challenges for businesses seeking to broaden their influence in the marketplace. Just as **take my job**, replace yourself with the heist cost job, and **look up** the line to the highest cost items in the supply chain, when **counting your pennies**.

Investments play a pivotal role in the growth and expansion of a business, acting as the lifeblood that fuels various initiatives and strategies. Both vertical and horizontal expansions are two distinct approaches to utilizing investments for business development, each with its own set of benefits.

Vertical expansion involves the expansion of a business along its supply chain, encompassing activities both upstream and downstream—Gobbling up the 5-fold rule. Investing in vertical expansion also allows a company to control more stages of the production or distribution process, enhancing efficiency, reducing costs, and ensuring a more streamlined operation. For instance, a manufacturing company might vertically expand by acquiring or investing in suppliers of raw materials or distributors.

On the other hand, horizontal expansion involves extending a business's reach within its existing stage of the supply chain. This can be achieved through diversification into related products or services, entering new markets, or acquiring competitors. Horizontal expansion allows a business to leverage its existing expertise and infrastructure, capturing a larger share of the market and potentially benefiting from economies of scale.

The benefits of vertical expansion include increased control over the production process, improved supply chain coordination, and the potential for cost savings through integration. Meanwhile, horizontal expansion offers opportunities for market share growth, increased brand visibility, and the potential to capitalize on synergies between similar product lines or services.

Hence, strategic investments in either vertical or horizontal expansion can contribute significantly to business growth by enhancing operational efficiency, market presence, and overall competitiveness. The choice between the two approaches depends on factors such as the nature of the industry, your **little ol' register's** capabilities, and its long-term strategic goals.

When you're ready to grow up or out, expand or diversify, the decision to invest in capital projects or ventures is a critical one that requires careful analysis and consideration. Capital budgeting and investment analysis are essential processes that help business owners and managers make informed decisions about allocating resources to various projects or investments. These decisions can significantly impact the financial health and long-term success of your **little ol' register**. Let's take a little field trip to better understand some of these concepts.

One of the key techniques used in capital budgeting is "Net Present Value" (NPV) analysis. NPV calculates the present value of all cash inflows and outflows associated with a project, taking into account the time value of money. By discounting future cash flows back to their present value using an appropriate discount rate, NPV helps determine whether a project is expected to generate positive or negative returns over its lifespan.[183] A positive NPV indicates that the project is expected to add value to the company, while a negative NPV suggests that the project may not be economically viable.

Imagine you're at a yard sale, eyeing a **little ol'** vintage toaster. NPV is like calculating whether buying that toaster now for $10 is worth it, considering how much toast it'll make you over the next few years compared to the cost of a new toaster. If the toast-to-price ratio is favorable, it's a good buy! Let's break this one down.

■ **The Vintage Toaster:** Imagine that vintage toaster sitting on the yard sale table, priced at a tempting $10.

■ **Cash Flows:** The NPV calculation involves estimating the cash inflows (in this case, the toast it'll make you) and the cash outflows (the initial cost of the toaster). These cash flows occur over a period of time.

■ **Discounting:** NPV accounts for the time value of money. It's like saying, "Hey, future toast isn't as valuable as today's toast." So, we discount those future toasts back to their present value.

■ **The Toast-to-Price Ratio:** Just like you'd compare the vintage toaster's toast-making potential to the cost of a new toaster, NPV compares the profitability of an investment or project to a minimum acceptable rate of return (the discount rate).

■ **Decision Time:** If the NPV is positive, it means the vintage toaster (or the investment) will yield more toast (or profit) than the cost. It's a "good buy"! If it's negative, well, maybe stick to regular bread for now.

So, next time you're at a yard sale, remember that NPV isn't just about toasters—it's a powerful tool for evaluating investments and making savvy financial decisions!

Another important metric used in capital budgeting is the "Internal Rate of Return" (IRR). IRR is the discount rate that equates the present value of a project's cash inflows with the present value of its cash outflows.[184] In simpler terms, IRR represents the rate of return at which the net present value of a project is zero. A higher IRR typically indicates a more desirable investment opportunity, as it represents a higher return on investment.

Think of IRR as the roller-coaster of investments. It's the same as evaluating whether that amusement park ticket for your **little ol' register** is worth it by calculating how many loops and twists you'll get for the price. If the ride's thrill factor matches or exceeds the ticket cost, it's a ride worth taking! Buckle up, and let's break it down:

■ **The Amusement Park Ticket:** Picture yourself at the ticket booth, eyeing that colorful roller-coaster. The price tag says $50.

■ **Cash Loops and Twists:** Just like the loops and twists of the roller-coaster, IRR evaluates the cash flows of an investment over time. These cash flows can be positive (like the thrill of a loop) or negative (like the stomach-drop feeling).

■ **The Thrill Factor:** IRR aims to find the discount rate that makes the present value of all those cash loops and twists equal to the initial ticket cost. It's like saying, "What rate of return would make this ride as thrilling as its price suggests?"

■ **Decision Time:** If the thrill factor (IRR) matches or exceeds the ticket cost, it's a ride worth taking! If not, maybe opt for the **shiny** Flamin' Hot Cheetos instead.

Now, next time you're crunching numbers, remember that IRR isn't just about roller-coasters—it's a financial loop-de-loop that helps you decide whether an investment is a wild ride or a snoozer!

Additionally, businesses often consider the "Payback Period" when evaluating capital investment projects. The Payback Period represents the length of time required for a project to recoup its initial investment through the net cash inflows it generates.[185] While the Payback Period is a straightforward metric that provides insight into how quickly an investment will pay for itself, it does not consider the time value of money or the cash flows beyond the payback period. Good investments often require patience.

The payback period is similar to waiting for your **little ol'** pet turtle to finish a marathon. You're timing how long it takes for your investment (the turtle) to "payback" the initial cost by crossing the finish line (achieving the desired returns). If your turtle can win the race in a reasonable time, it's a good investment in slow and steady wins!

Strategic investments are the lifeblood of expansion efforts, guiding decision-makers through the complex terrain of capital allocation. On this field trip, capital budgeting and investment analysis serve as indispensable compasses, providing clarity amidst uncertainty. Techniques like Net Present Value (NPV), Internal Rate of Return (IRR), and Payback Period analysis illuminate the path ahead, offering insights into the feasibility and potential impact of investment opportunities. Through meticulous evaluation of costs and benefits, your business can navigate the financial landscape with confidence, ensuring each investment decision contributes to the prosperity of your **little ol' register** and maximizes shareholder value.

No matter your direction, striving for perfection can often be a double-edged sword in the realm of business. While there's an undeniable allure to presenting a flawless product or service to customers, the pursuit of perfection can also exact a heavy toll. In the relentless pursuit of flawlessness, valuable time ticks away, and opportunities for growth and innovation slip through the cracks. Instead, a more pragmatic approach may yield greater dividends—taking your offering to market, even with its imperfections, allows for real-world feedback and iterative improvements based on genuine customer experiences.

In essence, the quest for perfection can become a quagmire, stifling progress and innovation. It's often better to embrace the mantra of "good enough for now" and refine your offering based on real-world feedback, rather than chasing an elusive ideal that may never materialize. Ultimately, the quest for perfection hangs on a knife's edge, and it's often more beneficial to embrace a pragmatic approach, taking products or services to market and refining them based on real-world feedback. By striking a balance between innovation and practicality, your **little ol' register** can navigate the complexities of growth and expansion while maximizing their long-term success. A sage fortune cookie, possibly cracked open by the venerable Confucius himself, may have revealed the timeless wisdom: "Everything is within reach, yet not all paths lead to the treasure."

Summing things up, binging into vertical and horizontal expansion strategies feels a bit like navigating a buffet line—you've got options, but you're not entirely sure which dish will satisfy your hunger best. Howard Hughes, amidst the chaos of building the Hoover Dam, must have felt a bit like a hungry diner eyeing all the choices. Should he stick to the tried-and-true meatloaf (vertical expansion) or venture into the unknown territory of sushi (horizontal expansion)? One thing's for sure: just like at a buffet, the interconnectedness of various aspects of business operations under one ownership umbrella, you'll want to avoid overloading your plate and ending up with a stomachache—or worse, a business flop!

Whether pursuing vertical expansion to gain greater control over the supply chain or opting for horizontal expansion to diversify product offerings and enter new markets, your **little ol' register** must carefully weigh the benefits and challenges of each approach. Regardless of choice, the **chicken** of the business will remain the same. So just remember, "everything is possible, just not so probable."

Summary and Conclusion

Summary and Conclusion

"I do not think that there is any other quality so essential to success of any kind as the quality of perseverance. It overcomes almost everything, even nature."

*–John d. Rockefeller,
Founder and CEO of Standard Oil Company*

LEARN, LEARN, AND CONTINUE TO LEARN.

Throughout the pages of this book, it becomes abundantly clear that business isn't just about numbers and strategies—it's deeply intertwined with the emotional and neurochemical dependencies that shape our perceptions and actions. From the dopamine rush of a successful deal to the cortisol spike of a looming deadline, these biochemical reactions wield tremendous power over our decision-making processes. Understanding and navigating these psychological currents is essential for anyone seeking success in the vigorous area of business. After all, it's not just about what we do, but how we feel and react that ultimately determines our outcomes.

I urge you, dear readers, to embrace the analogy of the **little ol' register** and apply its wisdom to your own business endeavors. Consider how every decision, every transaction, and every interaction contributes to the overall function and success of your enterprise Just as the parallels between fostering the growth and development of a new business and raising a child—both involving the delicate balance of meeting essential needs, facilitating learning experiences, and addressing evolving **wants-needs**. By viewing your business through this metaphorical lens, you can gain valuable insights into areas such as efficiency, organization, and customer experience.

Whether you're a seasoned entrepreneur or just starting, the lessons embedded in your **little ol' register's** narrative can illuminate pathways to success. Take heed of its insights on economic management, customer relations, and strategic decision-making. Let it inspire you to nurture your business with care and attention to detail, knowing that even the smallest of the **little ol' registers** can hold the keys to greatness.

Summary and Conclusion

From the **genesis** of our journey, through the adventures of **why** herein, we've gone through **100 pencils** in exploring the depths of your **little ol' register**, understanding how they operate in a world where **chicken is chicken** and **wants** blend seamlessly with **needs**. Along the way, we've encountered the **paradigm** of **blind men** grappling with **pushing paper** and driving the **vehicle**, realizing that in the grand scheme of **counting our pennies**, **nothing** truly remains **new** under the sun.

From the **blink** of **rich thinking** to navigating the **river for water**, we've learned the importance of keeping the **end in mind** and donning different **hats** to adapt to changing circumstances that **will take your job**. Whether we're playing **chess games** with your **sim** counterparts or navigating the ups and downs **at the bar** when **sh*t happens** from stepping on a **landmine**, we've come to realize the importance of staying grounded and vigilant, **looking up** at the **pyramid**, and embracing every challenge as **true powerful warriors**—a **system** for growth.

As the **mind-killer** path behind us fades, we take the reins as **kings of our own domains**, and off our **high horse**, we understand the power of **killing a tree** and the impact of **counting our steps** in our choices and on those around us. Never say no in **going vertical** even though you may be **broke til' midnight** and through **milking** it all, we've learned to push past the **shiny** distractions that **sounds good** and focus on what truly matters—our **customers**, our *values*, and our *vision*. So, let's raise a glass of **Kool-Aid** to **more money more problems**, sticking our **stickers** everywhere, and **never burning a bridge**, for in the end, it's not about the destination, but the journey we take to get there. Cheers to navigating the twists and turns of the entrepreneur's **dog and pony show** with humor, resilience, and a healthy dose of **peanut butter**—making the dream!

CLOSING THE REGISTER: REFLECTING ON BUSINESS SUCCESS

With formidable challenges, it's crucial never to lose sight of the grand *vision* that propels us forward. Dreaming big and creating something that transcends individual boundaries becomes our guiding light in the darkest moments. Acknowledging that there will be trials that nearly break us, the **true power** to choose greatness lies within us. Embracing the challenges without **mind-killer** fear and committing wholeheartedly reveals the astonishing resilience we possess.

Venturing into uncharted territories often yields surprising results. Commitment has the remarkable ability to propel us beyond our perceived limits. The journey we've traversed encompasses a vast expanse, highlighting the significance of expansive thinking and the resilience to overcome obstacles.

Success, as we've explored, is intricately linked to the expansive nature of our thoughts. The most valuable real estate is the space between our ears, housing the human brain—a wellspring of unlimited potential, creativity, and innovation. Recognizing the importance of *vision*, leadership, and accountability, we find the foundation for personal and professional growth.

This is a call to action, urging continuous learning and improvement. As we reflect on the immense value held within our minds, investing in education, honing skills, and prioritizing mental well-being emerge as pivotal strategies for maximizing the potential of our cerebral "real estate." In doing so, we pave the way for unparalleled success and fulfillment on the journey of your **little ol' register** and personal development.

DOG AND PONY SHOW

A "**dog and pony show**" is colloquially known for a presentation or seminar designed to showcase and market new products or services to potential buyers, yet we are steeped in the wisdom that **chicken is chicken**. While the term typically carries a negative connotation, implying overly dramatic or somewhat tedious presentations, it acknowledges the necessity of such events in the business world.

In the context of a business plan, or any type of **chicken**, engaging in a **dog and pony show** becomes essential when seeking investors or partners. It involves skillfully working the room, putting on a performance that may include serving metaphorical **Kool-Aid,** and presenting **shiny**, compelling aspects of the

Summary and Conclusion

company. While one may employ a certain level of theatrics, **Shiny** underscores the importance of effective and engaging presentations to attract attention and support in the competitive business terrain! Yet the work must be put in.

Once upon a time in the quirky town of Saleslandia, there was a renowned dog and pony show extraordinaire named Barney. Barney had an uncanny ability to turn any rejection into a comedy act that left clients in stitches. One day, armed with his trusty PowerPoint clicker and a toy pony named Sparkle, Barney set out for a sales pitch at the uptight offices of NoMoreNo Inc.

As Barney delved into his pitch about revolutionary paperclip technology, the stern-faced executives remained unimpressed. The lead executive, Mr. Stoneface, interrupted, "Sorry, but we're not interested in innovative paperclip solutions at the moment."

Without missing a beat, Barney whipped out a rubber chicken from his briefcase and exclaimed, "But wait, there's more! Introducing the Clip-a-Doodle-Doo!" He proceeded to demonstrate how the rubber chicken could miraculously hold papers together, turning the rejection into peals of laughter.

To everyone's surprise, Mr. Stoneface burst into laughter and declared, "Okay, you've got our attention. Tell us more about your poultry paperclip revolution!" And just like that, Barney's dog and pony show turned a sea of "nos" into a resounding "yes," leaving Saleslandia with a new champion of comedic salesmanship.

Revising the world of sales and business, the **dog and pony show** often comes with its fair share of rejection. The "Law of Numbers" teaches us that behind every resounding "yes" lies a trail of 99 "nos." It's a statistical reality that underscores the persistence and resilience required in the pursuit of success. Restated, having an order in hand is undeniably more valuable than the promise of a hundred potential deals in the future. The essence lies in pushing through the 99 rejections, learning from each one, and keeping the unwavering focus on that one elusive "yes" that can make all the difference. In this dog and pony

show of business, the journey through the "nos" is an indispensable part of the process, a testament to the tenacity needed to secure the coveted affirmation that propels your **little ol' register** forward and the internal growth of oneself.

The "Law of the Harvest" serves as a poignant reminder in the bustling world of business: you reap what you sow. It echoes the fundamental principle that effort, dedication, and strategic nurturing are prerequisites for yielding fruitful results. Yelling at a barren field, demanding it to produce crops, is an exercise in futility. The entitlement to a bountiful harvest arises only when one invests the time and energy to plant seeds, water them, and nurture their growth.

Impatience, our good old friend, often clashes with the "Law of the Harvest." In a society conditioned for instant gratification, the notion of waiting for the fruits of one's labor can be challenging. This impatience manifests in decision-making, as demonstrated by our simple thought experiment of marshmallows. Consider offering someone $10 today or $100 next week. Surprisingly, a considerable number of individuals opt for the immediate $10, despite understanding that it's a lesser amount. This impulsive choice contradicts the logic of delayed gratification.

Moreover, the experiment takes a fascinating turn when the time frame extends into the future. Presented with the choice of $10 in two years or $100 in three years, the majority opt for the higher amount. This shift highlights the inconsistency in decision-making, with individuals showing an unwillingness to wait for a larger reward when the temporal gap is extended. The juxtaposition of these choices serves as a microcosm of the clash between impatience and the "Law of the Harvest," emphasizing the need for a strategic, long-term perspective in the pursuit of success.

This concept is called hyperbolic discounting. The idea is that people make dramatically worse decisions when thinking of the present and short term, but their decision-making stabilizes over time.

Success requires diligent effort and the foresight to invest in the present for a bountiful harvest in the future. In the field of opportunities, you must persist through the 99 rejections, showcasing your strengths like a proud pony at each encounter, until you reach the envisioned destination, your **little ol' register end in mind**. It's a journey of determination and resilience, where each rejection serves as a stepping-stone towards the ultimate goal. So, saddle up your pony, navigate through the challenges, and plow through the fields of nos, knowing that each effort brings you closer to the fruitful "yes" awaiting at the end of the trail.

NEVER BURN A BRIDGE

In the deep ocean of business, we know the shark that perishes if it ceases to swim, constant innovation is our lifeblood. Embrace the art of daily innovation—address tomorrow's challenges today, avoiding mere reactions to the

Summary and Conclusion

issues of the present moment. Remember, burning bridges is a one-way journey; once ablaze, the path cannot be retracted.

Preserve lost leads for future opportunities, treat key performance indicators as vital tools for risk analysis and forecasting, and value the connections you've cultivated along the way. In the ever-evolving business environment, the bridges we build and maintain are essential for navigating the tides of success.

Establishing connections and networking in the business space goes beyond mere socializing; it's a strategic approach that can yield valuable benefits. Whether you're engaging in meetings or sales, every interaction offers an opportunity to glean something valuable. Consider each encounter as a potential resource, tapping into the concept of the "Six Degrees of Separation," where individuals are connected by a surprisingly small number of mutual acquaintances.

The business landscape is the same, the connections you make can open doors to unforeseen opportunities, collaborations, or insights where "chance favors the prepared mind."[66] Embracing the idea that it's a small world, fosters a proactive mindset, encouraging you to leverage relationships for mutual growth and success. So, rub elbows purposefully, for in the intricate existence of your **little ol' register**, every connection has the potential to lead to new horizons.

Staying in the area of your **little ol' register**, the adage "**Never Burn a Bridge**" holds profound significance. Burning bridges signifies irreparable damage to professional relationships, opportunities, and collaborations. In a dynamic and interconnected business landscape, maintaining positive connections is paramount. A bridge once burned may close doors to potential partnerships, collaborations, or valuable insights that could have contributed to future success. Instead, fostering positive and respectful relationships, even in challenging situations, establishes a foundation for future collaborations and opportunities. The preservation of bridges allows for the continuous flow of communication, trust, and support, creating a network that can prove invaluable over time.

Recognizing the various iterations of challenges and opportunities are essential. Businesses may take different forms, much like the various types of chicken, and vendors persist across different ventures. Even if a particular endeavor doesn't unfold as planned, the relationships formed with vendors may prove crucial in future ventures. Similarly, the value of a strong banking relationship transcends the status of an account—whether open or closed. The enduring benefits of these connections become apparent in the fluidity of business dynamics, showcasing the invaluable role that positive relationships play in navigating the intricacies of the entrepreneurial journey.

"Success is not final, failure is not fatal: it is the courage to continue that counts." — Winston S. Churchill. As we have been given sight to the blind, every venture is a learning experience, and even in the face of challenges or a bridge seemingly burned, there's always room for redemption, always room for improvement. The worst-case scenario is merely a stepping-stone to trying again, armed with the knowledge of what doesn't work. Each setback is a valuable lesson, contributing to the continuous refinement and growth of your business. So, **never burn a bridge**, for in the world of entrepreneurship, every interaction, every challenge, and every setback is an opportunity to learn, adapt, and eventually build a more resilient and successful **little ol' register**.

...the end? Well, see?
This is just the beginning of your entrepreneurial odyssey. Are you ready to take the next step? Remember that the true measure of just about success nor the destination, but the journey itself. Here's to our next chapters of life, and the countless adventures that await.

Summary and Conclusion

APPENDICES AND RESOURCES

Passion can be found in-abundance. Additional resources, templates, and tools can be found online at LittleOl.com for support materials discussed in the book. Below are some excellent starting points to further your **little ol' register's** education for personal and professional development:

■ **"The 7 Habits of Highly Effective People"** by Stephen Covey: This timeless classic provides practical guidance on how to cultivate habits that lead to success and fulfillment in both personal and professional life. Covey's principles, such as "Begin with the end in mind" and "Seek first to understand, then to be understood," offer valuable insights into effective leadership and interpersonal relationships.

■ **"Rich Dad's Cashflow Quadrant"** by Robert Kiyosaki: Building on the principles introduced in his bestseller "Rich Dad Poor Dad," Kiyosaki explores the different ways people earn income and how to transition from being an employee to becoming a business owner or investor. This book offers valuable lessons on financial literacy and wealth-building strategies.

■ **"How to Be a Winner"** by Zig Ziglar: Ziglar's motivational insights and practical advice inspire readers to adopt a winning mindset and achieve their goals. Through anecdotes and actionable strategies, he teaches readers how to overcome obstacles, develop confidence, and unleash their full potential.

■ **"How to Win Friends and Influence People"** by Dale Carnegie: A timeless classic on interpersonal communication and persuasion, Carnegie's book offers practical techniques for building rapport, resolving conflicts, and winning people over to your way of thinking. This book is essential for anyone looking to improve their social skills and cultivate meaningful relationships.

■ **"How to Read a Person Like a Book"** by Gerard Nierenberg: Understanding nonverbal cues and body language is essential for effective communication and interpersonal relationships. Nierenberg's book provides valuable insights into decoding the hidden messages conveyed through gestures, facial expressions, and posture, allowing readers to better understand and connect with others.

These books cover a wide range of topics essential for personal and professional growth, making them excellent starting points for anyone embarking on a journey of self-improvement. Happy reading!

ACKNOWLEDGMENTS

I hold the belief that who we are is a product of our past; our identities are shaped by the countless experiences that precede us, and none of what I present here is solely mine. It has been forged by the culmination of life's lessons, the wisdom imparted by those wiser, and the experiences others have shared with me. The tapestry of our lives is woven through the threads of our accumulated actions over time, intricately embellished by the gentle touch of humanity. Our lives are a tapestry, woven with threads of action and compassion, each stitch adding to the intricate pattern of our existence.

Nonetheless, I am immensely thankful and deeply indebted to the countless individuals whose wisdom and experiences have influenced my journey across four continents. Their impact on my life, coupled with their assistance, has shaped and culminated in the person I am today, and parts of their contributions are immortalized within the pages of this book.

CITATIONS

[1] J. G. Saxe, *The Blind Men and the Elephant*, 3rd ed. McGraw-Hill Book Company, 1963. [Online]. https://archive.org/details/blindmenelephant0000saxe

[2] Pali, "The Udāna, Inspired Utterances of the Buddha & the Itivuttaka, the Buddha's Sayings," ed. Kandy: Buddhist Publication Society, 1997, p. 266. [Online]. https://archive.org/details/isbn_9781681723402

[3] F. Nietzsche, *Beyond Good & Evil: Prelude to a Philosophy of the Future*. Createspace Independent Publishing Platform, 1909. [Online]. https://play.google.com/books/reader?id=KhdDAQAAMAAJ&pg=GBS.PP6&hl=en

[4] S. M. Ross, *A First Course in Probability*. London: Collier Macmillan, 1984. 1976. [Online]. https://archive.org/details/firstcourseinpro0000ross

[5] J. Surowiecki, *The Wisdom of Crowds: Why the Many Are Smarter Than the Few and How Collective Wisdom Shapes Business, Economies, Societies, and Nations*. Anchor, 2005. [Online]. https://archive.org/details/wisdomofcrowds0000suro

[6] G. Grimmett et al., *Probability and Random Processes*, 3rd ed. New York: Oxford University Press, 2001 1982. [Online]. https://archive.org/details/probabilityrando0000grim_r2s3

[7] S. Covey, *The 7 Habits of Highly Effective People*. New York: Free Press, 1989. [Online]. https://archive.org/details/7habitsofhighlye00cove_0

[8] D. J. Tarrnow, "Self Behavior," D. A. Suarez, Ed. The Tarrnow Center for Children with Learning Disabilities, 1991.

[9] J. J. Gross et al., "Emotion, Emotion Regulation, and Psychopathology: An Affective Science Perspective," *Clinical psychological science*, vol. 2, no. 4, pp. 387-401, 2014, doi: 10.1177/2167702614536164

[10] L. Karwoski, Garratt, G. M., & Ilardi, S. S., "On the Integration of Cognitive-Behavioral Therapy for Depression and Positive Psychology.," *Journal of Cognitive Psychotherapy*, vol. 20, no. 2, pp. 159-170, 2006.

[11] E. Harmon-Jones et al., *An Introduction to Cognitive Dissonance Theory and an Overview of Current Perspectives on the Theory*, 2nd ed. (American Psychological Association). 2019, pp. 3-24, doi: 10.1037/0000135-001

[12] USMC, "Recruit Depot," D. A. Suarez, Ed., San Diego, 1998.

[13] T. Fleming, "Mezirow and the Theory of Transformative Learning," 2018, pp. 120-136, doi: 10.4018/978-1-5225-6086-9
[14] J. B. Karl Fisch; Scott McLeod, "Did You Know?," in *Globalization & The Information Age*, ed: Sony/BMG, 2007. [Online]. https://youtu.be/16tgJFW1o7o?si=T-jWIXRiTypyRJrK
[15] Anonymous. "Facebook Users, Stats, Data, Trends, and More — Datareportal – Global Digital Insights." Kepios. https://datareportal.com/essential-facebook-stats (accessed 2024).
[16] J. Shaw, "Who Built the Pyramids?," *Harvard Magazine*, vol. 6, pp. 42-99, 2003.
[17] R. W. Morrow, *"Sesame Street" and the Reform of Children's Television*. Johns Hopkins University Press, 2006. [Online]. https://books.google.com/books?id=HZpIIYUrHp4C
[18] B. Oakley et al., *Learning How to Learn: How to Succeed in School without Spending All Your Time Studying; a Guide for Kids and Teens*. Penguin Publishing Group, 2018.
[19] M. A. K Alenizi, "Effectiveness of a Program Based on a Multi-Sensory Strategy in Developing Visual Perception of Primary School Learners with Learning Disabilities: A Contextual Study of Arabic Learners," *International Journal of Educational Psychology*, vol. 8, no. 1, pp. 72-104, 02/24 2019, doi: 10.17583/ijep.2019.3346
[20] IATSE. "Standard Agreement Working Conditions." https://iatse.net/wp-content/uploads/2021/10/2021.10.26-ASA-Negotiations-Working-Conditions-Fact-Sheet.pdf (accessed 2024).
[21] Anonymous, "Division of Labor Standards Enforcement (DLSE)," in *IWC Orders and Labor* vol. 512, ed. State of California, 2012. [Online]. https://www.dir.ca.gov/dlse/FAQ_MealPeriods.htm
[22] Anonymous, *Factors That Influence Consumers' Buying Behavior*: LibreTexts Business, 2019. [Online]. https://biz.libretexts.org/Bookshelves/Marketing/Principles_of_Marketing_(LibreTexts)/03:_Consumer_Behavior-_How_People_Make_Buying_Decisions/03.1:_Factors_That_Influence_Consumers_Buying_Behavior (accessed 2019-12-11).
[23] A. S. Robert Zemeckis, Alan Silvestri, William Ross, "Forrest Gump," USA, 1994. [Online]. https://youtu.be/H1nA1wanH2s?si=1om3UcHOYTEFjQ_h&t=77
[24] A. H. Maslow, "A Theory of Human Motivation," 1943. [Online]. https://archive.org/details/MaslowA.H.1943.ATheoryOfHumanMotivation.PsychologicalReview504370-396.
[25] theForm, "Freedom to Be and Freedom to Act," ed. Los Angeles: Landmark Education Business, 1993.
[26] R. I. C. Edelman. "Why So Many Lottery Winners Go Broke." https://fortune.com/2016/01/15/powerball-lottery-winners/ (accessed 2024).
[27] R. Kiyosaki, *Rich Dad Poor Dad: What the Rich Teach Their Kids About Money That the Poor and Middle Class Do Not!* TechPress, 1998. [Online]. https://archive.org/details/richdadpoordadwh00kiyo_0
[28] Anonymous, *Earth System Analysis for Sustainability*. The MIT Press, 2004, doi: 10.7551/mitpress/2548.001.0001
[29] B. Hyde. "Our Prussian Model of Public Schooling Controlling the Masses." St. George News. https://archives.stgeorgeutah.com/news/archive/2012/03/14/our-prussian-model-of-public-schooling-controlling-the-masses/ (accessed 2024).
[30] T. C.-P. Frankiewicz et al. "Does Higher Education Still Prepare People for Jobs?" Harvard Business Review. https://hbr.org/2019/01/does-higher-education-still-prepare-people-for-jobs (accessed 2024).
[31] M. Housel, *The Psychology of Money: Timeless Lessons on Wealth, Greed, and Happiness*. Great Britain: Harriman House, 2020. [Online]. https://www.google.com/books/edition/The_Psychology_of_Money/l81NzQEACAAJ?hl=en&gbpv=1
[32] D. J. S. PhD, *The Magic of Thinking Big*. New York: Simon & Schuster, 1987. [Online]. https://archive.org/details/magicofthinking000schw
[33] C. S. Dweck, *Mindset: The New Psychology of Success*. New York: Ballantine Books, 1956. [Online]. https://archive.org/details/mindsetnewpsycho0000dwec_g9z4
[34] R. Kiyosaki et al., *Rich Dad's Cashflow Quadrant: Rich Dad's Guide to Financial Freedom*. Warner Books, 1999. [Online]. https://archive.org/details/cashflowquadrant00kiyo
[35] T. WheelWright, *Tax-Free Wealth: How to Build Massive Wealth by Permanently Lowering Your Taxes*. Minden, NV: BZK Press, 2012. [Online]. https://archive.org/details/taxfreewealthhow0000whee
[36] Anonymous, "Holy Bible, New American Standard," in *Matthew 7:7-8*, 1st ed. LaHabra: The Lockman Foundation, 1995.
[37] B. Carson, *Think Big*. Zondervan, 1992. [Online]. https://archive.org/details/thinkbigunleashi00cars_2
[38] S. Bhogaraju. "Understanding Pepsico's Business Segments and More." MarketRealist. https://marketrealist.com/2014/12/understanding-pepsicos-segments/ (accessed 2024).

Summary and Conclusion

[39] PepsiCo, "Pepsico Reports Third-Quarter 2023 Results," 1st ed: 2024, doi: https://investors.pepsico.com/docs/default-source/investors/q3-2023/q3-2023-earnings-release_wlddafg8sim0xvmu.pdf

[40] (2024). *26 CFR § 1.110-1 - Qualified Lessee Construction Allowances. | Electronic Code of Federal Regulations (E-Cfr) | Us Law | LII / Legal Information Institute*. [Online] https://www.law.cornell.edu/cfr/text/26/1.110-1

[41] M. Ovens. "Improvise, Adapt and Overcome." Forbes. https://www.forbes.com/sites/michelleovens/2020/11/06/improvise-adapt-and-overcome/ (accessed 2024).

[42] J. Clear, *Atomic Habits: An Easy & Proven Way to Build Good Habits & Break Bad Ones*. Avery, 2018. [Online]. https://archive.org/details/atomic-habits

[43] AAF Group, *Ala-teen: A Day at a Time*, 1st ed. Al-Anon Family Group Headquarters, 1983. [Online]. https://archive.org/details/alateendayattime0000unse

[44] Z. Ziglar, *How to Be a Winner*. Nightingale Conant Corp, 1990.

[45] S. Johnson, *Who Moved My Cheese?* London, England: Vermilion, 1999. [Online]. https://archive.org/details/whomovedmycheese0000mdsp

[46] S. Hayes et al., "The Third Wave of Cognitive Behavioral Therapy and the Rise of Process-Based Care," *World Psychiatry*, vol. 16, pp. 245-246, 10/01 2017, doi: 10.1002/wps.20847

[47] Cherokee, "The Two Wolves," San Diego State University. [Online]. https://theacademy.sdsu.edu/wp-content/uploads/2015/06/two-wolves-cherokee-story.pdf

[48] Cherokee, "The Cherokee Myth: The White Wolf," ed. [Online]. https://www.ipl.org/essay/The-Cherokee-Myth-The-White-Wolf-PJS3Y3XGYT

[49] Z. Ziglar, *See You at the Top - Biscuits, Fleas, and Pump Handles*, 1st ed. Pelican Pub Co Inc, 1984. 1975. [Online]. https://archive.org/details/seeyouattopforme0000zigl

[50] F. Herbert, *Dune*, 15th ed. New York: Berkley Publishing, 1977. 1965. [Online]. https://archive.org/details/dune0000herb_f4t1

[51] J. B. Peterson, *12 Rules for Life: An Antidote to Chaos*. Random House of Canada, 2018. [Online]. https://archive.org/details/12RulesForLifeJordanB.PetersonAnAntidoteToChaos

[52] A. F. Cretenoud et al., "Individual Differences in the Perception of Visual Illusions Are Stable across Eyes, Time, and Measurement Methods," *Journal of Vision*, vol. 21, no. 5, 2021, doi: 10.1167/jov.21.5.26

[53] A. Hormozi, *100m Offers: How to Make Offers So Good People Feel Stupid Saying No*. Acquisitions.com LLC, 2021. [Online]. https://archive.org/details/100m-offers

[54] D. Ogilvy, *Ogilvy on Advertising*. New York: Vintage Books, 1985. [Online]. https://archive.org/details/ogilvyonadvertis0000ogil

[55] USMC, (2010). *Information Operations Training and Readiness Manual*. [Online] https://www.marines.mil/portals/1/Publications/NAVMC%203500.90.pdf

[56] E. A. David, "Should Legal Education Be Transformative?," *Journal of Christian Legal Thought*, 2023. [Online]. https://ora.ox.ac.uk/objects/uuid:6955ce99-3a48-4940-86f2-a52b3745c80e/files/s7s75dd98t.

[57] G. I. Nierenberg et al., *How to Read a Person Like a Book* Eighth ed. Great Britain: Woodnough Bookbinding, 1980. 1973. [Online]. https://archive.org/details/howtoreadpersonl0000nier

[58] A. S. Huddleston, "Hiding Behind the Title: Bridging the Gap between Identity and Leadership through Neuroscience, Emotional Intelligence and Ethical Management," 2022.

[59] J. O. Goh et al., "Neuroplasticity and Cognitive Aging: The Scaffolding Theory of Aging and Cognition," *Restorative neurology and neuroscience*, vol. 27, no. 5, pp. 391-403, 2009, doi: 10.3233/RNN-2009-0493.

[60] M. Geiser, "The Psychology of the Mind," D. A. Suarez, Ed., Las Vegas: University of Nevada Las Vegas, 2011.

[61] M. J. Naus et al., "Development of Memory Strategies: Analysis, Questions, and Issues," in *Trends in Memory Development Research*, vol. 9, M. T. H. Chi Ed.: S.Karger AG, 1983, p. 0, doi: 10.1159/000407963

[62] P. R. Pintrich et al., "Students' Motivational Beliefs and Their Cognitive Engagement in Classroom Academic Tasks," in *Student Perceptions in the Classroom*: Routledge, 2012, pp. 149-184.

[63] G. Schlaug et al., "Training-Induced Neuroplasticity in Young Children," *Annals of the New York Academy of Sciences*, vol. 1169, no. 1, pp. 205-208, 2009.

[64] M. Costandi, *Neuroplasticity*. MIT Press, 2016.

[65] D. Carnegie, *How to Win Friends and Influence People*. USA: Simon & Schuster Audio, 1999. 1982. [Online]. https://archive.org/details/howtowinfriendsi00carn

[66] R. M. Pearce, "Chance and the Prepared Mind," *Science*, vol. 35, no. 912, pp. 941-956, 1912, doi: http://www.jstor.org/stable/1638153.
[67] M. Hoffler, "Into to Biology," ed: Bishop Gorman College Prep., 1994.
[68] A. Christopher et al., *A Pattern Language: Towns, Buildings, Construction*. New York: Oxford University Press, 1977.
[69] C. Doctorow, *For the Win*. Booklassic, 2015.
[70] HSI, "USMC Commercial," D. A. Suarez, Ed., ed: HSI Productions, 2003.
[71] Anonymous, "The Empty Boat," ed: Taoist Parable.
[72] Anonymous, "Helping Small Business Owners and Entrepreneurs Pursue the American Dream," D. A. Suarez, Ed., Las Vegas: Small Business Administration, 1997.
[73] Anonymous. "A Guide for Small Businesses on Raising Capital and Complying with the Federal Securities Laws." https://www.sec.gov/reportspubs/investor-publications/infosmallbusqasbsec# (accessed 2023).
[74] B. Reinkensmeyer. "Trading Psychology: The 14 Stages of Investor Emotions." Investor.com. https://investor.com/trading-psychology-stages-investor-emotions (accessed 2024).
[75] C. Thompson, "Trading Psychology: Why Behavior Matters for Traders," 2024. [Online]. https://www.investopedia.com/articles/trading/02/110502.asp.
[76] A. Sax, "Soho Entertainment Group Inc. and ADL Services Inc. Join Greater Northwestern Research and Development Inc. and Studio 702 to Become Las Vegas' Entertainment Powerhouse," ed: Business Wire, 2002. [Online]. https://web.archive.org/web/20030205024237/http://gnrd.com/
[77] NOAA. "After the Big Spill, What Happened to the Ship Exxon Valdez?" https://response.restoration.noaa.gov/oil-and-chemical-spills/significant-incidents/exxon-valdez-oil-spill/after-big-spill-what-happened-s (accessed 2024).
[78] W. A. Lovett, "Exxon Valdez, Punitive Damages, and Tort Reform," *Tort Trial & Insurance Practice Law Journal*, vol. 38, no. 4, pp. 1071-1128, 2003. [Online]. http://www.jstor.org/stable/25763650.
[79] L. Z. Robert A. Klyman et al., "Strategies Regarding Corporate Veil Piercing and Alter Ego Doctrine," [Online]. https://www.gibsondunn.com/wp-content/uploads/2018/08/WebcastSlides-Alter-Ego-and-Veil-Piercing-2018-07-31.pdf
[80] "Winner Acceptance Corp. V. Return on Capital Corp," ed: Superior Court of the State of Delaware, 2008 No. 5352063, [Online]. https://courts.delaware.gov/opinions/download.aspx?ID=227750
[81] "Dole Food Co. V. Patrickson," ed: US Supreme Court, 2003 No. 538 U.S. 468, p. [Online]. https://supreme.justia.com/cases/federal/us/538/468/
[82] "SEC V. Homer T. Langrill and Thomas W. Becker," ed: United States District Court, 2002 [Online]. https://www.sec.gov/litigation/complaints/comp17822.htm
[83] M. Gladwell, *Blink: The Power of Thinking without Thinking*. 1st edition. New York: Little, Brown and Co., 2005. [Online]. https://search.library.wisc.edu/catalog/999992971702121
[84] B. A. O'Brien et al., "The Effect of Contrast on Reading Speed in Dyslexia," *Vision Research*, vol. 40, no. 14, pp. 1921-1935, 2000/06/01/ 2000, doi: 10.1016/S0042-6989(00)00041-9
[85] A. Mehrabian, *Silent Messages*, 1st ed. Belmont, CA: Wadsworth, 1971. [Online]. https://archive.org/details/silentmessagesim00mehr
[86] B. Gleeson. "9 Navy Seal Sayings That Will Improve Your Organization's Ability to Lead Change." Forbes. https://www.forbes.com/sites/brentgleeson/2018/07/23/9-navy-seal-sayings-that-will-improve-your-organizations-ability-to-lead-change/ (accessed 2024).
[87] Anonymous, "America's Most Wanted," [Online]. https://www.imdb.com/title/tt11710016/
[88] J. B. Shank, E. N. Zalta, Ed., *Voltaire*, Summer 2022 ed. (Stanford Encyclopedia of Philosophy). Metaphysics Research Lab, Stanford University, 2009. [Online]. https://plato.stanford.edu/archives/sum2022/entries/voltaire/
[89] P. A. M. Van Lange et al., *Handbook of Theories of Social Psychology*, London: Sage, 2011. [Online]. http://digital.casalini.it/9781446269008.
[90] Q. Zhang et al., "Enclothed Cognition: The New Perspectives on Embodied Cognition," 2015, doi: 10.1016/j.jesp.2012.02.008
[91] H. Adam, "Enclothed Cognition," *Journal of Experimental Social Psychology*, vol. 48, no. 4, pp. 918-925, 2012/07/01/ 2012, doi: 10.1016/j.jesp.2012.02.008
[92] L. Metrus. "This Is Why You Can't Stop Dyeing Your Hair." ByrdieBeauty. https://www.byrdie.com/hair-color-addiction (accessed 2024).
[93] E.-J. Li et al., "Effects of Hair Colors on the Optical Illusion of Body Types," *Journal of Fashion Business*, vol. 7, no. 3, pp. 14-23, 2003.

[94] R. B. Cialdini et al., "Social Influence: Social Norms, Conformity and Compliance," in *The Handbook of Social Psychology*, Fourth ed.: McGraw-Hill, 1998, ch. 151-192, doi: 10.1146/annurev. psych.55.090902.142015

[95] E. R. Smith et al., *Social Psychology*. Psychology Press, 2014.

[96] N. Zandan, "How to Stop Saying 'Um,' 'Ah,' and 'You Know'," 2018-08-01 2018. [Online]. https:// hbr.org/2018/08/how-to-stop-saying-um-ah-and-you-know.

[97] T. A. Pychyl, "Closing the Intention-Action Gap," *Psychology Today*, 2024. [Online]. https://www. psychologytoday.com/us/blog/dont-delay/200903/closing-the-intention-action-gap.

[98] F. Sniehotta et al., "Bridging the Intention-Behaviour Gap: Planning, Self-Efficacy, and Action Control in the Adoption and Maintenance of Physical Exercise," *Psychology and Health*, vol. 20, pp. 143-160, 04/01 2005, doi: 10.1080/08870440512331317670

[99] B. Jones, "How Disney Works to Eliminate the Words 'That's Not My Job' from Its Organization - Sponsor Content from Disney Institute," 2018-02-28 2018. [Online]. https://hbr. org/sponsored/2018/02/how-disney-works-to-eliminate-the-words-thats-not-my-job-from-its-organization.

[100] (2023). *Paying Yourself*. [Online] https://www.irs.gov/businesses/small-businesses-self-employed/paying-yourself

[101] E. M. Goldratt et al., *The Goal: A Proccess of Ongoing Improvement*, 3rd ed. The North River Press, 1984. [Online]. https://archive.org/details/goalprocessofong0000gold/mode/2up

[102] S. Tzu, "The Art of War," ed. London: Luzac & Co., 1910. [Online]. https://archive.org/details/the-art-of-war-by-sun-tzu-trans.-by-lionel-giles-m.-a.-1910

[103] W. Roberts, *Leadership Secrets of Attila the Hun*. First Warner Books, 1989. [Online]. https://archive.org/details/leadershipsecret00robe

[104] C. B. Bhattacharya et al., "Consumer–Company Identification: A Framework for Understanding Consumers' Relationships with Companies," *Journal of marketing*, vol. 67, no. 2, pp. 76-88, 2003, doi: 10.1509/jmkg.67.2.76.18609.

[105] J. T. Richardson, "People's Temple and Jonestown: A Corrective Comparison and Critique," *Journal for the Scientific Study of Religion*, vol. 19, no. 3, pp. 239-255, 1980, doi: 10.2307/1385862

[106] A. Dye, "Uncommon Grounds: The History of Coffee and How It Transformed Our World. By Mark Pendergrast. New York: Basic Books, 1999. Pp. XXI, 520. 18.00, Paper," *The Journal of Economic History*, vol. 61, no. 1, pp. 259-260, 2001, doi: 10.1017/S0022050701643171

[107] P. Peeling et al., "Influence of Caffeine Ingestion on Perceived Mood States, Concentration, and Arousal Levels During a 75-Min University Lecture," *Advances in Physiology Education*, vol. 31, no. 4, pp. 332-335, 2007.

[108] M. C. Severo et al., "Goals Matter: Amplification of the Motivational Significance of the Feedback When Goal Impact Is Increased," *Brain and Cognition*, vol. 128, pp. 56-72, 2018/12/01/ 2018, doi: 10.1016/j.bandc.2018.11.002

[109] K. C. Berridge et al., "What Is the Role of Dopamine in Reward: Hedonic Impact, Reward Learning, or Incentive Salience?," *Brain research reviews*, vol. 28, no. 3, pp. 309-369, 1998, doi: 10.1016/s0165-0173(98)00019-8

[110] Psycho, "America's Got Talent," in *Vegas - Night 1* vol. 4, R. Norman, Ed., Las Vegas, 2009. [Online]. https://www.imdb.com/title/tt1468409/?ref_=ttpl_ov

[111] M. H. Schneps et al., "History of Reading Struggles Linked to Enhanced Learning in Low Spatial Frequency Scenes," *PLOS ONE*, vol. 7, no. 4, p. e35724, 2012, doi: 10.1371/journal.pone.0035724

[112] E. Térouanne, "On a Class of "Impossible" Figures: A New Language for a New Analysis," *Journal of Mathematical Psychology*, vol. 22, no. 1, pp. 24-47, 1980/08/01/ 1980, doi: 10.1016/0022-2496(80)90045-0

[113] G. Geiger et al., "Peripheral Vision in Persons with Dyslexia," *New England Journal of Medicine*, vol. 316, no. 20, pp. 1238-1243, 1987, doi: 10.1056/nejm198705143162003

[114] M. H. Schneps et al., "Visual Learning and the Brain: Implications for Dyslexia," *Mind, Brain, and Education*, vol. 1, no. 3, pp. 128-139, 2007, doi: 10.1111/j.1751-228X.2007.00013.x

[115] V. Wang et al., "Transformative Learning," *International Journal of Adult Vocational Education and Technology (IJAVET)*, vol. 2, no. 4, pp. 58-66, 2011.

[116] K. K. Johnson, "Teaching Shakespeare to Learning Disabled Students," *The English Journal*, vol. 87, no. 3, pp. 45-49, 1998.

[117] E. L. Bernays, *Propaganda*. IG publishing, 2005.

[118] A. B. C. News, "Desert Inn Closes Its Doors after 50 Years," 2000. [Online]. https://abcnews.go.com/US/story?id=95995&page=1.
[119] S. D'Ambrogio et al., "How Celebrity Status and Gaze Direction in Ads Drive Visual Attention to Shape Consumer Decisions," *Psychology & Marketing*, vol. 40, no. 4, pp. 723-734, 2023, doi: 10.1002/mar.21772.
[120] A. Basiouny. "The Marketing Psychology Behind Celebrity Endorsements." A business journal from the Wharton School of the University of Pennsylvania. https://knowledge.wharton.upenn.edu/article/the-marketing-psychology-behind-celebrity-endorsements/ (accessed 2023).
[121] P. Kavilanz. "So This Is How the Tupperware Party Ends." CNN Business. https://www.cnn.com/2023/04/13/business/tupperware-history/index.html (accessed 2023).
[122] S. Kurt et al., "The Effects of Color on the Moods of College Students," *sage Open*, vol. 4, no. 1, p. 2158244014525423, 2014.
[123] A. J. Elliot et al., "Romantic Red: Red Enhances Men's Attraction to Women," *Journal of Personality and Social Psychology*, vol. 95, no. 5, pp. 1150-1164, 2008, doi: 10.1037/0022-3514.95.5.1150
[124] A. J. Elliot et al., "Color Psychology: Effects of Perceiving Color on Psychological Functioning in Humans," *Annual review of psychology*, vol. 65, pp. 95-120, 2014, doi: 10.1146/annurev-psych-010213-115035
[125] C. Money. "Green Ketchup?" CNN. https://money.cnn.com/2000/07/10/companies/heinz/ (accessed 2024).
[126] J. E. Grant et al., "Introduction to Behavioral Addictions," *The American Journal of Drug and Alcohol Abuse*, vol. 36, no. 5, pp. 233-241, 2010/08/01 2010, doi: 10.3109/00952990.2010.491884
[127] M. Moss, *The Extraordinary Science of Addictive Junk Food* (The Best Business Writing 2014). Columbia University Press, 2014, pp. 292-321.
[128] D. A. Zellner et al., "Color Affects Perceived Odor Intensity," *Journal of Experimental Psychology: Human Perception and Performance*, vol. 16, no. 2, p. 391, 1990.
[129] C. Spence et al., "Does Food Color Influence Taste and Flavor Perception in Humans?" *Chemosensory perception*, vol. 3, pp. 68-84, 2010.
[130] M. P. Narwal et al., "A Study on Challenges and Impact of Advertisement for Impulse Goods," *The international journal: Research Journal of Social Sciences & Management*, vol. 1, no. 6, 2011.
[131] M. Choy et al., "An Adaptive Network Model for Pain and Pleasure through Spicy Food and Its Desensitization," *Cognitive Systems Research*, vol. 66, pp. 211-220, 2021/03/01 2021, doi: 10.1016/j.cogsys.2020.10.006
[132] N. Fauzan, "Understanding the Neuromechanisms of Consumer Behavior in Advertising Industry," *Behavioral Sciences (Basel)*, 2021, doi: 10.3390/bs12120472
[133] N. Pornpattananangkul et al., "Motivated to Win: Relationship between Anticipatory and Outcome Reward-Related Neural Activity," *Brain and Cognition*, vol. 100, pp. 21-40, 2015/11/01 2015, doi: 10.1016/j.bandc.2015.09.002
[134] C. Voss et al., *Never Split the Difference: Negotiating as If Your Life Depended on It*. Harper Business, 2016. [Online]. https://archive.org/details/neversplitdiffer0000voss
[135] M. Ruiz, *The Four Agreements: A Practical Guide to Personal Freedom*. San Rafael, CA: Amber-Allen Publishing, 1997. [Online]. https://archive.org/details/fouragreementspr00ruiz/mode/2up
[136] B. Weiner, "Attribution Theory, Achievement Motivation, and the Educational Process," *Review of educational research*, vol. 42, no. 2, pp. 203-215, 1972.
[137] L. Tzu, "Tao Te Ching: The Classic Book of Integrity and the Way," 1st ed: Bantam Books, 1990 [Online]. https://archive.org/details/taotechinglaotzuvictorhmair_202002
[138] M. Miyamoto, "The Book of Five Rings," 1st ed. New York: Shambhala; Random House, 1993. [Online]. https://search.library.wisc.edu/catalog/9910563742202121
[139] T. Yamamoto et al., *Hagakure: The Book of the Samurai*, 1st ed. Tokyo, New York: Kodansha International; Distributed in the United States by Harper & Row (in eng), 1979. [Online]. https://archive.org/details/hagakure00yama
[140] R. Greene et al., *The 48 Laws of Power*. New York, New York, U.S.A. 3rd ed: Penguin Books New York, New York, U.S.A. (in eng), 2000. [Online]. https://archive.org/details/the48lawsofpower_201912/48%20Laws%20of%20Power%2C%20The%20-%20Robert%20Greene%3B%20Joost%20Elffers/
[141] E. M. G. J. Cox, *The Goal: A Process of Ongoing Improvement*, 3rd ed. The North River Press, 1984. [Online]. https://archive.org/details/goalprocessofong0000gold/mode/2up

[142] J. G. Bohanek et al., "Memories of Positive and Negative Emotional Events," *Applied Cognitive Psychology*, vol. 19, no. 1, pp. 51-66, 2005, doi: 10.1002/acp.1064
[143] A. Huberman. "ADHD, Drive and Motivation." Department of Neurobiology, Psychiatry and Behavioral Sciences at Stanford School of Medicine. https://www.hubermanlab.com/all-episodes (accessed 1,2,6,7,8,10).
[144] A. Westbrook et al., "Dopamine Promotes Cognitive Effort by Biasing the Benefits Versus Costs of Cognitive Work," (in eng), *Science*, vol. 367, no. 6484, pp. 1362-1366, Mar 20 2020, doi: 10.1126/science.aaz5891
[145] D.O.B.S. Center for Conservation Biology, "Notes on Butterfly Distributions in Southern Costa Rica," D. A. Suarez, Ed., Costa Rica: Stanford University, 1993.
[146] K. Hausken, "Principal–Agent Theory, Game Theory, and the Precautionary Principle," *Decision Analysis*, vol. 16, no. 2, pp. 105-127, 2019, doi: 10.1287/deca.2018.0280
[147] A. W. Gouldner, "The Norm of Reciprocity: A Preliminary Statement," *American Sociological Review*, vol. 25, no. 2, pp. 161-178, 1960, doi: 10.2307/2092623
[148] K.V.L. Rhoads et al., "The Business of Influence: Principles That Lead to Success in Commercial Settings," 2002: University of Minnesota Duluth. [Online]. https://www.d.umn.edu/~rvaidyan/mktg4731/Cialdini_InPress.doc
[149] H.V.D.I. Group;, "Interrogation: A Review of the Science," Federal Bureau of Investigation, 2016. [Online]. https://www.fbi.gov/file-repository/hig-report-interrogation-a-review-of-the-science-september-2016.pdf
[150] S. D. Couto. "Burgers, Fries and Robots: McDonald's Opens 1st Mostly Automated Location in Texas - National | Globalnews.Ca." Global News. https://globalnews.ca/news/9370313/mcdonalds-robots-automated-restaurant-texas/ (accessed 2024).
[151] K. Blanchard et al., *The One Minute Manager*, Reissue ed. New York: Berkley Books, 1983. [Online]. https://archive.org/details/oneminutemanager00kenn
[152] E. J. Masicampo et al., "Consider It Done! Plan Making Can Eliminate the Cognitive Effects of Unfulfilled Goals," (in eng), *J Pers Soc Psychol*, vol. 101, no. 4, pp. 667-83, Oct 2011, doi: 10.1037/a0024192
[153] TAMU. "Big Banana, Little Banana." Texas A&M University - College of Engineering. (accessed 2011).
[154] A. Reddy, *The Scrumban [R] Evolution: Getting the Most out of Agile, Scrum, and Lean Kanban*. Addison-Wesley Professional, 2015.
[155] B. Curtis, "Applying Lean to Cognitively Complex Work," *Industrial and Organizational Psychology*, vol. 12, no. 3, pp. 272-276, 2019, doi: 10.1017/iop.2019.85
[156] A. Nieoullon, "Dopamine and the Regulation of Cognition and Attention," *Progress in neurobiology*, vol. 67, no. 1, pp. 53-83, 2002.
[157] Anonymous. "1904.1 - Partial Exemption for Employers with 10 or Fewer Employees. | Occupational Safety and Health Administration." https://www.osha.gov/laws-regs/regulations/standardnumber/1904/1904.1 (accessed 2024).
[158] HSI Productions. Wynn Las Vegas Official Original TV Commercial with Steve Wynn. [Online]. https://www.youtube.com/watch?v=FPw7qdIzfVA
[159] HSI Productions. Encore Las Vegas Commercial. [Online]. https://www.youtube.com/watch?v=bSCiGL4y2Ow
[160] K. G. Cain, "The McDonald's Coffee Lawsuit," *Journal of Consumer & Commercial Law*, vol. 11, no. 1, pp. 14-19, 2007.
[161] R. Hartigan et al., "Critical Thinking and the McDonald's Hot Coffee Case: A Pedagogical Note," *Southern Law Journal*, vol. 24, no. 2, 2014.
[162] Á. Cain. "Geico May Have to Pay $5.2 Million to Woman Who Claims She Contracted Std in a Car Insured by the Company." Business Insider. https://www.businessinsider.com/geico-appeals-std-court-case-2022-6 (accessed 2024).
[163] Citi-Group, "Heath & Life Insurance," D. A. Suarez, Ed., Las Vegas: Primarica, 2000.
[164] E. S. Woolard Jr., "Taking Your Product to Market," D. A. Suarez, Ed., Houston, TX: Dupont, 1993.
[165] S. Reichelstein, "Providing Managerial Incentives: Cash Flows Versus Accrual Accounting," *Journal of Accounting Research*, vol. 38, no. 2, pp. 243-269, 2000.
[166] Mfr. Representative, ""3-Pulls" : Psychology, Friction Points, and Cost-Saving Implications," D. A. Suarez, Ed., ed: Georgia-Pacific, 2005. [Online]. https://www.gppro.com/gp/category/enMotion-towels-and-dispensers?query=%3Arelevance&searchText=

[167] P. Michalowski, *Early Mesopotamia* (The Oxford History of Historical Writing: Volume 1: Beginnings to AD600). Oxford University Press, 2011, p. 0, doi: 10.1093/acprof:osobl/9780199218158.003.0002
[168] FBI, "Al Capone — Fbi," (in en-us), Page 2022-05-24, 2022. [Online]. https://www.fbi.gov/history/famous-cases/al-capone
[169] P. Lotfus. "Accounting 101 for Government Contractors: Allocating Costs." CliftonLarsonAllen. https://www.claconnect.com/en/resources/articles/2019/accounting-101-for-government-contractors-allocating-costs (accessed 2024).
[170] DAU. "Indirect Costs." Defense Acquisition University. https://www.dau.edu/acquipedia-article/indirect-costs (accessed 2024).
[171] FAR (2017). *Chronology of Cost Principle Revisions Issued in Federal Acquisition Circulars (Facs) since 1984)*. [Online] https://www.dcaa.mil/Portals/88/FAR_Cost_Principles_Guide.pdf
[172] R. K. Gupta. Capitalization Tables: Who Owns What and How Much. Accessed 2024. [Online]. https://www.bu.edu/industry/files/2020/03/Capitalization-Table-tutorial.pdf
[173] DFARS-PGI. "PGI 204.7103 Contract Line Items. | Acquisition.Gov." Department of Defence. https://www.acquisition.gov/dfarspgi/pgi-204.7103-contract-line-items. (accessed 2024).
[174] Tax Expert. "Penalties for Missing the 1099-Nec or 1099-Misc Filing Deadline." https://turbotax.intuit.com/tax-tips/small-business-taxes/penalties-for-not-filing-a-1099-misc-irs-form/L4mwyM8Tk (accessed 2024).
[175] J. Davis. "Forgot to File Form W-2? Understand the Penalties and What to Do Next | Onpay." https://onpay.com/payroll/process/avoid-w-2-deadline-penalties (accessed 2024).
[176] P. Sarbanes, "Sarbanes-Oxley Act of 2002," in *The Public Company Accounting Reform and Investor Protection Act. Washington DC: US Congress*, 2002, vol. 55.
[177] J. C. Coates *et al.*, "SOX after Ten Years: A Multidisciplinary Review," *Accounting Horizons*, vol. 28, no. 3, pp. 627-671, 2014, doi: 10.2308/acch-50759.
[178] D. Curcic. "Reading Speed Statistics." Wordsrated. https://wordsrated.com/reading-speed-statistics/#:~:text=Average%20reading%20speed%20by%20page,contains%20800%20words%20per%20page). (accessed 2024).
[179] W. Kluwer. "The 5 Most Common Legal Risks That Can Impact Your Business - Lexology." Law Business Research. https://www.lexology.com/library/detail.aspx?g=1098aa11-e583-413a-8802-d2533ce87f69 (accessed 2024).
[180] "Rma Land Construction Inc V. Catering by Andre Inc, Et Al," ed: Nevada Superior Courts, 2007 [Online]. https://trellis.law/case/32003/05a511180/rma-land-construction-inc-vs-catering-by-andre-inc-linda-suarez-et-al
[181] X. S. Suarez *et al.*, "Don't Spill Your Trade Secrets: Protecting Your Competitive Advantage in the Food and Beverage Industry (Part 1 of 2)," *The National Law Review*, vol. XIV, 61, 2019. [Online]. https://www.natlawreview.com/article/don-t-spill-your-trade-secrets-protecting-your-competitive-advantage-food-and.
[182] F. McCabe, "Boulder City: Built by the Dam, for the Dam," in *Las Vegas Review-Journal*, ed: @ reviewjournal, 2014. [Online]. https://www.reviewjournal.com/news/boulder-city-built-by-the-dam-for-the-dam/
[183] A. Gallo. "A Refresher on Net Present Value." Harvard Business Review. https://hbr.org/2014/11/a-refresher-on-net-present-value (accessed 2024).
[184] T. Vipond. "Internal Rate of Return (IRR)." CFI_education. https://corporatefinanceinstitute.com/resources/valuation/internal-rate-return-irr/ (accessed 2024).
[185] R. Javed. "Payback Method - Formula, Example, Explanation, Advantages, Disadvantages | Accounting for Management." Accounting For Management. https://www.accountingformanagement.org/payback-method/ (accessed 2024).

Summary and Conclusion

PUBLISHER'S NOTES

■ **Marks Disclaimer:** All brands, trademarks, service marks, and company name mentioned in this book are the property of their respective owners. Any use of brand names, trademarks, or product names is solely for descriptive purposes and does not imply endorsement, sponsorship, or affiliation with this book. We acknowledge the rights of trademark owners and strive to respect intellectual property laws and regulations.

■ **Fair Use Disclaimer:** This book incorporates insights from various sources, all of which have been duly cited and may contain copyrighted material whose use has not always been specifically authorized by the copyright owner. We believe this constitutes a "fair use" of any such copyrighted material as provided for in section 107 of the US Copyright Law. Any such copyrighted material within this book falls under the guidelines of fair use, intended for purposes such as criticism, comment, news reporting, teaching, scholarship, or research. While we believe that the use of copyrighted material in this book constitutes fair use under U.S. copyright law, we understand that fair use is a complex legal doctrine. If you believe that any portion of this book infringes on your copyright, please contact us immediately. However, all original concepts, perspectives, and creative expressions within this book are the sole intellectual property of the author.

■ **Artificial Intelligence (AI) tools:** AI tools were used to assist with editing, proofreading, and image processing to enhance clarity, conciseness, and visual appeal. They did not contribute to the development of the core ideas or content. All ideas, concepts, and insights are original and solely the work of the author, who retains full ownership of the original work.

■ **Views Expressed Disclaimer:** The views, thoughts, and opinions expressed in the text belong solely to the author, not necessarily reflect the author's employer, organization, committee, or other group or individual. Any content provided by our authors are of their opinion and are not intended to malign or disparage any religion, ethnic group, club, organization, company, individual or anyone or anything else. Publisher remains neutral with regard to jurisdictional claims in published maps and institutional affiliations.

■ **Errors and Omissions Disclaimer:** The publisher or author takes no responsibility for the information provided and will not be liable for any errors or omissions in this content. This disclaimer serves as protection against legal claims.

■ **Use at Your Own Risk Disclaimer:** Use the information provided at your own risk. The reader assumes full responsibility for any consequences of using this information. Please note that the information provided in this book is for educational and informational purposes only.

■ **Investment Disclaimer:** The content herein is not intended as investment advice, an offer, or a prospectus for investment purposes. Past performance is not indicative of future results. The author encourages readers to conduct their own research and consult with qualified professionals before making any important decisions. Investing involves high risks, including the risk of losing your entire investment. The author does not guarantee any specific outcome or profit. The information provided is for educational purposes and is intended for accredited investors who understand and can bear the high risk of investments.

■ **Medical Disclaimer:** The health information provided in this book is intended for general informational and educational purposes only and is not a substitute for professional medical advice, diagnosis, or treatment. Always seek the advice of your physician or other qualified health provider with any questions you may have regarding a medical condition. Do not disregard professional medical advice or delay in seeking it because of something you have read in this book. The author and publisher do not claim to diagnose, treat, cure, or prevent any disease. Reliance on any information provided in this book is solely at your own risk.

All rights reserved.
The rights of Dimas Arquimedes Suarez as author and illustrator have been asserted in accordance with the Copyright, Design and Patents Act 1988.

By purchasing and reading this book,
you agree to the terms of these disclaimers.

You've made it this far, and that's a testament to your dedication; you must have had **purpose**. At the beginning of each chapter, a single word served as a sliver of shimmering insight. Those who were observant and attentive to the **little ol'** things would have discovered this inspiring message:

> "**Innovation and Resilience Illuminate the Path to Success; Every Challenge Unveils Opportunities to Grow and Achieve Dreams with Passion and Purpose.**"

Keep the flame burning—your journey has just begun.
The future is yours to shape!

www.ingramcontent.com/pod-product-compliance
Lightning Source LLC
Chambersburg PA
CBHW071628220526
45469CB00002B/528